The Huns

E. A. Thompson

Revised and with an afterword by
Peter Heather

Blackwell
Publishing

First edition published as *A History of Attila and the Huns*
by Oxford University Press, 1948

BLACKWELL PUBLISHING
350 Main Street, Malden, MA 02148-5020, USA
108 Cowley Road, Oxford OX4 1JF, UK
550 Swanston Street, Carlton, Victoria 3053, Australia

First published 1996 by Blackwell Publishing Ltd
First published in paperback 1999
Reprinted 2000, 2001 (twice), 2003, 2004

Library of Congress Cataloging-in-Publication Data

Thompson, E. A.
  The Huns / E. A. Thompson
    p. cm. – (The peoples of Europe)
  Rev. ed. of: A history of Attila and the Huns, 1948.
  Includes bibliographical references and index.
  ISBN 0–631–15899–5 (acid-free paper) — ISBN 0–631–21443–7 (pbk: acid-free
paper)
    1. Huns. 2. Attila, d. 453. I. Thompson, E. A. History of Attila and the Huns.
II. Title. III. Series.
  D141.T5   1996
  936–dc20

A catalogue record for this title is available from the British Library.

Set in 12 on 13½ pt Sabon
by Words & Graphics Ltd, Leicester
Printed and bound in the United Kingdom
by MPG Books Ltd, Bodmin, Cornwall

For further information on
Blackwell Publishing, visit our website:
http://www.blackwellpublishing.com

The Huns

The Peoples of Europe

General Editors
James Campbell and Barry Cunliffe

This series is about the European tribes and peoples from their origins in prehistory to the present day. Drawing upon a wide range of archaeological and historical evidence, each volume presents a fresh and absorbing account of a group's culture, society and usually turbulent history.

Already published

The Etruscans
Graeme Barker and Thomas Rasmussen

The Normans
Marjorie Chibnall

The Norsemen in the Viking Age
Eric Christiansen

The Lombards
Neil Christie

The Serbs
Sima Ćirković

The Basques*
Roger Collins

The English
Geoffrey Elton

The Gypsies
Second edition
Angus Fraser

The Bretons
Patrick Galliou andMichael Jones

The Goths
Peter Heather

The Franks*
Edward James

The Russians
Robin Milner-Gulland

The Mongols
David Morgan

The Armenians
A. E. Redgate

The Britons
Christopher A. Snyder

The Huns
E. A. Thompson

The Early Germans
Malcolm Todd

The Illyrians
John Wilkes

* Denotes title now out of print

Contents

Map 1   The Huns before Attila

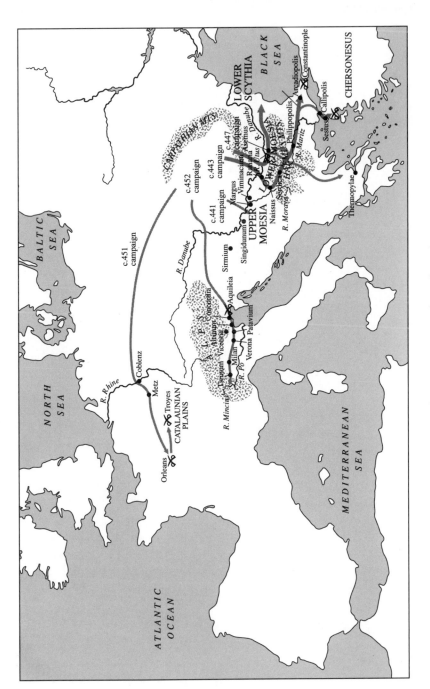

Map 2   The campaigns of Attila (after
Thompson's reconstruction)

Introduction

A student of the later Roman Empire who undertakes to write the history of the Huns must start with the admission that he is offering his readers a story that has neither a beginning nor an end, neither a head nor a tail. Every such history should begin with the question, are the Huns to be identified with the Hsiung-nu of whom the Chinese annals speak so often? The identification has been discussed endlessly since De Guignes first suggested it in the eighteenth century, but, without a knowledge of Chinese, one can do no more than say that most, but not all, competent authorities incline to accept it. On the other hand, the most recent inquirer[1] has built up what seems to the layman's eye a very strong case against the identification, and indeed many who have sought to follow the discussion must often have brought Bury's words to mind: 'It is a mortal leap from the kingdom of the northern Zenghi to the steppes of Russia, and he who takes it is supported on the wings of fancy, not on the ground of fact.'[2] At any rate, until the experts reach some agreement the student of the later Roman Empire is best advised to say nothing of the Hsiung-nu.

At the end of our story we should discuss the history of what is called the 'Attila legend'. Why was the Scourge of God never forgotten? Why did the Eastern Romans call by

Plate 1   *Attila – The Scourge of God.*
Copyright © Mary Evans Picture Library.

the name of Huns each successive wave of ferocious barbarians who descended upon them from the north-east?[3] Why do we ourselves, when we wish to vilify our enemies, apply to them the name of those poor nomads who lived in conditions of terrible hardship and poverty fifteen hundred years ago? An answer to these questions would imply a knowledge of Germanic saga and of medieval and modern literature to which the present writer can lay no claim. The task is not simplified by the fact that much of the discussion of the Attila legend has been conducted by Hungarian scholars in their native tongue: and Hungarian, like Chinese, lies beyond the powers of many classical students.

In the present book, then, we must content ourselves, as some of the Romans did, by beginning the history of the Huns not in Mongolia but in the basin of the river Kuban, and by confessing that nothing is known of them for certain until, towards the close of the fourth century AD, they fell upon the Ostrogoths. Our story will end with the collapse of the empire of Attila and with the immediate aftermath of that event. True, Huns are still found fighting in the armies of Justinian, but their significance in the sixth century is slight, and they were soon to be absorbed into the general population of Europe or replaced by other so-called Huns who were constantly streaming westwards across the steppe. Of Etzel, as of the Hsiung-nu, we shall have nothing to say.

Within these limitations then the plan of this book is as follows. In the first chapter a brief account is given of the principal sources from which we derive our knowledge of the Huns. Chapters 2 and 4–6 are entirely narrative and descriptive. They contain an account of the Huns' diplomatic relations with the Romans and of their victories and defeats in war. This is a story which has been told before, but the available English accounts are not altogether satisfactory. Gibbon's chapters on the fifth century are far from being among the best in his *Decline and Fall*. Hodgkin, in his *Italy and Her Invaders*, has written the fullest English history of the Huns, but his work, though of great value, is now old, and renewed study of the texts may elicit some facts which he passed by. More recent writers, such as Bury, the authors of the *Cambridge Medieval History*, and so on, have dealt with the Huns at greater or lesser length, but their purpose was to tell the history of the Roman Empire, a subject to which the career of Attila is only incidental. These chapters then do not seem to be entirely superfluous; at any rate, they contain an attempt to tell the story in considerably greater detail than will be found elsewhere. The reader should be warned, however, that the emphasis given to the various events recounted in these chapters is not such as the writer would have desired: it is entirely conditioned by the varying amount of evidence at our disposal. Thus, although we can give a full account of the inconclusive diplomatic mission of Maximinus, we can say very little of the great invasion of 447 and nothing at all of its causes.

The remainder of the book is devoted to an attempt to explain the narrative contained in these chapters. Why did the Huns act as they did? How were they able to accomplish their impressive deeds? What sort of people were they? In an effort to answer these questions I have devoted chapters 3 and 7 to an attempt to analyse the material civilization and social organization of the Huns. It becomes apparent at once that the society which Ammianus' informants observed had changed into something very different by the time Priscus visited it. If we wish to understand the society which produced Attila we must understand how that society had come to be what it was when he became its leader. No human community is, or ever has been, entirely static: the society of the Huns was more dynamic than most. No attempt has been made hitherto, I believe, to describe in detail the social history of the Huns, and it is therefore to be feared that the reader will find even more imperfections in chapters 3 and 7 than elsewhere in the book.

We next seek to understand why the Romans behaved as they did in their dealings with the Huns. Under what conditions was Roman foreign policy operating with regard to the new invaders? What judgement are we to pass on the respective policies of Theodosius II (aided by his minister Chrysaphius) and of Marcian? Modern historians from Tillemont and Gibbon to Bury and Ernst Stein have consistently condemned Theodosius as a weak and feeble prince and have praised Marcian as a tower of strength. But if we grasp the nature of Hun society, if we bear in mind some of the more obvious social divisions existing within the East Roman Empire, and if, further, we realize that Priscus was an author with strong prejudices, then I believe that we shall come to a different conclusion. Theodosius guided the Eastern Empire through one of the most violent storms of the fifth century in the best and most economical way open to him. It was Marcian's good fortune that, when he acceded to the throne, circumstances had altered and an entirely new situation had come into being. My excuse for adding this chapter is that, interesting as the Huns are in themselves, they are even more interesting in their relations with the Romans. And the present book is intended primarily for students of Roman history.

Finally, the reader will find in the last chapter a few general observations on the Huns and a tentative estimate of the significance for European history of their appearance on the Danube and the Rhine.

1

Sources

When the Huns first crossed over the Straits of Kerch into the Crimea and into the stream of European history they were illiterate. When they finally vanished in the turmoil of the fifth and sixth centuries, they were illiterate still.[1] The songs which Priscus heard them singing when the torches had been lit in the banqueting-hall, songs in which they extolled the warlike deeds of Attila, might in time have produced an epic record of some of their achievements. Certainly the Ostrogoths, among whom they lived for so long, remembered their own early history in a cloudy fashion 'in their ancient songs, in almost historic fashion', and used to sing of the deeds of their ancestors to the strains of the harp.[2] But the Huns vanished so quickly that if such epics began to develop among them they were never written down and did not survive the society which sang them. In fact, the Huns appear to have remained ignorant of their early history and could tell little of it to the Roman travellers who came among them.

I

Primitive peoples, however, can leave behind them other

records than epic poems and literary histories. But Hun society by its very nature was such that we can never expect to discover many traces of it in the archaeological record. The difficulties of working metals on a large scale in the conditions of steppe nomadism are overwhelming. The nomad could only carry with him a limited supply of his raw material – whether metal, wood, or textile – as he rode from pasture to pasture. He could obtain an abundant quantity of his raw material only if he settled down at the source of supply, if, that is, he detached himself altogether from the society of which he formed part. The manufactured commodities, therefore, which the steppe society used were for the most part acquired by trade or plunder, and were not the handiwork of the nomads themselves.[3] 'I do not think', writes Minns (p. 56), 'that the nomads worked metals themselves. Metal-work, if not all art-work, was for slaves, tributaries, and neighbours to supply', and it is certainly difficult to imagine one of Attila's henchmen spending his time on artistic metal-working. There is no inherent reason, however, why a nomad should not be able to carry about with him a few tools and a limited quantity of his raw material. Indeed, he has much freer access to materials that are not available everywhere than has the smith of a settled society. The point is that his products must of necessity be very few in number and can at most leave only a faint trace in the archaeological record.

It is true that several objects have been found which archaeologists ascribe with confidence to the nomadic peoples who swarmed into Europe in antiquity and early medieval times. Unhappily it does not seem to be possible in the present state of our knowledge to say whether these objects were all imported into the steppe, and, if not, whether any of them should be attributed specifically to the Huns. Professor Alföldi produced in 1932 a considerable volume entitled *Funde aus der Hunnenzeit und ihre ethnische Sonderung*, in which he claimed that at least four groups of objects can be regarded as exclusively Hunnic. In 1935

Plate 2   Hunnic bronze cauldron (c. AD 400).
Nationalmuseum Budapest. Photograph: AKG London.

another Hungarian scholar, Zoltàn de Takàcs (p. 177 n.), declared that 'the Hunnic objects discussed by Alföldi are in reality late Roman export goods known also from Untersiebenbrunn in Austria, Airan in Normandy, Southern Russia and Kudiat Zateur'. Recent discoveries and further study of the objects available to Alföldi have introduced such

uncertainty into the subject[4] that even an expert archaeologist, if he were to undertake to write of the Huns, could
scarcely make any profitable use of the finds. Certainly, no
use will be made of them by one who has never inspected the
kettle found at Dessa in Little Wallachia,[5] and to whom the
Pecsüszög and Nagyszeksos finds are only names.

Similarly, since the Huns minted no coins, it might
reasonably be expected that the numismatic evidence would
be slight. This is indeed the case, but from the distribution of
Roman coins found in some of the territories once ruled by
the nomads it does seem possible to draw one or two
inferences. These inferences, however, are of a tentative
character and serve, if at all, only to confirm an occasional
conclusion already suggested by the literary evidence.

II

It is clear then that at present the history of the Huns
depends exclusively on what we are told by Greek and
Roman travellers and historians.

It may well be that, when the Huns began to expand
westwards in the seventies of the fourth century, Ammianus
Marcellinus had already decided to write the history of his
age. At any rate, when he composed his thirty-first book
about the year 395, he found it necessary to take account of
the new-comers and to offer his readers a description of
them. But he had no literary authorities to draw upon, for no
account of the history of the seventies of the century,
comparable in scale with Ammianus', had been published
before his own. Therefore we need have no hesitation in
supposing that, as he himself hints,[6] his description of the
Huns is something more than a re-hash of an earlier account.

The description is in fact justly famous and well worthy of
the great historian who wrote it. Its defect – if that be the
right term – is that, since Ammianus himself in all
probability had never in his life laid eyes upon a Hun, he

could not rely here upon his own observations. The chapter
therefore summarizes information which the historian had
obtained at second hand from military officers, civilian
officials, and others who had come in contact with the
strange new barbarians. These informants were not
infallible, and, although Ammianus doubtless relied on
witnesses as trustworthy as those who supplied him with
the information contained in the rest of his history, he is not
entirely free from error in his account of the Huns (xxxi. 2).
To take a notorious example, he tells us that the Huns ate
raw meat which they warmed a little by carrying it between
their saddles and their horses' backs as they rode on their
journeys. Although this story was long believed and is also
told of the Tartars of Tamburlaine's day, it is now known to
be false. This is an honest mistake, however, for the
historian's informants were misled by a deceptive custom of
the steppe horsemen, the nature of which has only been
elucidated in comparatively recent times.[7]

Ammianus has been accused of a more sinister type of
error. Since he loves to scatter throughout his work phrases
and sentences taken from earlier writers, and since such
flosculi occur in the chapter in question, it has been
concluded that he 'adhered to the traditional picture of the
Scythians and northern barbarians in general. He transferred
to them not only the stock epithets; he took also the
primitive traits which the Stoics found ennobling, and used
them as evidence of Hunnish savagery.'[8] Thus he attributes
to the Huns qualities which Pompeius Trogus had applied to
the Scythians,[9] and even ascribes to them a trait which Livy
had given to the Africans.[10] All this cannot be denied, but
what conclusion are we to draw from it? Let us beware of
blaming upon the historian the fact that many nomadic tribes
have many customs and attributes in common. Ammianus is
a candid writer, and where his information failed him, as in
his effort to solve the problem of the origin of the Huns, he is
not afraid to say so frankly. Moreover, he took the utmost
pains to procure accurate information on the various peoples

and provinces that he describes elsewhere in his book, and he included the results of his extensive reading as well as of his personal observations. There is no reason whatever to suppose that his account of the Huns is a solitary exception and that here alone he was indifferent to the accuracy of his narrative. The *flosculi* may or may not deserve criticism on literary and stylistic grounds: to the historian in this case they are immaterial. The portrait of the Huns which emerges from his chapter, although incomplete, as we shall see, is highly vivid and consistent, and Rostovtzeff is justified in calling it 'a masterly, entirely realistic description of their lifestyle'.[11] In the present book Ammianus' statements will be accepted as valid, except in the few instances (like that of the raw meat) where they can be proved false.

III

The information contained in Ammianus xxxi. 2 relates to Hun society as it existed between *c*.376, when they first came in contact with the Ostrogoths, and *c*.395, when Ammianus published the last instalment of his history. The first traveller whom we know to have published an account of a personal visit to the Huns is Olympiodorus of Egyptian Thebes. He served on an embassy sent out from Constantinople to the Hun king Donatus about the year 412, and when he came to write the history of his age some years later, he included in it a description of his mission and, apparently, an excursus on the Huns (frag. 18). The loss of Olympiodorus' work is a disaster for our knowledge of the nomads. He may indeed have displayed marked prejudices in narrating some controversial episodes of internal Roman history, but he had a passion for statistics and for geographical and chronological accuracy, and possessed a keen eye for social distinctions. Even in his meagre fragments we can detect traces of his precise terminology. He seems to have distinguished carefully between the military commander of a confederacy of barbarian tribes and the military leader of an individual tribe, calling the former φύλαρχος (ruler of a people) and the latter ῥήξ(king): the ῥῆγες (kings) of the Huns will present us with a problem later on (pp. 63–4 below). Furthermore, Olympiodorus was intimately acquainted with the affairs of the Western Roman Empire and knew the Latin language. These are facts of importance, for during the years covered by his work (407–25) the Huns devoted more of their unwelcome attention to the Western Empire than to the Eastern. It is clear then that his book, if it had survived, would have been of fundamental value.[12] However, we need not merely be content with the brief paraphrase of his description of the Huns which Photius has preserved for us. Zosimus and the ecclesiastical historian Sozomen fortunately made extensive use of his work, so that parts of their narratives are of extreme importance, coming as they do from so talented a source. We should remember, however, that Zosimus also made use of the history of Eunapius, who was endowed with more than a due share of human frailties. We must therefore be careful to distinguish between those parts of Zosimus' work which are based on Eunapius and those which paraphrase Olympiodorus.[13] Of Eunapius himself we need say nothing here: would that we could avoid him throughout.

IV

The last visitor to the Huns with whom we are concerned here is incomparably the most important for the study of Attila, but to understand the work of Priscus of Panium we must be clear as to one or two facts relating to the circumstances in which the late Greek historians produced their works. Their books were intended to be read only by the narrow circle of the educated, and, for reasons which we shall indicate later (p. 23 below), these educated readers expected certain canons of composition to be observed. Thus the conventional prose style, at the time when Priscus wrote, insisted on the avoidance of the expressions of the spoken tongue. In particular, masses of figures and technical terms of all kinds were to be excluded as being ruinous to a good style. It is Olympiodorus' merit to have discarded this convention and to have spoken boldly, for instance, about the ῥῆγες (kings) of the Huns. Unhappily Priscus did not follow him, and has thereby introduced an element of vagueness into his work where we should have liked him to be more specific.

On the other hand, citations of classical authors were regarded as an essential quality of a good style, and here Priscus gave his readers full measure. When his information failed him – and this was particularly the case with the movements of distant tribes and with the course of military operations[14] – he fell back on his reading and introduced into his work phrases and sentences culled from his favourite authors which were designed to tide him over his difficulties. It does not follow that every borrowed phrase to be found in his work – and a thorough search would reveal dozens – conceals a fact or series of facts which the historian was unable to discover from his informants and such documents as he was able to use. Nevertheless, the accounts of the siege of Naissus, the cause of the movements of the steppe tribes of the Saraguri, and so on (frags. 1 *b*, 30), show us that his work contained weaknesses. The reader will notice the sharp contrast with the methods of Ammianus. A *flosculus* in Ammianus' writings is merely an indication of his stylistic ambitions: he knew what he wanted to say, but he did not know how to express it and went to Livy or Tacitus for help. Priscus, on the other hand, quoted Herodotus or Thucydides when in fact he had nothing to say at all.

Some of these *flosculi* have misled recent historians. Thus there is a widespread view that in the fourth century and the early years of the fifth it was not the Huns as a whole who pushed westwards and subdued the Goths, but only their 'royal' families. Alföldi, for instance, writes: 'Here [in

Wallachia in 380] the flow of the people as a whole came to a halt; only the ruling clan moved itself forward thirty years later still further in a westerly direction and came as a result of this advance into direct contact with the Western Roman Empire.'[15] Now the only evidence for such a view is the recurrence of the phrase 'royal Scythians' (οἱ βασίλειοι Σκύθαι) in Priscus. It is exceedingly hazardous to base such a theory on this phrase. It is, of course, a mere *flosculus* taken indirectly from Herodotus, and a glance at Zosimus (iv. 20. 3) will show that it was Eunapius who first suggested the identification of the Huns of central Europe with the 'Royal Scythians' (βασίλειοι Σκύθαι) of Herodotus (iv. 20). That the phrase should be found in Priscus is merely one of several indications of his *literary* debt to Eunapius and Herodotus. As used by Priscus, the phrase refers to Attila and Bleda with or without their great lieutenants, and is never used as a collective term for *all* the Huns in central Europe.

Again, Priscus' use of the term 'Scythian' has introduced no little confusion into modern works, but here, I believe, the truth was found by Bury.[16] Bury pointed out that there is a distinction between Priscus' use of the terms 'Scythian' and 'Hun'. 'Scythian' was a generic term for all nomadic nations, and, as a great many different nomadic nations were united under the sovereignty of Attila, it was a very convenient term to apply to his subjects: the Huns were Scythians, but all Scythians were not Huns. Most scholars, however, reject this distinction and believe that the term 'Hun' is used indiscriminately for any northern nomadic barbarian. But this shows a misunderstanding of the canons of historiography in the time when Priscus was writing. At that date the term 'Hun' had not yet been sanctified by use in the classical historians. It was still a new and barbarous name which no one would introduce into his work if he could avoid it. Later on, when the works of Priscus and the like became classics in their turn, we find historians using the word 'Hun' precisely as Priscus uses the word 'Scythian': it had then become a term sanctified by long usage and was familiar to every reader, and so could be employed in place of such new and uncouth names as Turk, Khazar, Petcheneg, and the like.[17] We must assume then that when Priscus says 'Hun' he means it, and accordingly we cannot follow those numerous scholars who believe that the Acatziri were not Huns and that Edeco was a German, despite Priscus' statements to the contrary.[18]

From what sources did Priscus receive his information? We do not know whether he was able to use written authorities for the earlier period covered by his book. Evagrius (ii. 1; cf. v. 24) tells us that the history of Marcian's reign was written by 'others' in addition to Priscus, and one or several of these unknown historians may have published before him. At any rate, his accurate knowledge of the many treaties made with the Huns would seem to show that he was able to draw on official records for information about them. He might also have derived more or less valuable information from the countless speeches, panegyrics, pamphlets, historical and other poems, and the like, which were turned out on so many occasions. But on the whole it is safest to assume that Priscus gathered most of his information painfully from interviews with participants in the events which he describes, in so far as he was not an eyewitness himself. Thus Bigilas, the interpreter, must have been his source for the highly secret conversations between Chrysaphius and Edeco, whom the eunuch tried to induce to murder Attila; we know that Bigilas was present at these conversations and that he afterwards spoke of the matter to the historian.[19] If we grant that oral sources supplied him with most of his information it follows that we must treat his references to the history of the far West with especial caution.[20] The famous account of his own journey to Attila, of course, falls into a category of its own. This account is so detailed and minute that few will disagree with Hodgkin's assertion (p. 60, n. 1) that Priscus was jotting down notes from day to day and almost from hour to hour while the embassy was still in progress. It would have been all but impossible for him to have remembered the incidents of the journey so vividly and in such detail had he not written down copious notes on the spot.

It may be that Bury has overstated the virtues of Priscus when he claims him as the greatest historical writer of the period.[21] The fact that so few chronological indications have survived in his fragments is a sinister sign. His lack of exact specification in the matter of Greek renderings of Roman official titles, his more or less inadequate geographical data, his incompetence as a military historian, the fact that he approved, as we shall see, of the disastrous social organization of the later empire – all these features of his work combine to give the *Byzantine History* a lower place in our estimation than the *Raw Materials for a History*. (῞Υλη Συγγραφῆς) of Olympiodorus. None the less, his merits are striking. There is no need to emphasize the vigour and lucidity of his narrative. He is, as Bury says, a master of narrative. Nor need we dwell on his qualities in expounding the course of East Roman diplomacy, or on the vast mass of reliable facts which his work contained when it existed in its entirety. The history of eastern Europe in the middle of the fifth century is a subject of great difficulty: without the fragments of Priscus we should be lost. Other writers tell us isolated facts pertaining to secular affairs in that age: Priscus alone gives us a history.

V

Apart from the chroniclers, all later historians who supply us with information of interest about the Huns derived their knowledge from the work of Priscus. Hence they require little comment here.

Published soon after 476 – frag. 42 could not have been written until Basiliscus had fallen – Priscus' book won immediate fame even in the West. It was heavily drawn upon by Cassiodorus, the primary source of Jordanes. The latter names Priscus half a dozen times, and Mommsen[22] has well analysed his debt to him. He points out that Jordanes has nothing to say about Attila which is not taken from Priscus, and that there are no traces of Priscus in him save those which refer to Attila. The first passage of the *Getica* (§§ 178–228), which is taken from Priscus, contains a sketch of Attila's character and a narrative of his expedition to Gaul, while the second (§§ 254–63) tells of Attila's death and burial and of the dissolution of his empire. Mommsen has admirably illustrated the superiority of Jordanes' style in these parts of his work – the vivid characterization of the Huns, the beautiful song sung at Attila's funeral, the scrupulous motivization of events, the care with which conjecture is said to be such, the admirable *sententiae*, the happy similes. When we reach these two passages of Jordanes' work, says Mommsen, 'from the world of the barbarian we appear to return to civilization, and to hear educated tones in place of the stilted monk of Moesia'. This praise, of course, is only relative: Mommsen is thinking of Jordanes' achievements in the other parts of his work. Even in the passages which are based on Priscus Jordanes displays his genius for misunderstanding the most straightforward narrative his source could supply to him.

In the Eastern Empire John Malalas was among those who knew and valued the work of Priscus, but he had read it to such purpose that he believed Attila to have been, not a Hun, but a Gepid.[23] Evagrius pays tribute to the accuracy of Priscus' account of Attila's career,[24] and although he says that the period was covered by other writers, too, it was to Priscus that he went for most of his facts pertaining to the secular history of the mid-fifth century.[25] Unfortunately, the epithets which he uses of Priscus' style are applied by him indiscriminately to so many other writers (including himself) that we do not know what specific features of the work appealed to him particularly. Finally, John of Antioch used the *Byzantine History* as one of his sources, and three of his fragments overlap three of the fragments of Priscus. This is fortunate, for John simply transcribed his authorities' works, so that he preserves the actual words of Priscus, and thereby helps us to solve an important chronological problem.[26]

What is truly surprising is the fact that Procopius went elsewhere for his knowledge – such as it is – of the mid-fifth century,[27] a fact which has had an unfortunate effect on some parts of his work. Thus he places the great Hun advance of *c*.376 *after* the settlement of the Vandals in Africa, and he dates Attila's siege of Aquileia *after* the death of Aetius, which, as Gibbon justly says, is 'an inexcusable mistake'.[28] The student of the Huns can hope for little help from Procopius.

Such, in brief, are our main authorities for reconstructing the history of Attila and the Huns. It is to be hoped that, after further study, the archaeologists will be able to contribute appreciably more to our knowledge.[29] But it may be urged that we do not merely require to be told whether such and such an article was used by the Huns. We also want to know whether it was *made* by them, and, if so, where the raw material came from, in what circumstances the Huns acquired it, and in what conditions they worked it into the finished article. Even in the present state of our knowledge, however, we should indeed be fortunate if we were as well acquainted with the other barbarian invaders of the fifth century as we are with Attila and the Huns.

2

The History of the Huns before Attila

I

'The nation of the Huns, scarcely known to ancient documents, dwelt beyond the Maeotic marshes beside the frozen ocean, and surpassed every extreme of ferocity.'[1] Ammianus makes no attempt to derive the Huns from the depths of Asia. He offers no wild equation of them with any of the barbarous peoples who had been known long ago. In the course of his wide reading he had rarely, if indeed ever, come across their name. He may have had his private view as to their origin, but, if so, he could base it on no satisfactory evidence, and he therefore says simply that they dwelt in that region in which they had been living when they first became known to history. For him their story began in eastern Europe, north or north-east of the Sea of Azov, and they lived near the Northern Ocean. Why they left this home he does not even conjecture.

Where Ammianus had feared to tread, Eunapius did not hesitate to rush in. There is a story, professing to explain the first appearance of the Huns, which can be read in every age of East Roman historical literature. It is to be found in

Sozomen and Zosimus, in Priscus, and, after him, in Jordanes. It reappears in Procopius and Agathias. Its course was not stopped by the Arab invasions. It may be read in Simeon the Logothete, both in the Slavonic version and in the Greek versions of Leo Grammaticus and Theodosius of Melitene. Thence it passes to Cedrenus and is finally found at the beginning of the fourteenth century in the *Ecclesiastical History* of Nicephorus Callistus Xanthopoulos.[2] Few stories of equal value have had so long a life.

According to this tale, the Goths and the Huns had long lived side by side without either knowing of the other's existence. They were separated by the Straits of Kerch, and each nation thought that there was no land over the horizon. But one day it happened that a heifer belonging to the Huns was stung by a gadfly and fled through the marshy water to the opposite shore. Its herdsman followed it, and, finding land where it was believed that none existed, he came back and told his fellow countrymen. The story offered an alternative. According to the second version, some Hunnic huntsmen in pursuit of a stag were led across the straits by the flight of their quarry. They were amazed by the mild climate and fertile soil of the land to which they had come, and returned with the good news of its existence to their fellow Huns. Whether a heifer or a stag were the guilty party, the Huns soon after crossed the straits in force and attacked the Gothic inhabitants of the Crimea.[3]

Now this story originated in the history of Eunapius, and we are fortunate in possessing a fragment of the part of his work where he was discussing the origin of the Huns.[4] He states frankly that no one can give any clear account of their origin or of the country in which they were living when they set out on the conquest of Europe. In these circumstances, he says, he had recourse at first to τὰ παλαιά, and gave as plausible an account as he could at the beginning of his work. Later, however, he revised his opinion in the light of τὰ ἀπαγγελλόμενα, and this second account he believed to be the more satisfactory. What are we to understand by these terms? Vasiliev (pp. 24ff) is too kind to Eunapius, for he paraphrases τὰ παλαιά as 'the information about the Huns given by ancient writers from whom he borrowed data, in his opinion, reliable'. Alas, τὰ παλαιά means no such thing, as Vasiliev himself has enabled us to see. When Eunapius turned to τὰ παλαιά, it was not the historians to whom he had recourse, but the poets. Vasiliev (pp. 29ff) draws attention to a sentence which occurs in Sozomen's version of the story: 'And when it chanced that a heifer ran across the marsh stung by a gadfly, its herdsman followed it.' The word οἰστροπλήξ, 'stung by a gadfly', is taken from Aeschylus in his story of Io, who had herself crossed this very strait 'stung by a gadfly'. We must agree with Vasiliev that the story is merely an adaptation of the old tale of Io as Aeschylus had told it.[5] Eunapius then had placed at the beginning of his work an invention of his own to explain the first appearance of the Huns, and there it remained and was read, although he himself subsequently changed his opinion in the light of τὰ ἀπαγγελλόμενα, the reports about the Huns which later reached him. It would be unnecessary to add that the tale throws no light on the Huns' attack on the Crimea, were it not that some scholars assume from it that the nomads crossed over the Straits of Kerch in winter when the water was frozen.[6] The only legitimate conclusion we can draw is that, even in the earliest years of the fifth century, no one knew precisely how the Huns had come to attack the Ostrogoths.

From later versions of Eunapius' story we can see that he made several attempts to identify the Huns with various peoples known in antiquity. Thus Zosimus says on his authority that we must identify the Huns either with the 'Royal Scyths' or with the 'Snub-nosed men', both mentioned by Herodotus, or else we must simply suppose that they originated in Asia and crossed thence to Europe.[7] Philostorgius reports an additional speculation which we can scarcely doubt is also drawn from Eunapius. He is inclined to equate the Huns with the Nebroi of old, whom

Herodotus had mentioned as an all but mythical people living at the extreme edge of Scythia.[8] Of Eunapius we can say at any rate that he did his utmost for his readers. At least four suggestions as to the origin of the Huns – three of them based on Herodotus – were offered by him, and those readers who were not satisfied by at least one of them must have been, by Eunapius' historical standards, very difficult persons indeed.

The Eunapian theories, although they dominated later thought on the subject, did not entirely exclude other speculations. Quite apart from them stands the view of Orosius. He mentions the Huns as living in the neighbour-hood of the Caucasus, and he believes that the reason for their descent upon the Goths and the Romans was no mystery but a thoroughly obvious and well-deserved punishment for the sins of the world. The Huns had long been shut up in inaccessible mountains, but God sent them forth as a punishment for our iniquities.[9] Many Christians must have believed likewise, but a greater Christian than Orosius went back to Herodotus for information about the Huns. Jerome equates them with those Scythians who, according to Herodotus, held the East captive for twenty years and exacted an annual tribute from Egypt and Ethiopia.[10] Procopius added to the cloud of conjectures by proposing that the new invaders were no others than the Cimmerians.[11] This was exact historical inquiry in compar-ison with what was to come, for as time went on, scholarship went to more and more desperate lengths in its effort to solve the mystery. It was a small matter that Constantine VII Porphyrogennetos thought that Attila was the king of the Avars and that his conquests resulted in the foundation of Venice.[12] Even more curious was the view of Constantine Manasses, himself a poet. According to Manasses, Sesostris, king of Egypt, made allies of the Huns, and, after subduing Asia, gave them the land of Assyria and changed their name to 'Parthians'.[13] This train of thought was pushed to its logical conclusion by John Tzetzes in the twelfth century:

according to this scholar the Huns fought in the Trojan war, for Achilles had come to Troy leading an army of Huns, Bulgars, and Myrmidons.[14]

Leaving aside these later fancies, let us return to the earlier speculations, for they call for some comment. Did Eunapius and his followers really believe that the Huns were identical with the Nebroi, the Simoi, and the others? Did one of the most eminent bishops of the fifth century, whom we shall discuss presently (p. 41), really believe that the Huns ate their parents? It may be doubted. Greek inquirers at that time did not consider it their duty to venture out into the steppe and discover the exact truth about the ferocious barbarians who roamed there. An Ammianus or an Olympiodorus might have somewhat higher standards than their contemporaries; in general, however, neither the historians nor their public demanded the precise truth in descriptions of the northern nomads. But every writer considered it his duty to display his knowledge of the classics which were the heritage of his class. It was their possession of the classical authors which distinguished the educated class from the other inhabitants of the world. 'You know well', writes Libanius to the Caesar Julian in 358, 'that if anyone extinguishes our literature, we are put on a level with the barbarians', and a century later the same sentiments are current among the well-to-do. Sidonius writes to a correspondent: 'When the grades of office have been taken away from us, by which the highest used to be distinguished from the lowest, then the only indication of nobility will be a knowledge of literature.'[15] To equate the Huns with the Massagetae, to believe of them what Herodotus had believed of the nomads of old, to decorate one's account of their wars with the phrases of Thucydides, was not a sign of childish credulity or indescribable stupidity. It was an indication that the writer belonged to that social class which Sidonius equates with the community of Rome, 'the only community in the whole world', he says, 'in which slaves and barbarians are the only strangers'.[16]

Let us turn to the Goths. They did not possess the works of an Aeschylus or an Herodotus upon which to base their speculations. Instead there circulated among them a folk-tale which has survived in Jordanes.[17] According to this tale there was once a Gothic king called Filimer, who ruled over his people in the fifth generation after they had emigrated from Scandinavia. Among his subjects he discovered certain witches, who were called in the Gothic language 'Haliur-unnae'.[18] These he expelled from among his people and drove them far into the solitude of the Scythian desert. Some evil spirits, who were wandering about the wilderness, saw these witches and fell upon them, so that they brought forth this most ferocious of all races, 'a race of puny, offensive, and poverty-stricken half-men'. Whatever the source of Jordanes, few will doubt that this was a story told by the horrified Goths, amazed at the ferocity of their masters.[19]

In view of all this wild sea of speculation it is difficult not to admire the restraint of Ammianus: 'The nation of the Huns, scarcely known to ancient documents, dwelt beyond the Maeotic marshes beside the frozen ocean, and surpassed every extreme of ferocity.'

II

It was the practice then for those historians who wrote for an educated public to substitute the old familiar names given by Herodotus and Thucydides in place of the uncouth names of contemporary barbarians. The reverse was customary among those historians whose works were intended to be read only by humble monks and laymen. It was idle to speak to them of Nebroi and Simoi and Neuroi, of whom they had never heard. But everyone knew of the Huns, the Gepids, and the like, and so we often find John Malalas and other writers whose works were read by the uneducated calling earlier barbarian peoples by the names of tribes dreaded in their own day – even if the latter had been quite unknown at the time spoken of.[20] This is why we read in John Malalas that Lucius Verus and the Emperor Carus met their deaths when fighting against the Huns.[21] So, too, we hear from an anonymous popular writer that Constantine the Great crossed the Danube and conquered the land of the Huns.[22] Such statements we may confidently ignore. But it used to be held by modern scholars that when Dionysius Periegetes mentions the 'Tocharoi, Phrounoi, and barbarous nations of Seres'[23] he means by Phrounoi the Hsiung-nu, who are often equated with the Huns. This view has now been exploded and abandoned.[24] Dionysius, in his editions, also mentions the Οὗννοι as living near the Caspian Sea, but it has now been proved that in fact he there wrote Οὐίτιοι, a name which soon became meaningless and was altered by scribes to one of which the meaning was only too well understood.[25] We are left with a passage of Ptolemy (iii. 5. 10), where we read that 'between the Bastarnae and the Roxolani [are] the Chuni', Χοῦνοι or Χουνοί. On the basis of this text it is confidently asserted that early in the second century AD the Huns were already settled in the Pontic area, perhaps between the Bug and the Dniester. But it seems very doubtful whether they could have survived there for two hundred years without becoming known in any way to the Romans. If, in fact, they were close neighbours of the Bastarnae and Roxolani, why did their appearance towards the close of the fourth century cause so much surprise? Again, they are placed by Ptolemy in a very unexpected area if in fact they were the ancestors of the Huns, who, beyond all question, were settled in or near the basin of the Kuban when they first became known to the Goths. It may be suggested that the similarity of the names Χοῦνοι and Οὗννοι is merely a coincidence; and it should be noted that, although West Roman writers often refer to the *Chunni* or *Chuni*, no East Roman ever has the guttural at the beginning of the name.[26]

Whatever be the truth of Ptolemy's Χοῦνοι, we need have little hesitation in rejecting Seeck's suggestion that the Persians and the Romans had already encountered the Huns

in the year 363. In that year Jovian signed his notorious truce
with Sapor, the Persian king, and in the treaty it was
stipulated that the Romans and the Persians should unite in
building fortifications in the passes of the Caucasus so as to
prevent Armenia being overrun by the incursions 'of those
barbarians who are unknown both to us and to the
Persians'.[27] These barbarians were not the Huns who later
invaded Europe, but the Kidarites or Black Huns who were
to preoccupy the Persian kings throughout the course of the
following century. Not only the origin of the true Huns, but
also their movements and activities before the last quarter of
the fourth century, remain as profound a mystery to us as
they were to Ammianus.

III

In the year 376 reports reached the Roman officers
commanding the Danube garrisons that new and unusually
large movements had begun among the northern barbarians.
It was said that all the peoples between the Theiss and the
Black Sea were in commotion. A savage people of great
ferocity had struck the nations with terror and sent them
fleeing from their homes. The officers received the news with
indifference. They rarely heard of barbarian wars beyond the
great river until the fighting had completely died down or
had at least come to a temporary close. Their experience told
them that no exceptional events could be expected. But the
rumours persisted, and then the first refugees appeared on
the northern bank, begging to be taken into the safety of the
empire. The first fugitives were joined by others and yet
others, until an immense multitude crowded on the bank of
the river.[28] The officers had been mistaken. The Gothic
kingdom of Ermanarich had fallen before the Huns.

Ermanarich was not the first victim. Before him, the Alans
had been reduced to subjection. The western frontier of this
people was the river Don; the eastern lay beyond the

knowledge of Roman inquirers and was said to be outside Europe altogether.[29] The Alans were typical nomads, and drove their flocks and herds to new pastures every spring and autumn. They had no temples, but worshipped a naked sword stuck in the ground. Otherwise they were not remarkable, except that at one time they had not known the institution of slavery.[30] They had often attacked Bosporus in the Crimea, and even Armenia and Media, so that the Romans knew them, like other nomads, as unconquerable warriors. But they had been conquered now. At a date and in circumstances which have not been recorded, they became the subjects of the Huns. We only know that vast numbers of them were slaughtered before the nation submitted.

It seems to have been soon after the year 370 that the Huns, accompanied by contingents of their Alan subjects, began their assault on the rich villages of the great Ostrogothic kingdom. This newly built empire stretched from the Don to the Dniester and from the Black Sea to the Pripet marshes.[31] It was attacked first by small parties of the Huns, but soon had to bear their full assault.[32] The aged Gothic king, Ermanarich, although unnerved by the rumours of the Huns' savagery which had reached him, was able to maintain himself for a considerable time, but then in despair he committed suicide and was succeeded by his great-nephew Vithimiris.[33] The Alans were being made to fight in the van of the Huns, and Vithimiris met them with an army composed partly of some Huns whom he had hired to fight for him against their countrymen. With these and his own followers he went into battle again and again, but each time met with a severe and bloody defeat. Finally, in a battle said to have been fought on a certain river Erac, somewhere between the Dnieper and Dniester, when he had reigned only about a year, he was killed.[34] Most of the Ostrogothic nation now submitted to the nomads, but the story that was told afterwards, that they voluntarily abandoned the struggle, is only a Gothic fable designed to explain away their crushing defeat.[35]

The remainder were now ruled by Vithimiris' son Viderichus, but, as he was still a child, the command of the army was entrusted to Alatheus and Saphrax. Despite the skill and courage of Alatheus and Saphrax, the Goths were gradually forced back behind the river Dniester.[36]

This brought the Huns to the frontiers of Athanaric, the chieftain (*iudex*) of the Visigoths. Athanaric determined to resist the new invaders if he too should be attacked, and he established himself on the banks of the Dniester not far from Alatheus and Saphrax. His first move was to send some of his chief men, led by one Munderich, at the head of a considerable force, some twenty miles beyond the river, with instructions to report on the movements of the enemy and to screen the main body of the army as it prepared its defences. The Huns at once realized that Munderich's force was but a fraction of the Gothic army, and decided to ignore it. Riding hard through a moonlit night, they completely outmanoeuvred and eluded Munderich, and, before he could even discover their whereabouts, they had forded the Dniester twenty miles in his rear. Athanaric had no suspicion of his danger. He and his army were stunned by the surprise of the Huns' attack. There was no resistance: the Goths scattered to the Carpathian foot-hills behind them with slight losses.[37] Alatheus and Saphrax appear to have been crushed simultaneously.

Athanaric next decided to build and defend a wall between the Gerasus (Pruth) and the Danube. The work was hurried on with skill and vigour; but again the troops were surprised and would have been massacred, had it not been for the weight of the Huns' booty, which prevented them from carrying out their usual swift manoeuvres.[38]

The Goths were panic-stricken: they could resist no longer. They melted away from Athanaric, and with their families and their goods began to stream towards the Danube. In the fertile fields of Thrace, secured by the broad Danube and the strength of the Roman garrisons, they would escape from this 'race of men, which had never been seen before . . . , which had arisen from some secret corner of the earth, and was sweeping away and destroying everything that came in its way'.[39]

As more and more of them reached the Danube, the Roman officers on its southern bank began to realize that the reports, which they had heard with contempt,[40] were nothing more than the truth.

IV

In the autumn of 376 the Goths, said by contemporaries to number 200,000, were permitted to cross the Danube, and two years later, on 9 August 378, they engaged the Emperor ·Valens on the plains outside Adrianople.[41] Did the Huns take any part in this greater Cannae?

In the autumn of 377 the Goths were penned in among the defiles of Mount Haemus in Thrace by a Roman army.[42] Their position was desperate. They had no food, and all their efforts to break through the ring formed by the Romans had been beaten back. When they were reduced to the last extremities some of their number managed to slip through the enemy lines and arrange an alliance with a body of Huns and Alans who were roaming the land north of the Danube. The Gothic emissaries held out hopes of immense booty if the nomads would rescue them from their critical position in Thrace. The effect of this alliance was striking. As soon as the Roman commanders heard of it, they at once began to withdraw their men cautiously. The Goths escaped from the trap in which they had been caught, and began once again to devastate the unlucky countryside of Thrace.[43]

Now the band of Huns which thus dramatically rescued the Goths is not reported to have left them before the battle of Adrianople. Immediately after the battle, when the Goths had made a vain effort to surprise Adrianople itself, we hear of these same Huns again: a few days after the great victory they are found still in the company of the Goths.[44] We cannot doubt that they had been with them all the time, and it is not impossible that the cavalry charge which decided the greatest disaster in Roman military history was headed, not by only Goths, but by Huns. That our sources say nothing of this is not surprising: the Roman disaster was so complete that no one could afterwards give a clear or accurate account of what had happened.[45]

We hear little of the Huns in the years which immediately followed. We are assured explicitly, however, that they took their full share in the plundering and devastation of the north Balkan provinces in the period after Adrianople.[46] Theodosius I was proclaimed emperor on 19 January 379, and in his first year, we are told, he defeated several bands of Huns, Alans, and Goths, who were still devastating the Balkans, and was able to proclaim considerable victories on 15 November. It would seem that companies of the Sciri and Carpodacae were serving in a subordinate position, like the Alans, under the Huns,[47] who themselves behaved with their usual ferocity: they were 'more violent in every destruction', according to a contemporary.[48] It is said by a later authority that in the year 427 the Huns had been in occupation of Pannonia for fifty years.[49] The statement has been vigorously denied,[50] but if we remember that a few years after the accession of Theodosius I a company of Huns is found approaching the frontiers of Gaul, it seems reasonable to suppose that on the morrow of Adrianople great tracts of Pannonia, especially the eastern regions, had already fallen under their sway.[51]

Although we hear once or twice of the 'roving fierceness of the Huns' in the years which followed,[52] it was not until 395 that the new barbarians launched their first great invasion of the Roman Empire, and their raids of that year seem to have been conducted on a bigger scale than any others until the days of Attila. In the winter of 395 the Danube was frozen, and the Huns took the opportunity of crossing into the Roman provinces and renewing the devastation which Theodosius had barely managed to check. Once again

Thrace bore the brunt of the suffering, but Dalmatia, too, feared an invasion.[53] Claudian maliciously suggests that the Huns were actually invited into the empire by the praetorian prefect Rufinus, whose position was being violently assailed by Stilicho. But this is merely the propaganda of the poet in favour of his patron, and we know that Rufinus did what he could to alleviate the fearful hardships of the peasants of Thrace.[54]

The Huns put out their greatest effort, however, far to the east. Pouring over the passes of the Caucasus, their bands overran Armenia and made for the richest provinces of the Eastern Empire. The smoke rose from the villages of Cappadocia. The invaders were said to have approached the Halys. Areas of Syria itself were devastated, and Antioch looked to her defences: 'the enemy's cavalry thunders along the banks of the Orontes, home hitherto of dance and a happy people's song'.[55] Crowds of captives and great herds of cattle were led away north of the Caucasus. 'Beyond the Cimmerian marshes, defence of the Tauric tribes, the youth of Syria are slaves.'[56] In Armenia the Huns reached the city of Melitene; thence they overran the province of Euphratesia and even galloped into Coele Syria and Cilicia.[57] Jerome writes vividly of this raid:

Behold, the wolves, not of Arabia, but of the North, were let loose upon us last year from the far-off rocks of Caucasus, and in a little while overran great provinces. How many monasteries were captured, how many streams were reddened with human blood! Antioch was besieged, and the other cities washed by the Halys, Cydnus, Orontes, and Euphrates. Flocks of captives were dragged away; Arabia, Phoenicia, Palestine, and Egypt were taken captive by their terror. Not even if I had a hundred tongues and a hundred mouths, and a voice of iron could I recount the name of every catastrophe.

And again:

Lo, suddenly messengers ran to and fro and the whole East trembled, for swarms of Huns had broken forth from the far distant Maeotis between the icy Tanais and the monstrous peoples of the Massagetae, where the Gates of Alexander pen in the wild nations behind the rocks of Caucasus. They filled the whole earth with slaughter and panic alike as they flitted hither and thither on their swift horses. The Roman army was away at the time and was detained in Italy owing to the civil wars. . . . May Jesus avert such beasts from the Roman world in the future! They were at hand everywhere before they were expected: by their speed they outstripped rumour, and they took pity neither upon religion nor rank nor age nor wailing childhood. Those who had just begun to live were compelled to die and, in ignorance of their plight, would smile amid the drawn swords of the enemy. There was a unanimous report that they were making for Jerusalem and that they were converging on that city owing to their extreme greed for gold. The walls of Antioch, neglected in the idle times of peace, were hastily patched up; Tyre wished to break away again from the land and looked for her ancient island. Then we ourselves were forced to make ships ready, to wait on the shore, to take precautions against the enemy's arrival, to fear the barbarians more than shipwreck even though the winds were raging.[58]

As Jerome says, there was no regular army to meet them: Theodosius, at his death, had left the armies of the empire in the West. An important officer in the East was suspected of cowardice and of indifference to the lot of the country under his command.[59] At any rate, the invasion was unopposed[60] until the eunuch Eutropius, hastily assembling a few Gothic troops[61] and whatever Roman soldiers he could lay hands on, succeeded in taking the field against them.[62] He failed to recover the booty they had taken,[63] but peace was restored to the East at the end of 398,[64] and the world saw a eunuch as consul in 399.

For some thirteen years the Huns do not appear to have raided the Eastern provinces again, but in the first years of the new century they seem to have undertaken a tremendous drive through central Europe towards the West from their recently conquered homes in the northern Balkans. Scenes similar to those of 376 were witnessed again. In the closing months of 405 Radagaisus broke into Italy, and terrified contemporaries said that he headed 400,000 men, though more sober judgements put the figure far lower. On 31 December 406 swarms of Vandals, Sueves, and Alans broke the Rhine frontier for ever and crowded into Gaul. These movements, it is agreed,[65] were caused by a westward expansion of the Huns, but only one hint has survived in our authorities of the fierce battles by which the Germans were dislodged from their homes and sent fleeing into the provinces of the Roman Empire. Orosius, in reference to this period, writes: 'I say nothing of the many internecine conflicts between the barbarians themselves, when two divisions of the Goths, and then the Alans and Huns, destroyed one another in mutual slaughter.'[66]

Attacks on the lower Danube provinces were resumed in 408. In that year a certain Uldin, the first Hun whom we know by name and one whom we shall have to mention frequently again, crossed the Danube and captured Castra Martis, a fortress lying well back from the river in the province of Moesia.[67] He took this place by treachery, and unhappily we do not know who it was that co-operated with him and betrayed the fort. Uldin then proceeded to overrun Thrace, and, when the Romans tried to buy him off, he rejected their offer: when the Roman officer commanding the army in Thrace made his proposals to him, the Hun merely pointed towards the rising sun and said that, if he so wished, he would find it easy to subdue all the land which the sun looked upon. He demanded an impossible sum as the price of peace, but the Roman officer was not at a loss. He prolonged his conversations with Uldin, and entered into secret negotiations with the subordinate leaders in the enemy's army. He emphasized the great humanity of the Roman Emperor and the very acceptable gifts which that Emperor was accustomed to offer to brave men. His suggestions were agreeable. Many of Uldin's followers deserted, and he himself only escaped across the Danube with difficulty. He lost many Huns and a considerable number of Sciri who were serving under him in much the same capacity as we have seen the Alans serving in other Hun armies.[68]

We have more than one memorial of the East Roman government's efforts to repair the damage done by Uldin and to prevent the recurrence of such raids as his. Herculius, the praetorian prefect of Illyricum, a patron of letters and the arts, was instructed to force everyone, without distinction of rank, to take part in the rebuilding of city walls and in the collection and transport of food to the ruined areas. The emperor, instructed by his praetorian prefect Anthemius, expected that many would endeavour to evade this work, and he therefore repeats: 'this burden will apply to all from the highest to the lowest'. The raid may be repeated: the moment is critical.[69] Anthemius issued further orders. Every possible method of entering the Eastern Empire is to be scrutinized; every place where the provinces can be approached – 'all naval bases, harbours, shores, all points of departure from the provinces, even remote places and islands' – is to be guarded closely because of the barbarous savagery.[70] Specific measures were taken for the strengthening of the Danube fleet. A seven-year programme of shipbuilding was published on 28 January 412. In the provinces of Moesia and Scythia, which bordered on the great river, a stated number of vessels, both warships and supply ships (*naves agrarienses*, as they are called), were to be built every year and a stated number of old ships to be repaired. Over two hundred vessels were to be in service at the end of seven years, and local officials were to be heavily fined if the programme was not fully carried out each year.[71] But Anthemius' greatest achievement in these years was the construction of the Theodosian walls on the land side of Constantinople, which had long since extended beyond the original wall of Constantine. The need for them had been felt as early as the time of Theodosius I,[72] but it was not until 4 April 413 that the government could refer to the completion of the new wall, 'which has been constructed for the defence of this most splendid city'.[73] Who can doubt that it was Uldin's raid that impressed upon Anthemius the urgent necessity of the defence of the capital? Bury justly says that 'in planning the new walls of the capital, he was preparing consciously for the Hunnic war which he foresaw'.[74]

After the defeat and disappearance of Uldin we come to one of the obscurest incidents in the history of the Huns. Priscus heard of it from a West Roman, Romulus, whom he met in Attila's encampment in 449 and of whom he held a high opinion. Romulus told him that the Huns had once, πάλαι, sought to attack Persia at a time when famine prevailed in their own country and the Romans were engaged in a war. Under two leaders named Basich and Cursich, who afterwards went to Rome to obtain an alliance, a large Hun army entered a desert country, passed a certain lake, which Romulus thought might be the Maeotic Sea, and after fifteen days crossed some mountains and found themselves in Persia. After devastating the land, they encountered a Persian army which filled the air over their heads with arrows. The Huns were beaten back and recrossed the mountains with only a little of their booty, for the Persians succeeded in recovering most of it. Fearing a pursuit, Basich and Cursich returned home by a different route, which appears to have led them past the oil country of Baku.[75] This expedition seems to have taken place about the period 415–20 or a little later.

In 420 the Eastern Roman Empire went to war with Persia. The Persians had been taking the merchandise from the Roman traders in their dominions and had refused to return the Roman gold-miners whose services they had hired. In addition, they had begun a general persecution of the Christians in Persia.[76] As the Roman armies became more and more deeply involved in the East, the northern frontier seems to have been stripped of its defenders, and this was doubtless the reason why the Huns in 422, after a long interval, again launched a plundering raid on Thrace.[77] We have no details and know nothing of how they were expelled. We hear of no further hostilities on the northern frontier of the Eastern Empire before the appearance of Rua, the uncle of Attila.

V

The little that our authorities enable us to say about the wars
between the Romans and the Huns before the days of Attila
has been summarized above. But in the early days of their life
in Europe the Huns by no means appear exclusively as the
enemies of the Romans, Goths, or Persians. We have already
seen that, although Huns destroyed the kingdom of the
Ostrogoths, Huns also fought in its defence. In their first
great achievement in Europe the new barbarians were
divided against themselves. So it continued throughout the
entire period at present under review, a fact which was noted
by contemporaries with surprise and satisfaction.[78]

We have seen that Theodosius I, in his first year as
emperor, managed to drive the Hun raiders from the
northern Balkans and that his reign was frequently troubled
by them thereafter. But he also used them as allies. When he
engaged the army of the usurper Maximus on the river Save
in 388, his very swift cavalry victory was won by Hunnic
horsemen serving in his army.[79] It may well be, as Seeck
suggests, that, after the victory over Maximus' brother
Marcellinus at Poetovio in that same year, it was Hunnic
cavalry that inflicted the heavy losses suffered by the fleeing
enemy.[80] Again, towards the end of the eighties officers of
Valentinian II beat back a party of Huns who were
approaching Gaul, while at the same time Bauto, the
Master of the Soldiers, succeeded in inducing an army of
Huns to attack the Juthungi, who were then devastating the
Roman province of Raetia.[81]

We have already mentioned the defeat of Uldin in 408. But
Uldin's history had a beginning and a middle as well as an
end. In the year 400 the German rebel Gainas attempted to
cross into Asia Minor, but was deterred by the warships of
the imperial fleet. He therefore retreated northwards and
crossed the Danube with a small body of followers. Here he
was met by Uldin, who decided to attack him for two

reasons. He did not wish an independent barbarian army to roam at large north of the Danube, and he believed that, by chasing away Gainas, he would do a service to the Eastern Emperor. He therefore collected his forces and fought the German, not once but many times, before he succeeded in slaying him. Gainas' head was displayed to view in Constantinople on 3 January 401, and in return Uldin demanded 'gifts', which, in fact, he received. An alliance was thereupon concluded between him and the East Romans, and it may be supposed that it involved the payment of an annual tribute to this body of the nomads.[82] The credit for the overthrow of Gainas did not belong exclusively to the Hun. The reason why the Germans had to turn northwards towards the Danube in the first place lay in the initiative of the local city magistrates and of the urban population of Thrace. Foreseeing the arrival of Gainas' band, the citizens hastily repaired the defences of their cities, and themselves manned them with their weapons in their hands. 'Owing to previous raids', says our authority, 'they were not unpractised in warfare, and applied themselves to the struggle with all their strength. Gainas found nothing outside the walls except grass,' he goes on, 'for everyone had taken care to bring inside the walls all the crops and the livestock and all the furniture and equipment of the farmsteads.' Evidently the events of 395 had taught the townsmen of Thrace a lesson which they were not slow to learn. Neither were they quick to forget it, as Attila many years later had good reason to observe when his horsemen were beaten back by the initiative and courage of the citizens of Asemus.[83]

Uldin next appears in the service of West Rome. At the end of 405 Radagaisus and a huge throng of Germans, fleeing before the Huns, as we have seen, descended into Italy. The cities of the peninsula were panic-stricken, but Stilicho, as well as mobilizing the forces at his disposal in Italy, managed to make an alliance with a body of Huns and Alans: these Huns were the followers of Uldin. In the battle of Faesulae early in 406 they showed their mettle. They first prevented the Germans from collecting provisions, and then in the conflict itself a swift outflanking movement by their cavalry enabled Stilicho to encircle the enemy and destroy them with the utmost carnage. Uldin's men sold off their prisoners at one *solidus* a head.[84] They had rendered considerable service, then, to both Eastern and Western Rome before they invaded Thrace in 408.

The measures which the Western government took against its German mercenaries after the fall of Stilicho in 408 rendered it essential to obtain military assistance from some non-Germanic source in future. They therefore turned to the Huns and obtained assistance from them by a treaty which seems to have involved the giving of hostages: one of the hostages was a young man named Aetius.[85] Many years later his panegyrist magnified the results of Aetius' life among the Huns: 'The Caucasus has granted repose to the sword, and its savage kings renounce combat.' Indeed, Rome would otherwise have fallen before the 'shafts of the North': 'When the world was going down before Scythian swords, and northern spears were overwhelming Tarpeian axes, he broke the enemy's mad attack, and became the guarantee of a proud treaty and the ransom of the world.'[86]

At any rate, we find that when Athaulf, the brother-in-law of Alaric, appeared south of the Julian Alps in 409, leading an army which included a number of Huns, Honorius' minister Olympius was able to meet him at the head of a little band of 300 Huns, and at a cost of seventeen dead slew 1,100 of the enemy.[87] Later in that same year, 409, as the relations of the West Roman government with Alaric grew steadily worse, a force of 10,000 Huns was brought into Italy from Dalmatia by the imperial government. Their presence seems to have weighed with Alaric, who at once abandoned his plan of an immediate march on Rome.[88] More than thirty years after their first appearance in Europe the name of the Huns struck terror even into the bravest of those who heard it.

In 412 we find the East Roman government again in

Plate 3   An early nineteenth-century vision of Alaric.

diplomatic relations with the Huns, or at any rate with some
of them. We learn from a fragment of Olympiodorus that in
that year he himself served on an embassy which was sent
out from Constantinople to the barbarians. In order to reach
their destination the ambassadors had to sail northwards
across the Black Sea and were almost lost in a storm on the
way. They eventually reached a Hun king named Donatus,

whose sphere of activity was obviously far from that in which Uldin had held sway. On their arrival the ambassadors successfully achieved what one of Priscus' companions failed to do in similar circumstances many years later: after exchanging oaths of friendship with Donatus they treacherously murdered him. Perhaps his realm had recently grown to dangerous strength and the East Roman government, which was still controlled by the prefect Anthemius, saw a cheap way of dispelling the danger. But a certain Charato was chosen to succeed Donatus, and, not without reason, he entertained feelings of some hostility towards Olympiodorus and his friends. But the ambassadors had come prepared to deal with such a situation, and costly presents given in Theodosius' name induced the barbarian to remain at peace (frag. 18).

In 425, when the usurper John was fighting for his life against East Roman forces at Ravenna, he sent Aetius to the Huns to hire an army and bring it to Italy as quickly as possible. But Aetius returned too late. When he appeared in Italy John had been three days dead. Nevertheless, he engaged Aspar, the commander of the Eastern forces, in a stubborn but apparently indecisive battle, and finally induced the Huns to leave Italy and return home. The Huns, we are told, laid aside their anger and their arms for gold, gave hostages, and exchanged oaths. Aetius' achievement in getting rid of them was considered to be so great that Placidia and Valentinian III made their peace with him and gave him the rank of count. It was said that the number of Huns whom he had sent home was 60,000.[89]

VI

Thus the Huns were not only the foes of the Romans towards the close of the fourth century and in the opening years of the fifth; also to some extent they were their friends, and served not without effect as mercenaries in the imperial armies.

It was not only the Roman government which profited from their services: wealthy private individuals did so too. We hear of only two cases, but there is no reason to doubt that in fact there were others. Claudian tells us that Arcadius' praetorian prefect Rufinus maintained a personal guard of barbarians, and we hear from another source that this guard was composed of Huns.[90] Rufinus' great rival Stilicho also sought to ensure his own safety by hiring a private army of Huns, and before his enemies could set about murdering him they had to deal with these retainers. Consequently, at the head of an army they made a sudden descent upon them while they were asleep and slew them as they lay.[91] Since Rufinus' Huns are mentioned in one of our meagre chronicles, it would seem that the force was of considerable dimensions.

If a few of the great potentates of both the East and the West relied on Huns for their personal security, many of the population were willing to believe the new barbarians capable of the utmost atrocities. Claudian does not hesitate to tell his readers not only that the Huns slew their parents but that they delighted to swear oaths by their bodies thus slain. This was a belief that did not soon die out: had not Herodotus said that the Massagetae sacrifice their old men? Indeed, half a century later, Theodoret is prepared to go considerably farther. According to him the 'Massagetae', as he terms the Huns, not only made a regular practice of killing off their old men but actually ate their bodies.[92] All alike agreed that they lived the life of wild beasts. They descended upon the Goths like wolves, according to Priscus. 'Though by nature they lived the life of wild animals', writes an ecclesiastical historian, a missionary changed them to milder ways. Even the sober Ammianus says that you could take them to be two-footed animals, and to Jerome also they were wolves and wild beasts. In the sixth century Jordanes considered them to be 'a race almost of men', and Procopius notes that the Ephthalites, alone among the Huns, do not live the life of animals. Indeed, Zachariah of Mitylene at the end

of the fifth century represents some Huns as referring to themselves as 'barbarians, who, like rapacious wild beasts, reject God in the North-West region'.[93]

Unspeakable hardships were caused to the people living in the actual areas devastated by the raids of the Huns. We can say little of the sufferings of the Goths when this new nation of barbarians descended upon them as unexpectedly and suddenly, in Ammianus' words, as a storm from the high mountains.[94] But we have a little information from Thrace. When St Hypatius was twenty years of age (*c*. 386), he visited the monks of that area and found that, since Hun bands were roaming the countryside and plundering everywhere without hindrance, the brethren had been compelled to build forts, καστέλλια, wherein they might live in comparative security. Hypatius himself and eighty of the brethren proceeded to build a big fort, καστέλλιον μέγα, for themselves so that they might continue their devotions without interruption. Evidently there was no organized defence left in the province.[95] Many years afterwards Hypatius used to tell his disciples of how the Huns surrounded his καστέλλιον in Thrace, but God protected His servants and put their enemies to flight. 'They had a hole, τρυμαλιά, in the wall', he said, 'through which they hurled out a stone and dealt a blow to one of the foe, so that the others saw it, and, waving their whips, φραγέλλια, as a signal, they mounted their horses and retreated. When a stop had been put to the fighting, the people of the countryside, who had been plundered and had nothing left, ran to the monastery, seeking their sustenance.' The head of the monastery, he went on, Jonas, an Armenian, thereupon went to Constantinople and told the great men there, τοῖς ἰλλουστρίοις, that the poor in Thrace were starving. When this became known, Rufinus and the other officials 'filled ships with grain and with pulse' – presumably communications by land were broken – 'and sent them to Jonas that he might distribute them to the poor'.[96] The central government no doubt did what it could to relieve the suffering, but its means were limited, and little or no help can have reached the most exposed districts immediately behind the frontier and far from the sea.

The church was not daunted by the fury and savage reputation of the new invaders, and very soon after their first appearance on the frontier, Christian missionaries went among them. At the turn of the fifth century they were visited by Theotimus, bishop of Tomi and Scythia. The Huns on the Danube held him in high respect, we are told, and called him 'God of the Romans', Θεὸς ʿΡωμαίων.[97] It was said that Theotimus had performed wondrous deeds among them, but the ecclesiastical historian who tells us of them seems to have had his doubts as to the truth of the stories.[98] It was said that as he journeyed one day through enemy territory, Theotimus saw a band of Huns riding towards him on their way to Tomi. The bishop's companions were dismayed and began to lament that they would be put to death at once; but Theotimus dismounted from his horse and began to pray, whereupon he and his companions and their horses became invisible and the Huns rode by without seeing them. On another occasion a Hun, who thought the bishop to be a rich man, plotted to take him prisoner and hold him to ransom. He therefore prepared a lasso, such as the Huns often used in warfare, and tried to entangle him in its coils. But as he raised his hand to cast the noose around the bishop, he became as it were petrified and could not lower his arm again. He remained as though tied by invisible ropes until, at the request of his companions, Theotimus prayed to God to release him from his predicament.[99]

Despite such prodigious works Theotimus does not seem to have met with any success in converting the Huns. All that our authority can claim is that he changed them from their bestial manner of life to milder ways, and this he accomplished by the procedure, not unusual in a bishop of those times, of inviting them to banquets and presenting them with gifts.[100]

At approximately the time when Theotimus was active, other missionaries were sent to work among the Huns. John

Chrysostom, we are told, dispatched them to some 'of the nomadic Scyths who were encamped along the Danube'. The term 'nomadic Scyths' is one which our authority uses elsewhere of the Huns and of no one else,[101] and we can have no doubt that the great patriarch of Constantinople had endeavoured to have the new barbarians converted. But again no claim is made that the missionaries met with the slightest success. One of their greatest difficulties must have been that of language. John Chrysostom himself could find an interpreter easily enough when he wished to preach to the Goths in the capital; but, as we shall see later, the number of Romans who knew the Hun language was exceedingly small (p. 109 below), so that churchmen qualified to preach among them can only have been acquired with the utmost difficulty, if, indeed, at all.

None the less, there were not wanting enthusiasts within the Roman Empire who believed that the task of converting the Huns was all but accomplished. 'The Huns are learning the Psalms', cries Jerome in a letter written in 403, only eight years after he had trembled in his cell in Bethlehem. Orosius in 417 observes that 'the churches of Christ everywhere throughout the East and the West are filled with Huns, Suevi, Vandals, Burgundians, and innumerable other peoples of believers'. In the very heyday of Attila, Theodoret considered that the Huns had abandoned with loathing the custom of eating their old men because they had now heard the gospel, and he mentions their name in a list of those who profit from the good works of the martyrs.[102] Unhappily, more sober witnesses had to admit the complete failure of the church's efforts, and towards the middle of the fifth century, in the great days of Attila, Salvian classes them without qualification among the pagans. Prudentius, far away in Spain, although he thought that the 'bloody ferocity' of the Huns had been tamed somewhat – they no longer drink blood, he says – can do no more than look forward to the day when they will drink the blood of Christ.[103] Even in the sixth century their wanton cruelty, their readiness to rape nuns

and to massacre those who had taken refuge at the altars of
the churches, shocked even the barbarous armies of
Justinian.[104] It is possible that individual Huns, particularly
among those living in the Roman Empire as captives or
exiles, had been converted to Christianity; but if so, we hear
of none of them until long after the death of Attila.
Thereafter, those few whom we know to have been
converted had especially close relations with the Romans,
like that Sunica whom Zachariah of Mitylene describes as 'a
general, who was a Hun, and, having taken refuge with the
Romans, had been baptized'. Zachariah, then, pictured only
the truth when he made the Huns describe themselves as
'barbarians, who, like rapacious wild beasts, reject God in
the North-West region'.[105]

Such was the impression which the Huns, in their early
days, left upon those Romans whose literary works have
come down to us. But they, the educated, the comparatively
well to do, were a small minority in the empire. We cannot
doubt that this impression was shared by all, high and low
alike, who lived in the areas actually devastated, who saw
their hovels burnt and their sons and daughters led away into
a bitter slavery. We shall try in later pages to discover the
sentiments of the vast bulk of the population of the European
provinces, that is, the peasants living far from the frontiers,
both those who sweated in the fields of their masters, and
those who had been entirely expropriated and lived as
brigands in the mountains and forests. Attila, it has been
said, was only the Scourge of God for the Roman priests and
administrators interested in keeping the nations under the
domination of Rome.[106]

3

Hun Society before Attila

An attempt has been made in the previous chapter to outline
the military exploits of the Huns and the wars which they
fought for and against the Romans and Goths before the
days of Attila. But it is clear that many problems arise from
our narrative and demand explanation. Before we approach
them the reader may be urged to bear constantly in mind the
rapidity with which the Hun empire rose and fell. When
Priscus crossed the Roman frontier and entered the
dominions of the Huns in 449 he passed into a world
which a generation before his birth had not yet come into
existence, and which had utterly disappeared by the time his
book was published. If we are to understand the strange
phenomenon presented by the great nomad empire we must
never forget that their society was not static but dynamic.
History is no longer satisfied to ascribe so striking a
movement as the rise of the Hun empire to the genius of a
single man, and in fact, as we shall see, there is not much
evidence to show that Attila was a genius. It is only in terms
of the development of their society that we can explain why
the Huns attacked the Roman Empire at all, why they as
often defended it, how they came to build up so vast an
empire of their own, and yet proved unable to hold it for
more than a few years. We must therefore examine their

society, and we can only hope to succeed if we are clear as to the productive methods at their disposal. In no part of our study shall we have more reason for gratitude to Ammianus than here.

I

In material civilization they belonged to the Lower Stage of Pastoralism as defined by Hobhouse, Wheeler, and Ginsberg (pp. 26, *et passim*). The herds which they had driven before them over the steppes of southern Russia consisted, according to Ammianus, of all kinds of domesticated animals[1] – cattle, horses, goats, and, above all, sheep, which, although unmentioned by our authorities, are more essential to the steppe nomad even than horses.[2]

Their clothing was made either of linen or of the skins of *murinae* (marmots?) stitched together, and some of the steppe tribes were famed in the Roman Empire for their trade in such skins.[3] Owing to the hard conditions of their life the Huns wore their clothes on their backs, we are told, until they disintegrated and fell off bit by bit, a fact which reminds us that in the law code of Chinghis Khan it was made obligatory for the Mongols to wear their clothes without washing them until they should be worn out.[4] The Huns wore leggings of goat-skin, and round caps on their heads, but of what material these were made we do not know.[5]

Although they derived the bulk of their food from their herds, it is quite certain that, like all other nomads of the steppe, they had to augment their supply by hunting. While Ammianus, oddly enough, mentions hunting only in connection with the Alans, Priscus appears to have thought that, when the Huns were settled in the Kuban (immediately before they began their attacks on the Ostrogoths), their whole food-supply was obtained by hunting.[6]

Finally, they had to rely on food-gathering, and Ammianus

tells us that they collected the roots of wild plants to supplement their diet.[7] The fact that he mentions this at all in such a comparatively brief account of their way of life suggests that food-gathering played a very important part indeed in their economy. We need scarcely add that agriculture was entirely unknown.[8] Their linen clothing, then, must have been acquired by barter, for a people which knows nothing of agriculture does not grow flax.

The productive methods available to the Huns were primitive beyond what is now easy to imagine. When Ammianus says that they were accustomed to endure hunger and thirst from their very cradles, he reminds us that their own economy was simply *unable* to support them unaided. Without the assistance of the settled agricultural populations at the edge of the steppe they could not have survived. They were therefore compelled to have continuous intercourse with these peoples, and the question of their trade will occupy us at length later on.

II

From this description of their primitive methods of producing and appropriating food it will be evident that a very large area of pasture land was necessary to support a comparatively small number of Huns. Hence they must not be pictured as wandering over the steppe in one enormous multitude – Hunnic 'hordes' and their *unzählige Schwarmen* (innumerable swarms) are misleading terms. Rather, a large number of comparatively tiny groups drove their herds hither and thither in search of pasture and water, and, within limits, the smaller the groups the more secure was their food-supply. What can we learn of these groups? It is unfortunate that Ammianus omits to tell us anything of the tribal organization of the Huns. We know from Priscus and other writers that they were organized in tribes, and we have a number of their tribal names. Ammianus' remark that they entered battle in wedges (*cuneatim*) reminds us of the *cunei* in which the Germans fought, according to Tacitus, of whose chief works Ammianus was writing a continuation.[9] But whether the *cunei* of the Huns were formed likewise of *familiae et propinquitates* (relatives and neighbours) we do not know. There is no direct evidence to support the suggestion, but, although tribes and confederacies were easily broken up in the unstable conditions of steppe life, clans and families tended to survive,[10] so that the conjecture may not be incorrect. However that may be, scholars appear to agree in making deductions as to the Huns from what is in general customary on the steppe. Thus Bury accepts Peisker's statements to the effect that the basic unit of Hun society was formed by the five or six persons of one family who lived in one tent. 'Six to ten tents formed a camp, and several camps a clan. The tribe consisted of several clans and the highest unit, the *il* or people, of several tribes.'[11] If we equate the word 'several' in this quotation from Bury with the figure 10, we may conclude that the average Hun tribe consisted of about 5,000 persons all told. But not all pastures and hunting-grounds would support 5,000 persons with their flocks and herds if they moved about in one group; and that is why Peisker tells us that the camps, that is the groups of about fifty persons, wandered about separately. Priscus says that the Acatziri, a people whom he declares to be Hunnic, were divided into several tribes and clans under their own leaders.[12] We may suppose that the clans, γένη, which he mentions correspond to the groups of about 500 persons of whom a clan, in Peisker's terminology, was composed. The organization in households may be taken as certain, for it still existed in Attila's day, as we shall see (p. 187 below).

Something can be learned of the social organization of these tribes at the time of which we are speaking. When every male was engaged in the day-long task of looking after the herds, and when even then famine conditions very often prevailed among them – 'they learn from the cradle to endure hunger and thirst'[13] – a leisured or even a semi-leisured class of nobles could not fully emerge. Ammianus explicitly notes the absence of kings from their society, 'they are not subject to the authority of any king'.[14] Instead of kings, he says, each group was content with the improvised leadership of their leading men (*tumultuario primatum ductu*). Who these chief men (*primates*) were he does not say, but it is clear from his language that their leadership (*ductus*) existed only in time of war. Indeed, we may guess that even in war-time they could not so much exercise any legal or traditional power as merely use personal influence: they had, one may suspect, little or no right of coercion. It is known that the Mongols had no king until 1206: when Chinghis was proclaimed Khan a few years previously, in 1203, he had not been vested with any royal power, but was merely the leader of a little band of adventurers – his followers swore to obey him in war, but in peace merely to refrain from 'harming his affairs'.[15] Ammianus' *primates* may well have been in some such position within their own tribes. As among the Alans,[16] they were, no doubt, simply those who had won the greatest reputation as military leaders, and in time of peace their power will have been little greater than that of any other adult male Hun: for in peace-time the clans scattered to their various pastures and the basis of a ruler's existence was gone. It would appear instead that all the adult Huns – or at any rate the heads of the households – met together in a form of council to discuss matters of general interest, and we are told that, when they came together thus, they carried on their discussions on horseback.[17]

Ammianus omits to say on what basis property rested, whether it was held privately, by the clan, by the family, or by some other unit. There was certainly no private ownership of land, for that was impossible among the pastoral nomads.[18] But what of the herds? We know that among the Mongols of Chinghis Khan's time each nomad household owned its own herds, tents, and accoutrement,[19] and it is perhaps safest to assume that this was also the case among the Huns; it will scarcely be doubted that Onegesius, whom we shall meet in the sequel, owned all the property used by the persons of his household. It may be pointed out, however, that if private property, as we understand the term, were highly developed in the period that Ammianus is speaking of, we should find ourselves in some difficulty with the *tumultuarius primatum ductus*; for if the *primates* were simply those who had inherited or acquired most property it is all but inconceivable that their *ductus* should have been practically non-existent in times of peace. A propertied class is never slow to make full political use of its economic and social advantages. It follows that the military leadership of the *primates* was not strictly hereditary, although the prestige of a father who had held the leadership might well give some indefinite advantage to his son when a new leader was to be chosen. Finally, we may safely assert that slavery was but little developed in Hun society. That it did exist at this time is indicated not only by what we know of other pastoral peoples at the same stage of material culture as the Huns,[20] but also by Ammianus' failure to say that it did *not* exist – for in the case of the Alans, who had once had no slaves, the historian is careful to point out the absence of the institution. The function of the slaves of the Huns will have been to carry out menial work at the great hunts and to act as shepherds and stable boys, as among the early Mongols.[21] They were completely at the mercy of their masters, who could put them to death without scruple or hindrance, and Priscus saw two of them crucified on a charge of having killed their masters. The sole source of slavery seems to have been warfare: we hear of no native Hun slaves.

III

Such being the material civilization of the Huns in the later fourth century, let us turn now to the question of their numbers and their military strength.

It has been pointed out above that the present writer

cannot pass judgement on De Guignes's identification of the Huns with the Hsiung-nu of the Chinese annalists. Now the Chinese, when they deal with the steppe nomads, speak with embarrassing frequency of nomad armies numbering 100,000, 200,000, 300,000, and even 400,000 men. Thus Parker, whose narrative in *A Thousand Years of the Tartars* is closely based on the original authorities, writes, '[Baghdur] had 300,000 troops under his command', 'Baghdur let loose 300,000 of his best troops', '[Merchö] had a standing army of 400,000 horse-archers always ready', and so on.[22] It may seem impertinent for one who knows nothing of the Chinese authorities to criticize the historians who follow them, but we may be permitted to ask (1) how the extremely primitive nomadic pastoralists of Mongolia could possibly feed three hundred thousand men concentrated into one body, and (2) how their society could function at all if even one hundred thousand men were withdrawn from production and from the business of tending and protecting the flocks and herds for an entire campaigning season. Indeed, even when we find the view[23] that in 430 Attila's Huns numbered some 600,000 or 700,000 persons, we cannot but wonder how such an enormous multitude managed to feed itself in Pannonia and on its long journey thither, even if they had come from no more distant spot than the Kuban basin.[24]

The statistics given by our fifth-century Greco-Roman authorities indicate a very different state of affairs. In 409 Honorius employed 10,000 Huns against Alaric.[25] It is significant, however, that the excellent authority from whom we derive this information, Olympiodorus, himself a first-hand observer of Hun life, immediately goes on to describe the extraordinary efforts which the emperor found it necessary to make in order to collect food to support this force: he brought both livestock and grain from Dalmatia into Italy for the purpose. As Zosimus puts it, 'the emperor . . . summoned ten thousand Huns as allies, and in order to have supplies for them when they came, ordered the Dalmatians to contribute corn, sheep, and oxen'. From the fact that Zosimus, or rather Olympiodorus, thought this information sufficiently important to include in his history, it is clear that it was quite exceptional and that the feeding of 10,000 Huns for a campaigning season was considered to be no ordinary task. In fact, one might reasonably suspect that only the commissariat of the imperial government was at this period in a position to concentrate so large a force of Hun warriors in one spot. In view of what we have seen above, it is highly unlikely that the Huns themselves, in the years immediately after their first appearance in Europe, could produce a sufficient surplus of food to feed so large a body throughout a campaign: certainly there could be no question of living off the land after the devastating invasion of Radagaisus a few years earlier. It is true, however, that at the end of the period under review Octar's Huns, who were defeated by the Burgundians, are said by Socrates to have numbered 10,000 (p. 74 below). But at that time circumstances had changed: whole nations of agricultural peoples were then working perforce to feed their masters. Moreover, it suits Socrates' *Tendenz* in that passage to make the Huns as numerous as possible: they may therefore have numbered far fewer than 10,000. Indeed, when ancient authors give us figures relating to the size of barbarian armies operating beyond the frontier against other barbarians, they are hardly ever right: it was nearly always impossible for them to obtain reliable information on such matters.

Next, we are told by Olympiodorus[26] that the Hun force which defeated Athaulf's Goths in the interests of Olympius in 409 numbered 300. In view of the supply difficulties which we have already mentioned this is the sort of figure that we should expect. In the time of Procopius, when the Huns had reverted, as we shall see (pp. 201–2 below), to a kind of social organization similar to that in which they were living *c.*376, their armies nearly always appear to number between 200 and 1,200 men, and the expedition of Zabergan, which caused so much alarm in Constantinople in 558 and was composed of 7,000 Kotriguri, was noted as altogether exceptional.[27] We shall not be very likely to err then if we assume the average Hun raiding party, which harried the Roman provinces at the beginning of the fifth century, rarely if ever to have numbered more than about 1,200 warriors. We may assign the same sort of figure to the average body of Hun mercenaries employed by the Roman government at the same period.

According to Ralph Fox (p. 39), who had first-hand experience of Mongolia, the nomads living there under the old tribal society went from pasture to pasture in companies of several hundred tents. This suggests that each company could muster approximately a thousand warriors; presumably, when a raid was undertaken, some grown men were left behind to protect the women and children, and to look after the flocks and herds. Further, we have already seen that the tribal unit in our period may well have consisted of about 5,000 persons all told. This again points to a field force for each tribe of about the figure we have suggested, and it indicates that the smaller Hun forces which harried the Roman provinces on so many occasions and the bodies of Hun mercenaries hired out by the Roman government were, not random groupings, but tribal levies. In this fact we have the answer to many of our questions. Since each tribe sought out its pastures and hunting-grounds in comparative isolation, the tribal forces could act with complete independence, the one of the other, and we may be sure that rivalry and hostility were as common among them as friendship and co-operation. This is the fundamental reason why, when some Huns were attacking Vithimiris' Goths, others played a considerable part in the Gothic defence (p. 27 above). This is why the Huns as often defended the Roman Empire as they attacked it. Again, the Huns had a reputation for extreme faithlessness in making and breaking treaties.[28] The reason why they should have acquired such a reputation lies in their tribal organization: a treaty made by one group in no way bound another. Finally, this is the explanation of the fact that no major battles between the Huns and the

Romans are reported for many years after the first appearance of the former across the Danube frontier.

The preceding discussion throws considerable doubt, I think, on the last figure at our disposal, the 60,000 Huns whom Aetius is alleged to have brought into Italy in 425.[29] A force of 60,000 warriors implies a total population of at least a quarter of a million Huns, and when we consider that only a fraction of the Huns in Europe were united in the confederacy which supported Aetius, and when we further take into account the fact that neither Aetius nor the Western government could possibly have paid or fed 60,000 mercenaries, we cannot but conclude this figure to be an exaggeration. In all probability, if we may risk a guess, Aetius' force was about one-tenth of the figure given by Philostorgius. Quite apart from the fact that Aetius, like other commanders, will have exaggerated the size of his army for purposes of propaganda, it cannot be sufficiently emphasized that the astounding mobility of the steppe horsemen has always led contemporary historians to believe them much more numerous than they actually were. It should be remembered that our best authorities rarely, if ever, attempt to assess the numbers of the armies of the Huns in their greatest days. It is to Priscus' credit that he gives no such figures in the extant fragments. Attila, he says, took Margus 'with a large force of barbarians':[30] the men of Asemus fought 'against an overwhelming force'.[31] But such terms are elastic: for instance, the Huns ferry a 'barbarian multitude' across a stream, and Attila's tent, he observes, was surrounded 'by a multitude of barbarians'.[32] Again, Basich and Cursich are said to have been 'leading a huge force'.[33] Unfortunately in a lost part of his work, Priscus, if we can trust Jordanes, appears to have given it as his opinion that Attila's army in 451 numbered 500,000 men, a figure that outdoes even the Chinese annalists; but the historian was careful to point out that this figure was conjectural.[34] How could he find out the truth? It is unlikely that Attila himself knew even approximately the number of men in his army on that occasion, or that he was less willing than Geiseric to exaggerate the size of his force.[35] In view therefore of the direct evidence of our sources together with what is known of nomad empires in general, we may safely conclude that the enormous conquests of the Huns were carried out by 'a ridiculously small band of horsemen'.[36]

IV

It was not because of superiority in numbers that the Huns were so often able to defeat the Roman and Gothic armies. What of their armament? No one can read the relevant chapter of Ammianus (xxxi. 2) without feeling something of the profound horror which their appearance in south-eastern Europe stirred in this capable officer: as Peisker (p. 350) says, they froze the blood of all peoples. We may confidently deny the view[37] that 'at the time of the death of Theodosius [the Great] they were probably regarded as one more barbarian enemy, neither more nor less formidable than the Germans who threatened the Danubian barrier', for it was precisely at the time of Theodosius' death that Ammianus was writing his thirty-first book. Even Seeck, who limits this growth of confidence to the East Romans, is scarcely correct: 'in the East', he writes, 'where Romans and Germans had already fought with them often enough, sometimes as enemies, sometimes as allies, the initial shock must have been gradually neutralized by familiarity.'[38]

But several passages in Procopius and Agathias show that even in the sixth century the Huns still aroused exceptional terror.[39]

It is curious that Ammianus, Claudian, Sidonius, and Jordanes, when they first turn to describe the Huns, at once speak of their loathsome personal appearance. These writers can find no words strong enough to express their horror of the new barbarians. The Huns, says Ammianus, are 'so prodigiously ugly and bent that they might be taken for two-legged animals or the figures crudely carved from stumps, which are seen on the parapets of bridges'. Claudian introduces his description of them with the words 'their bodies are obscene to look at'. Sidonius, in his panegyric of Anthemius, assures us that 'truly the very faces of their infants have a gruesomeness all their own'. Jordanes develops the theme. They caused excessive panic, he says, by the terror of their faces; they put men to flight by their 'terrifying appearance, which inspired fear because of its swarthiness, and they had, if I may call it so, a sort of shapeless lump, not a head'. Jerome puts the matter in a nutshell: 'The Roman army', he says, 'is terrified by the sight of them.'[40] Evidently the facial appearance and tattered marmot-skin clothing of the new invaders unnerved the soldiers of the empire, accustomed as they were to fight opponents who at least looked and dressed like themselves. This psychological weapon must have been of great military value at first, and seems to have declined very slowly later.

There is no need to labour the point that the Huns all but lived on horseback, and in sheer horsemanship they far surpassed the best Roman and Gothic cavalry. They are, says Ammianus, 'almost glued to their horses.' 'They are unable to plant their feet firmly on the ground', says Zosimus, 'they live and sleep on their horses.' Jerome observed that the Romans are defeated by men who are not able to walk, men who think themselves dead if they touch the ground. Suidas glosses the word $\dot{\alpha}\kappa\rho o\sigma\phi\alpha\lambda\epsilon\tilde{\iota}\varsigma$ as 'persons who trip up when walking, i.e. the Huns'. Priscus tells us how they even carried on their negotiations with the Romans on horseback, and he himself saw Attila eat and drink when mounted.[41] The Romans could never produce such cavalrymen because they could not abandon their agricultural economy. 'The Chinese', writes Lattimore (p. 65), 'took over the whole of the technique of mounted archery, but without subordinating their agricultural economy to the nomadic economy. This meant that both their horses and their archers were inferior to those of the nomads, except in abnormal periods when

Plate 4   Artificially deformed skull of a noblewoman (c. AD 450), found at Ladenburg (Baden). Lobdengaumuseum, Ladenburg. Photograph: AKG London.

years of consecutive campaigning, at ruinous cost to their settled economy, produced a professional cavalry that could match the "natural" cavalry of the steppe.' The Romans did not imitate this desperate policy, not because they were too wise, but because they were too weak.

It is easy to under-estimate the military strength of nomadic mounted archers, especially those of a nation which had so recently emerged from tribal society and was still endowed with all the courage engendered by the free institutions of the tribes. As late as the mid-nineteenth century the fighting qualities of the mounted archers of a tribal society, even when faced with modern fire-arms, were demonstrated on more than one occasion in more than one part of the world.[42] The horses of the Huns were of a hardy though ugly breed, and when Jerome contrasts their 'nags' (*caballi*) with the 'horses' (*equi*) of the Romans, we must not forget that their pasture-fed horses could do less work than the stall-fed horses of the Romans which had their hay and grain brought to them.[43] But the Huns were not long in mounting themselves on Roman horses,[44] so that this disadvantage quickly disappeared. The complete command of horsemanship possessed by these unsightly beings, and the ferocious charges and unpredictable retreats of their cavalry,[45] the clouds of arrows which they discharged from their dreaded bows and which never missed the mark,[46] the astounding speed of their strategical manoeuvres,[47] were too much for the cruelly exploited and dispirited infantrymen of the declining empire.

Ammianus speaks of iron swords, and these must have been obtained by barter or capture from the peoples with whom the Huns came in contact, for metal-working on more than a minute scale was impossible in the conditions of nomadic life:[48] their arrows consequently were tipped with bone. In close fighting, however, they did not rely on the sword alone. They also used a lasso or net wherein they entangled their opponent, whether horseman or on foot, and in fact we hear of several other northern peoples in antiquity who used the lasso without any knowledge of the sword at all.[49] When Sozomen tells of the Hun who tried to ensnare the bishop Theotimus in a lasso, it is noteworthy that the nomad whom he describes has no sword, although he does carry a shield.[50]

But the Huns were mounted archers (ἱπποτοξόται) above all, and the bow was by far their most characteristic weapon. Both Darkó (p. 449) and Lattimore (pp. 465, 466) agree that the superiority of the nomads was due to their peculiarly powerful bow. The compound bow of the steppe horseman, according to Lattimore, 'is notably short for its great power and is made of horn – a steppe material – and short pieces of wood spliced double'. Alföldi argues that the Hun bow was not short: the types of bow used in northern Asia, he says, are in general very long. But this information must be rejected in view of the testimony of Lattimore, whose knowledge of steppe conditions is unsurpassed. It should be remembered that a horseman would find a short bow less unwieldy than a long one – and the steppe was treeless.[51] The accuracy with which the Hun archers used this formidable weapon never failed to astonish Greco-Roman observers.[52] Aetius, who had been a hostage among them, became, we are told, 'a fine horseman, and a sure shot with an arrow'. The Romans were always glad to capture these 'Scythian bows', and when Vegetius, who seems to have written during the reign of Valentinian III, says of the Romans of his day that they 'have improved the weaponry of their cavalry [*equitum arma*] after the example of the Goths, Alans, and Huns', he may well mean by *equitum arma* the dreaded bow of the Huns.[53] In all, when we bear in mind that the Huns possessed horses which were at least equal to those of the Romans in performance, and that they also seem to have adopted some Roman defensive armour,[54] we can see that their horsemanship and above all the extreme mobility of their entire society gave them a decided tactical and strategical advantage over their opponents. 'The whole people', writes Minns (p. 51) of the steppe nomads in general, 'is a ready-made army, easily marshalled, self-supporting, capable of sudden attacks, of long-distance raids. In the steppe the nomad is always on a war footing.'

The Romans, however, could scarcely have been defeated for long were it not that they fought with a hostile rear. Ralph Fox writes that 'It is doubtful if even the Mongol military genius could ever have conquered China completely . . . without the help of great sections of the population who were full of hatred and contempt for their degenerate and greedy rulers' (p. 142). The same is true of the Huns and the Eastern Roman Empire. Zosimus says that in 400, when Thrace was in a state of utter confusion following the defeat

and death of Gainas at the hands of Uldin's Huns, runaway
slaves and 'others who abandoned their posts' in the Roman
caste system gave out that they were Huns and proceeded to
devastate the Thracian countryside until they were defeated
by Fravitta.[55] These slaves presumably said that they were
Huns because they knew that this name would cause more
terror and confusion than any other; the Huns, then, be it
noted, were at this time more dreaded by those Romans, who
still had something to lose, than were the Goths (p. 56
above). More important, the incident shows us clearly that
the coming of the Huns, like that of many other barbarians
hostile to the imperial government, was greeted by the
depressed classes in the empire with enthusiasm: it meant a
chance to throw off the burden of their servitude. It was a
symptom of the times that, as early as 408, an important
frontier fortress should have been betrayed to Uldin (p. 33
above), and we may be sure that the treachery at Castra
Martis could be paralleled many times if our sources for
early-fifth-century history were less unsatisfactory.

The condition of the army too was disastrous from the
point of view of the Roman government. Admittedly
Vegetius finds one matter to the credit of the high
command: the equipment of the cavalry had been improved
as a result of study of the weapons of the Goths, Alans, and
Huns, and we have seen that the Roman cavalrymen may
have been equipped with the 'Scythian' bow.[56] In the
Problemata of Leo VI, who is drawing on Urbicius, who in
turn is based on the accumulated experience of the fifth and
sixth centuries, we find another illustration of the observa-
tional powers of the Roman high command. Leo puts his
information in the form of question and answer, and writes
as follows:

Q. 'What must the general do, if the nation [of the enemy] be
Scythian or Hunnic?'
A. 'He should attack them about the month of February or March,
when their horses are weakened by the hardships of winter.'[57]

V

Such in brief was the material civilization and the military potential of the Huns when they first came in contact with the Romans. The reader will note, on the one hand, their crushing poverty and the extreme primitiveness of their productive methods, and, on the other hand, their immense potential military strength. But the Huns could never seriously threaten the Roman Empire as a whole so long as their primitive economy rendered any kind of political integration and any united military action impossible. So long as the Hun tribes and clans sought water and pasture-lands as isolated units, they could never develop sufficient political coherence to threaten more than isolated districts of the empire. Yet there must have been from the very beginning a strong tendency for these nomads, who 'learn from the cradle to endure hunger and thirst', to take what they could from the provinces of the empire, which to them appeared a paradise of riches and prosperity. 'In your empire', says a Hun to Justinian many years later, 'there is a superabundance of everything, including, I suppose, even the impossible.'[58] The tendency to take what they could, or, failing that, to hire themselves out as mercenaries to the imperial government or even to individual Roman ministers, must have laid the seeds of endless conflicts. That this was the sole reason for their contacts with the Roman Empire would seem to be indicated by Ammianus when he speaks of them as 'burning with an immense desire for gold' and 'aflame with an inhuman desire for plundering other people's property'.[59]

It is time now to point out that even before Ammianus published his work the state of affairs which he depicts was coming to an end. In Jordanes' mythical account of the Hun conquest of the Ostrogoths we find a king named Balamber, who is mentioned as leading the nomads in the years immediately preceding the battle of Adrianople. It seems reasonably certain that Balamber never existed: the Goths invented him in order to explain who it was that conquered them.[60] Nevertheless, the Huns at this time achieved one great victory: they subdued, as we have seen, a 'great part' of the Ostrogoths. This suggests that they were operating on that occasion with a much larger force than any one of their tribes could have put in the field. Ermanarich, Vithimiris, and Viderichus were not successively beaten by a body of about 1,000 Huns – the approximate size of a tribal muster. It seems then that we are dealing here with a confederacy of a group of tribes. From a sentence of Sozomen[61] it would seem that the first minor attacks of the Huns on the Ostrogoths were carried out by tribal forces, and, when these attacks proved lucrative, the tribes coalesced into a confederacy so as to launch the main invasion. But this confederacy can only have existed for a very short time, for we do not hear of its accomplishing any further exploits. Also, Ammianus is an excellent authority, and his express statement that the Huns were not ruled by kings forbids us to posit several 'Balambers' or more than one confederacy.

Some light is thrown on the development of Hun society by what is known of the first historical kings whose names have come down to us. We hear that Uldin defeated and killed Gainas in 400. In 406 he was in Italy helping Stilicho to defeat Radagaisus. In 408 he is found in Thrace attacking the Roman dominions (pp. 37, 33 above). In the last of these campaigns the Roman officer opposing him detached many troops from the Hun after negotiations with his 'retainers and captains' (οἰκεῖοι καὶ λοχαγοί). A fragment of Olympiodorus throws some light on these subordinate commanders in this Hun army. During his visit to the Huns Olympiodorus was greatly impressed by the archery 'of their kings' (τῶν ῥήγων αὐτῶν), and met Charato 'the first of the kings' (ὁ τῶν ῥήγων πρῶτος). Now we have seen that Olympiodorus was extremely careful in his use of such terms,[62] and it is clear that among the Huns whom he visited there were several 'kings' and one 'first king'. The latter position was filled by Donatus and after his death by Charato. From his usage elsewhere it seems that Olympiodorus drew a distinction between the military leader of a confederacy of tribes, the 'tribal leader' ($\phi\acute{v}\lambda\alpha\rho\chi o\varsigma$) or first king, and the military leader of a single tribe, the 'king' ($\acute{\rho}\acute{\eta}\xi$). From this we can deduce that in Uldin's confederacy the leaders of the individual tribes, doubtless the 'leading men' (*primates*) of whom Ammianus had spoken, retained a position of authority and responsibility even when serving under a 'tribal leader' ($\phi\acute{v}\lambda\alpha\rho\chi o\varsigma$). It should further be noted that after his defeat in 408 Uldin is never heard of again and would appear to have lost his command. This is no coincidence. The military leader retains his position only as long as he fulfils the function for which his position came into being, that is, the collection of food and plunder and the defence of his people's flocks and herds. That this last was also part of the military leader's function, incidentally, is explicitly stated by one of our authorities in the case of Uldin himself. Zosimus, following Eunapius, tells us that Uldin attacked Gainas in 400 'because he did not think it safe to allow a barbarian with an army of his own to take up his dwelling across the Danube'.[63] The disappearance of Uldin as soon as he was unsuccessful in war is one more sign of that democratic character of primitive kingship which historians too often overlook. The kingship, however, seems to have become a permanent institution among at least one body of Huns by the year 412; for when Olympiodorus visited them he found that as soon as Donatus was murdered, Charato was appointed immediately to fill his place.

What are we to say of the continuity of the confederacies led by Uldin, Donatus, and the others? Are we to picture a Hun empire founded by Uldin or a predecessor of his, and surviving as a political entity until the death of Attila? Kiessling, for instance, speaks of a Hun empire stretching from the Carpathians to the Don in the seventies of the fourth century, the political unification of which was

Plate 5 Hunnic period sword from Bátaszék, Hungary.
Nationalmuseum, Budapest.

confirmed by Uldin, who was followed as its leader by Octar (Uptar), then by Rua, and finally by Bleda and Attila.[64] This view, it may be suggested, is unlikely. After their conquest of the Goths there is no reason to believe that the Huns maintained in its entirety such political unification as they had achieved. The various tribes would seem to have relapsed to a large extent into their original state of mutual

independence, each controlling a specific portion of the
subject Goths and Alans.[65] Their raids during the closing
decades of the fourth century and the first years of the fifth
were carried out by independent tribes without any central
direction. There is no reason to suppose, for instance, that
the raid across the Danube in 395 was timed to coincide with
that launched over the Caucasus in that same year (pp. 30ff
above). Two unrelated groups of Huns simply took
advantage simultaneously of the absence of the Roman
armies in the West. Such independent tribes at times
coalesced into confederacies, of which we hear about those
led by Uldin and by Donatus and Charato and by Basich and
Cursich. But we have no evidence to show that there existed
one single, continuously growing confederacy of which
Uldin, Donatus, and the others were the successive military
leaders. There is evidence, on the other hand, which seems to
show that some of the Goths were in a position at times to
act independently of the Huns in the period before Rua, that
is, before *c.*430; for about the year 418 the Goth Thorismud
was able to win a victory over the Gepids, and our sources
give us no hint that he was acting under Hunnic orders.[66]
This could scarcely have happened under an empire that was
in any way centralized.

Much confusion has been caused by the scanty data
concerning Uldin. Many scholars believe that it was he who
led the great westward advance of the Huns in the opening
years of the fifth century. Alföldi thinks that it was Uldin
who first fixed the residence of the Hun kings on the bank of
the Danube opposite Margus and that it remained there
without interruption until the forties of the century.[67] Seeck
actually inclines to the view that Rua and Octar were the
sons and successors of Uldin.[68] Bury states that 'it is
uncertain whether Uldin . . . was king of all the Huns or only
a portion'.[69] But indeed Uldin was clearly a minor figure in
Hun society – the mere fact that he was reduced to seeking
service in the Roman armies of both the East and the West
shows that he was not the ruler of a great state north of the

Danube. Moreover, Zosimus tells us that he had great difficulty in defeating Gainas in 400; he had to engage him in several battles before he could dispose of him. Yet Gainas was leading a very weak force which had already been defeated by the Romans (p. 36 above). We may believe then that Uldin was the leader of a mere fraction of the Huns, and that it is quite certain that he did not lead them all. That the family of an unsuccessful leader should have retained the command of the Huns for fifty years is impossible at this stage of the development of Hun society. We may safely conclude that the confederacies of Uldin, Donatus, and the rest had little interconnection and that it was not until about 420, if even then, that the confederacy which Rua subsequently led came into existence.

VI

When the nomadic Huns, living in the conditions of desperate hardship which we have outlined above, came into contact with the higher material civilization of the agricultural peoples on both sides of the Danubian frontier, it was inevitable that they should try to ease the harshness of their lot by collecting as much food and plunder and as many primitive luxuries as they could from the Goths and Romans. In times of drought particularly, attacks on their rich neighbours must have been a matter of life and death for them. At first they carried on the struggle under their tribal *primates*, although even in the seventies of the fourth century the increased food-supplies won by their superior military strength and their subjugation of agricultural peoples in southern Russia enabled larger concentrations of warriors to be made. This fact resulted in the appearance of a confederacy of some of their tribes which was able to overpower the Ostrogoths. But on the whole at this time there were only tribal ῥῆγες, and these in time of war alone. When war became the normal state, however, 'kingship'

became a more or less permanent institution; and as their
military ability brought them more and more success, greater
and greater forces of warriors could be concentrated and
confederacies grew larger and larger. Apparently, however,
the *primates* of Ammianus' day still continued to function
inside the confederacies as late as the time of Uldin and
Donatus. Clearly then it is scarcely true to say that the Huns
rose to power as rapidly as they afterwards fell from it:
Attila's position is now seen to be the culmination of a
process which had been gathering strength for half a century.

The turning-point in their history in the period under
review would seem then to have been their move from the
country east of the Black Sea into what is now the Ukrainian
Republic. This was not a mere geographical move, an
exchange of neighbours. It was a move from an area where
there was no surplus of food to an area where there was a
surplus of food. East of the Black Sea the Huns could exploit
only the Alans, a race of nomads as primitive as themselves,
whereas the Ostrogoths were agriculturists, living in rich
villages.[70] It was the possibility of wresting their food-
surplus from the Ostrogoths that enabled Hun society to
develop on the lines which it eventually followed.

It will be seen in the sequel that we have neglected an
important factor in this summary of the process by which the
Huns developed their strength – the factor of trade. It will be
more convenient to discuss it at a later stage. A
contemporary of Attila, who also tried to summarize the
process, omits it likewise. Nestorius, the heresiarch, writes as
follows:

For because the people of the Scythians were great and many and
formerly were divided into peoples and into kingdoms and were
treated as robbers, they used not to do much wrong except only as
through rapacity and through speed; yet later they made them a
kingdom and, after they were established in a kingdom, they grew
very strong, so that they surpassed in their greatness all the forces
of the Romans.[71]

4

The Victories of Attila

The *Byzantine History* of Priscus began with the year 434, the year in which Attila acceded to the leadership of the Huns. In this chapter, then, we have the invaluable aid of his work. But his book has survived only in fragments, so that in our journey through the history of these years we pass in rapid succession from periods of bright sunshine to periods of total darkness. When discussing incidents related in his fragments we can enter into great detail; when his help is lacking we are reduced to conjecture or to blunt confession of our ignorance. Moreover, it could probably be shown that his work did not include a consecutive narrative of Western affairs; our sunny moments, then, are restricted to the frontier history of the Eastern Empire.

I

In the early twenties of the fifth century a certain Rua obtained the military leadership of the last and greatest of the Hun confederacies. He was not its only leader, for we hear that he shared the position with his brother Octar; he also had a third brother, Mundiuch, the father of Attila and Bleda, who is not said to have shared in ruling.[1] Presumably

Plate 6   Medallion portrait of Attila. Certosa di Pavia.
The Mansell Collection, London.

each of the brothers ruled over a specific portion of the Huns and their subject nations, for joint rule of a common territory seems to have been a principle unknown to this people. We have no information as to the father or forebears of Rua and Octar, nor do we hear how they came to acquire their positions of authority. We can only say that Octar died some years before his brother, for Rua was the sole military leader of the confederacy when he first appears in history in the year 432.

In that year Aetius had been defeated by Boniface, count of Africa and master of the soldiers, in a battle fought at the fifth milestone from Ariminum. After the battle Aetius had retired to one of his estates, where he was too strong to be attacked openly; but Sebastian, Boniface's son-in-law, made an unexpected and unsuccessful attempt to have him murdered. Aetius realized his insecurity, went to Rome, and embarked on a ship bound for the Dalmatian coast. He then travelled through the provinces of Pannonia and reached the Huns, whom he had long counted as his friends: he had been their hostage more than twenty years before and they had helped him in the crisis of 425.[2] The Huns, who were now led by Rua, proved faithful to him once again, but at a price. In 427 Pannonia Secunda, including the great city of Sirmium, had been recovered from the Huns by the forces of East Rome, which now occupied all the powerful Danube fortifications lying in that province;[3] but during the year 433, as a result of a treaty between Aetius and the Huns, Pannonia Prima was surrendered to the latter by the Western government.[4] The province was in a difficult position: there were no natural boundaries between it and the even more exposed Valeria, and its loss was in any event merely a matter of time. The fact remains that Aetius voluntarily surrendered to the barbarians a province of the Roman Empire. It may have been in connection with this agreement that his son Carpilio followed in his footsteps by serving as a hostage among the nomads.[5]

Whatever the precise terms of the treaty, Aetius was able to re-establish his position in Italy with the aid given him by Rua. It may well be that he once again led a force of Huns into Italy, but our sources do not indicate that he found it necessary to fight a battle with the Gothic troops whom Sebastian and the Empress Placidia had summoned to their help from Gaul.[6] Aetius became a patrician and Sebastian fled to Constantinople. For a decade and a half thereafter Italy and the Western Empire remained undisturbed by the Huns, and it was contingents of their cavalry that enabled

Aetius and the Gallo-Roman landlords to maintain themselves with such success in Gaul throughout the years which followed. The enemies whom the Huns, supplied by Rua, helped them to withstand in Gaul were three-fold, and it was the Burgundians who first engaged their attention.

The Burgundians seem to have been among the Germanic peoples driven across the Rhine by the great westward expansion of the Huns in 405–6.[7] They were a powerful nation, numbering, according to Jerome, no less than 80,000 souls and stated by Ammianus to be a terror to their neighbours.[8] In 413 they had been settled on the left bank of the middle Rhine as allies (*foederati*) of the Romans, and their new kingdom, centred on Worms, seems to have included the territories of Mayence and Speyer.[9] For over twenty years we hear little of them, but at the beginning of the thirties their vigorous and growing population seems to have demanded an increase of land, and, taking advantage of the weakness of the Romans, they followed their King Gundahar in 435 in an invasion of Upper Belgica (the area around Trier and Metz).[10] But they under-estimated their adversary. They were crushed in a battle by Aetius and begged for a peace which they obtained but did not enjoy for long.[11] In 437, for a reason which can no longer be determined, Aetius induced his Hun friends to assail them. The result was devastating. According to one authority 20,000 Burgundians were massacred. Another says that almost the whole race was destroyed, and we know that the king Gundahar was among the slain.[12] This was the end of the Burgundian kingdom of Worms: it had lasted less than a generation, and in 443 its survivors were settled in Savoy. The destruction of their realm caught the imagination of contemporaries. Alone among the events of this period of Burgundian history it is mentioned by no less than four of the chroniclers, and it provided the historical basis of the epic of the *Nibelungen*. It was indeed a *bellum memorabile*: yet the reason for it is, to us, an utter mystery.

It may be, however, that the Huns had an account to

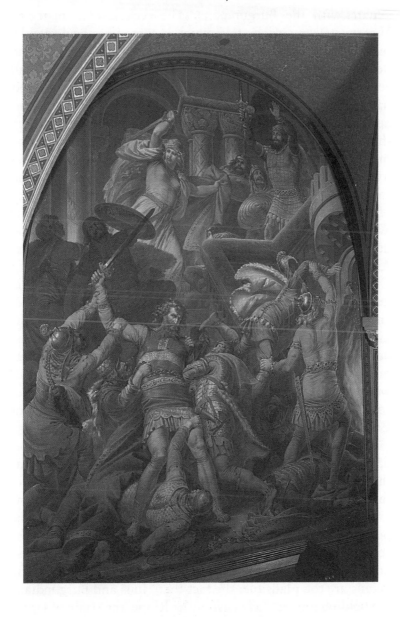

*Plate 7 The massacre of the Nibelungs. Nineteenth-century
painting, Neuschwanstein.
Ancient Art and Architecture Collection.*

square with the Burgundians. The ecclesiastical historian Socrates tells a curious tale which is sometimes neglected by modern writers.[13] Some of the Burgundians, he says – and here he is supported by independent sources[14] – had remained east of the Rhine when the majority of their nation had fled into Gaul in 406. The eastern Burgundians appear to have lived on the right bank of the Rhine, between that river, the Main, and the Neckar, in the neighbourhood of the Odenwald.[15] 'These men', Socrates goes on, 'always live an idle life, for they are practically all carpenters and they support themselves by their earnings from this craft.' (The East Romans held many curious beliefs about the West.) The Huns used to assail them continually, and devastate their land, and often slay large numbers of them. As a counsel of despair the Burgundians embraced Christianity, for they understood that the Christian God helped those who feared him. They were not disappointed, and the immediate result of their conversion was striking: the king, βασιλεύς, of the Huns, Uptar by name, burst open during the night as a consequence of his gluttony, and left his men without a leader. They numbered about 10,000, but were routed by 3,000 Burgundians. 'As a result', Socrates concludes, 'the nation of the Burgundians became ardent Christians.'

What are we to make of this tale? Fortunately, Socrates dates it with some precision to the year 430. The name Uptar therefore takes on a new interest: as Valesius pointed out in the seventeenth century, Uptar is none other than Octar, the brother of Rua, who outlived him, as we have seen. The purpose of Socrates' story, of course, is to explain the conversion of the eastern Burgundians, but it is nevertheless unlikely that every incident of the tale is a fabrication. The details are too plausible: the fact that Huns and Burgundians are fighting immediately east of the Rhine, the name of Uptar and the date of his death, the numbers of those engaged in the battle – none of these matters bears the stamp of an ecclesiastical historian's invention. We may safely conclude that seven years before the destruction of the kingdom of Worms Rua's brother Octar had been operating somewhat east of the Rhine, that he died in the middle of a campaign, and that some thousands of his men were surprised and defeated by the eastern Burgundians. The Huns who fell upon the kingdom of Worms, then, must have done so with particular relish; but, of course, that does not explain why Aetius unleashed them in the first place.

One of the officers who fought under Aetius against the Burgundians was Avitus, the future Emperor of the West.[16] After the campaign he retired to his estate of Avitacum, in Auvergne near Clermont-Ferrand. But his repose was soon rudely interrupted. Litorius, the principal lieutenant of Aetius and perhaps master of the soldiers in Gaul, marched hastily past the future emperor's estate on his way to Narbonne. This city was being besieged by the Visigoths of Theodoric I, who were making full use of Aetius' difficulties with the Burgundians in Upper Belgica. Litorius' army consisted of Huns – presumably those lent by Rua – and as they passed by the estate of Avitacum they behaved as though they were the enemies rather than the friends of the Gallo-Romans: 'with raid and fire, and sword and barbarity, and pillage, they were destroying everything in their path, betraying and making void the name of peace'.[17] One of them, more savage than his companions, cut down one of Avitus' servants for no reason that has been recorded. The news was brought to Avitus, busy with the defences of his estate, the inhabitants of which had been thrown into a panic by the news of their allies' approach. Avitus put on his armour, mounted his horse, galloped after the host of Litorius, and in single combat avenged his murdered servant.[18] None the less, Litorius proceeded to Narbonne, where the Huns, each of whom had been directed to carry two bushels of wheat with him, drove away the Visigoths after a vigorous charge and replenished the starving town.[19] In the years which followed, Litorius and his Huns maintained their offensive against the Visigoths. In 437, we are told, the war was continued 'with the aid of the Huns'.[20] Roman successes in 438 are also recorded, and, although the Huns are not mentioned, we need have no doubt that the successes were due to them.[21] Aetius himself, now freed from his entanglements in the north, slew 8,000 Goths in this year; but we have no information as to the nationality of the troops he was leading.[22] The crisis was reached in 439, when the Huns of Litorius laid siege to Theodoric's capital at Toulouse. The Goths had been discouraged by their losses in three successive years. They sent certain bishops as ambassadors to Litorius to beg for terms; but, says a contemporary, 'while they laid their hopes in God, we laid ours in Huns'. Litorius, anxious to eclipse the glory of Aetius, contemptuously rejected their embassy.[23] Outside the city walls he made a concession to his pagan troops: for the last time in Roman history a Roman general performed the ancient sacrifices and consulted the soothsayers on the result of the forthcoming battle. But the gods betrayed him when he engaged the army of Theodoric. At first the Huns inflicted fearful losses on the Visigoths, but at the height of the battle Litorius himself was taken prisoner by the enemy. The scales were turned and the Huns were destroyed to a man.[24] Litorius was brought into Toulouse and put to death. 'Whoever exalts himself', said Salvian, quoting Luke xiv. eleven, 'will be humbled, and whoever humbles himself will be lifted up.'[25] After a few months Aetius arrived upon the scene and engaged in a drawn battle with the exhausted Visigoths, after which peace between the Romans and Goths was arranged by Avitus, and the patrician returned to Italy to deal with a greater crisis.[26]

When Litorius led his undisciplined army past the estate of Avitus on his way to Narbonne he was coming from an encounter with the third of Aetius' enemies in these years. This third enemy was greater and of more interest than the Burgundians of Gundahar or Theodoric's Visigoths, for it consisted of the peasants, slaves, and brigands of north-western Gaul, the Bagaudae. As usual, our authorities tell us practically nothing of them, but two entries in a Gallic chronicle indicate the immense extent of their movement in these years. We are told that in 435 the Bagaudae of the *tractus Armoricanus* detached themselves entirely from the Western Empire and proclaimed themselves an independent state. Now it must be remembered that the *tractus Armoricanus* covered a far greater area than the modern Brittany. It consisted of the vast stretch of land between the mouth of the Garonne and that of the Seine, including the provinces of Poitou, Brittany, Anjou, and Normandy, with the cities of Tours, Orleans, and even Auxerre.[27] In this enormous tract of land then the slaves and peasants rose in rebellion against the oppression of their Roman and Gallic masters. Even in the third century the Gallic Bagaudae had succeeded in setting up two emperors of their own, Aelianus and Amandus, a fact which suggests that the political, like the social, organization of their independent state was a mere replica of that from which they seceded.[28] It is mere prejudice to characterize it as a robber state (*Räuberstaat*), a term which would more aptly describe the empire which they sought to leave.[29] At any rate, that the Bagaudae should have sought independence was, save in the case of newly conquered territories, an almost unique event in Roman imperial history: the closest parallel was furnished by their ancestors in the third century who, before setting up Aelianus and Amandus, seem to have supported Postumus and Tetricus.

In 435 the leader of the Bagaudae was Tibatto, of whom we know nothing: even his name is unique. We can only say that, soon after he rose, he was joined by practically every slave in Gaul.[30] For two years Tibatto and his men held their own, but in 437 Litorius and his Huns fell upon them. We have no details of the struggle which ensued. The chronicler merely tells us that 'when Tibatto had been captured, and some of the other leaders [*principes*] of the uprising had been thrown into chains, and others slaughtered, the disturbances of the Bagaudae came to rest'.[31] Litorius, the proud

Plate 8   Attila and the Huns in a nineteenth-century representation, 1891. Photograph: AKG London.

conqueror, had seen himself compelled, as Bury puts it, 'to reimpose upon them the "liberty" of Imperial rule'.[32] The court poet, Merobaudes, who was himself to smash an uprising of the Bagaudae in his native Spain a few years later, sings thus of the suppression of Tibatto: 'A native dweller, now more gentle, traverses the Armorican wilds. The land, accustomed to conceal with its forests plunder obtained by savage crime, has lost its old ways, and learned to entrust grain to its untried fields. The hand which long fought against the efforts of Caesar upholds the laws received under our consuls.'[33] Litorius thereupon galloped light-heartedly at the head of his unruly followers towards Narbonne, but the road led him in the end to Toulouse (p. 76 above). We shall see in the sequel that a solitary Hun campaign had not been sufficient to crush the Bagaudae of the *tractus Armoricanus*: the economic condition of the empire called for something more constructive than a massacre of the peasants. We shall also see that the Huns were not to continue for ever in the role of henchmen to the Gallic landlords.

From the time when Aetius negotiated his treaty with Rua in 433 until Litorius' disaster before Toulouse in 439, the Huns were the main prop of the vanishing dominion of the Gallo-Roman aristocracy in Gaul. But in 439 they were massacred (p. 76 above): brutal and senseless oppression exercised in the interests of great landowners is rarely successful for long.[34] The Huns do not appear to have reinforced Aetius after 439, for their forces were required elsewhere. It is time now to return to Rua and to consider events on the lower Danube frontier of the Eastern Empire.

II

In the opening months of the year 434 Esla, the principal diplomat of Rua, appeared in Constantinople. He came with a blunt demand. The Romans must return to Rua's dominions certain peoples who had fled from it; otherwise, Rua would declare war.

The Hun had chosen his time well. The great raids of 395 were only carried out when the Roman armies were assembled in Italy and the East was helpless. The attack of 422 was launched when the Eastern armies were at grips with the Persians (p. 35 above). Now too, in 434, the East was short of troops. Five years before, East Rome had been alarmed by the news that large tracts of Africa had been conquered by the Vandals. The loss of Africa was to the Roman Empire – so men said in Constantinople – what the Sicilian expedition had been to Athens.[35] So steps were taken at once to help the Western government. Aspar commanded the combined Eastern and Western forces in North Africa, but suffered a grievous defeat and lost the entire province, apart from the cities of Carthage and Cirta. When Boniface went home to Italy in 432 to fight Aetius (p. 71 above), Aspar and the Eastern forces continued the struggle alone, and the commander was appointed Western consul for the year 434. It was a golden moment for an enemy on the Danubian frontier, and Rua was prepared to use it.

The peoples whose return Elsa demanded were the Amilzuri, Itimari, Tunsures, Boisci, and others whose names are not given by our authorities. Their habitation seems to have lain near the Danube, but otherwise nothing is known of them. It seems very reasonable to suppose, however, as several scholars have done, that they were Hunnic tribes who refused to recognize the overlordship of Rua. He had doubtless sought to compel them to join his confederacy, but the old freedom of the steppe was strong in them, and they had preferred the comparative independence of service under their own chiefs in the imperial army. In any event, it is clear that the Huns were not yet a political unit.[36]

The Eastern government, always glad of recruits for its army, and especially so when its regular forces were away in Africa with Aspar, prepared to negotiate, and two diplomats showed some anxiety to undertake the task of appeasing Rua. In 418 Plintha, a Goth, had suppressed a rebellion in Palestine and had been made consul for the following year.[37] He was quickly appointed master of the soldiers, and, despite his ardent Arianism, was at one time recognized as the most powerful person in the court of Theodosius.[38] He and a certain Dionysius, the consul of 429 and master of the soldiers in the East, volunteered to travel to Rua, and Plintha sent out one of his henchmen named Sengilachus to urge the Hun to open negotiations with himself and not with any other Romans.[39] It would seem that it was a sort of Gothic clique in East Rome which tried to monopolize these negotiations with Rua; but it is not easy to see who were the 'other Romans' whom they wished to exclude from the negotiations. This is one of our tantalizing glimpses into the internal political struggles of Theodosius' reign upon which we have too little information to pass a judgement.

Whatever the intrigues which lay behind Plintha's moves, in the event it proved unnecessary to send any embassy to Rua; for, on the eve of the campaigning season of 434, the Hun leader suddenly died.[40] His death gave great relief to the

East Romans, who had been thoroughly alarmed by his
warlike attitude, and the Patriarch Proclus (434–47) preached
a sermon of thanksgiving when the news arrived, taking as
his text Ezekiel xxxviii. 2 and 22,

Son of Man, set thy face against Gog, the land of Magog, the chief
prince of *Rosh*, Meshech, and Tubal, and prophesy against him.
And I will plead against him with pestilence and with blood; and I
will rain upon him, and upon his bands, and upon the many people
that are with him, an overflowing rain, and great hailstones, fire,
and brimstone. [Rosh, 'Ρώς, is omitted from the Authorized
Version.]

The archbishop was highly commended for his adaptation of
Ezekiel's words, and the sermon became the universal topic
of conversation in Constantinople. But men soon became
somewhat confused as to the precise order in which the
events had taken place. It was believed that, when the people
were still *expecting* the attack, Proclus had assured them that
God had expressly announced his intention of destroying
Rua with a thunderbolt, and his people with fire and
brimstone from heaven. It was further believed that the
prediction had been confirmed in as much as Rua had never
come near the capital. The final stage in the growth of the
miracle was that which is still preserved in three of our
sources, two Greek and one Ethiopian. Socrates, Theodoret,
and John of Nikiu combine to tell us that, when Rua was
about to launch an attack on the Eastern Empire, God
destroyed him and his followers in accordance with the
prophecy contained in Ezekiel xxxviii. 2 and 22.[41]

But no miracle prevented the ominous event which
followed: Rua was succeeded by his two nephews, of whom
the elder was named Bleda, and the younger Attila.[42]

III

We know little of the rough, boisterous character of Bleda,

except that it was very different from his brother's. After the
great invasion of 441 we find him in possession of a Moorish
dwarf named Zerco, the very sight of whom Attila was
unable to endure. But Bleda was amused beyond all measure,
not merely by Zerco's stammering talk, but particularly by
his twisted and painful walk. He kept him by his side both at
his banquets and on his campaigns: he even made him a little
suit of armour to increase the grotesqueness of his figure.
Once Zerco escaped with a number of other Roman
prisoners. Bleda cared nothing for the others, but he was
wild with rage at the loss of Zerco. Horsemen scoured the
countryside until the dwarf was found, and Bleda roared
with laughter when he saw him brought back in chains. He
asked him why he had tried to escape. Zerco, in his strange,
halting speech, said that it was because Bleda had never given
him a wife. The Hun laughed more loudly than ever. He
swore that he would give him one of the ladies-in-waiting
from the empress's palace in Constantinople.[43]

No one could have formed a greater contrast to Attila.
When we follow Maximinus and Priscus to his camp in a
later chapter, we shall see something of his unbending, but
not pitiless, character. The portrait of him which has
survived in Jordanes is based on Priscus, who had seen him
more than once, and Gibbon's paraphrase of it has rendered
it famous.[44] No period of his manhood is as obscure as his
first years after he and Bleda had succeeded Rua. We know
only the circumstances and terms of his first treaty with the
East Romans, and then for some five years all is dark. The
Senate decided that Plintha's embassy should be sent,
notwithstanding the death of Rua and the accession of new
rulers among the barbarians. Plintha brought with him a
certain Epigenes, who was a noted speaker and whose
eloquence, it was hoped, might prove effective with the
Huns: he had until recently been engaged on the commission
which drew up the Theodosian Code.[45]

Plintha and Epigenes travelled to the city of Margus in
Moesia Superior, where, more than a century and a half

before, an obscure soldier named Diocles had sprung to fame by defeating the Emperor Carinus. Its situation near the mouth of the river Morava made it an important trading-centre,[46] and its bishop was soon to play an ignominious part in the wars of the Huns and Romans. Bleda and Attila met the Roman ambassadors outside the walls, and throughout the conversations which followed remained seated on their horses. The Romans considered that it would be unsuited to their dignity to stand on the ground and look up at the Huns as they talked, and they therefore sat painfully on horseback throughout the negotiations.[47] But an agreement was eventually reached. The Romans were to receive no further fugitives from the dominions of the Huns, and they were at once to return those whom they had already admitted into the empire. They were also to send back escaped Roman prisoners or were instead to pay 8 *solidi* for each of them, a sum which, in this period, in normal times and places, would buy almost 100 *modii* of corn. It was further stipulated that the Romans should make no alliance with any people with whom the Huns went to war. The Huns' trading rights were also reaffirmed: they were to trade on equal terms with the Roman merchants and in complete security. Rua's treaty had also bound the East Roman government to pay him the sum of 350 lb of gold per annum, a fact which perhaps explains the peace that prevailed on the Danube frontier for the first few years after Aspar had departed to Africa with large Eastern forces in 431: it may well have been in that year, and as a result of Aspar's departure, that Rua had extorted this treaty. At any rate, Attila's price was higher. Plintha was obliged to agree that the annual tribute payable to the Huns should be doubled, and that henceforth 700 lb of gold should cross the Danube every year. On these conditions the Roman government signed what we may call the Peace of Margus in the year 435.[48]

At this point the darkness descends. What occupied Attila between the years 435 and 439? A sentence in Priscus seems to hint at the answer. After signing the Peace of Margus, says the historian, Bleda and Attila 'went on subduing the nations in Scythia and made war upon the Sorosgi'.[49] It would seem then that in these obscure years Attila completed the task of extending his frontiers to the limits which they finally attained.

These limits cannot be exactly determined, and the direction in which Attila now turned cannot even be guessed at, for the Sorosgi are mentioned nowhere else. The western boundary of the Huns did not reach the Rhine, for, as we have already seen, the independent eastern Burgundians lay between them and the great river. Nor did the Burgundians stand alone: the Ripuarian Franks were also independent (p. 147 below), and there were doubtless many others. Octar had clearly ruled the westernmost territories of the Huns in the early days of Rua, and at the end of his life he had apparently been thrusting towards the Rhine, but he died before his task was finished. Towards the north, Priscus heard from a very reliable authority that Attila ruled 'the islands in the Ocean'.[50] Historians now agree that the islands ruled by Attila were those of the Baltic Sea, but Mommsen (p. 539, n. 5) thought that Britain was intended. In fact, Priscus himself may well have thought that his informant meant Britain: probably the historian's knowledge of the geography of north-western Europe was so limited that, knowing certain islands to be subject to Attila, he assumed them to be the British Isles. Gibbon believed very plausibly that the Huns derived a tribute of furs from these northern regions.[51]

Priscus says that Attila ruled 'all Scythia'.[52] How far did his dominions extend towards the east? Kiessling supposes that the Alans between the Don and an area somewhat west of the Aral Sea also recognized without qualification the overlordship of Attila. This seems scarcely likely to be correct. True, the Alans had never won their independence, but they would appear to have been ruled by Huns who owed little, if any, allegiance to Attila. We shall see that the Hun tribe of the Acatziri, who lived east of the Black Sea, were leading an independent life under their own chieftains until the year 448 (pp. 104ff below), and there is no reason to suppose that they stood alone.

We may conclude then that all the Germanic and other nations between the Alps and the Baltic, and between the Caspian (or somewhat west of it) and a line drawn an unknown distance east of the Rhine, recognized Attila and Bleda as their masters. Although the two brothers always acted in concert, so far as we know, and regarded their empire as a single property, they divided it between them and ruled separately;[53] but we do not know which portion was allotted to each.

In the years from 435 to 440 East Rome seems to have enjoyed an uneasy peace on her northern frontier. In the case of the Western Empire Attila, it will have been observed, continued the policy of his uncle. The troops whom Rua had lent to Aetius continued to serve the landowners of Gaul until the Visigoths destroyed them outside Toulouse in 439 (p. 76 above). But Litorius' force was not replaced, for by the year 440 a critical position had come about on the Danube.

When Theodosius ratified the treaty which Plintha had negotiated in 435, it would seem that he did so with little intention of carrying out its terms. True, his government did not hesitate to make a show of doing so. They at once surrendered the barbarians who had fled to them for refuge, among them two boys of the royal clan named Mama and Atakam, who are otherwise unknown. They had been kept by the Romans in a fort called Carsum in the Dobrudja near Troesmis, and, as soon as they had been handed back, they were crucified without delay.[54] Yet it would seem that, in the years which followed, Theodosius omitted to pay the 700 lb of gold which he had stipulated to send across the Danube. It is quite certain that he found the fugitive tribes far too valuable as soldiers in his army to send them back to their master.[55] He must have realized fully the danger of his policy, for in 439 he took a significant step. We have seen that after Uldin's raid into Thrace in 408 the prefect

Anthemius had refortified Constantinople, building the great Theodosian wall some distance to the west of that of Constantine. But this did not fully secure the capital, for the sea-shore at either end between the two walls remained open, and these two gaps would be a standing invitation to Vandal sea-raiders, who might well become the allies of the Huns. Therefore, in 439 Theodosius instructed the prefect Cyrus to complete the fortification of the capital.[56] The imperial government was not without its internal troubles. At some date in these years a certain Valips, a chieftain of a body of Rugi settled within the empire, who had caused trouble before, now rose in open rebellion, and, appealing to the innumerable discontented persons in the European provinces to join him, managed to seize the city of Noviodunum on the Danube, and compelled the government to give him terms.[57] None the less, the forces of East Rome were substantially unimpaired: the forts were manned and Anthemius' warships still actively patrolled the Danube.[58] There was no chance for Attila, still busy with his conquests in the north, to collect the 700 lb of gold which each year failed to arrive. The East was too strong: the opportunities of 395, 422, and 434 seemed unlikely to recur. But in fact an unparalleled chance presented itself in 440.

IV

In the year 440 the resources of East Rome were as severely strained as they had ever been hitherto during the long reign of Theodosius II. Shortly before, the tremendous news had arrived in Constantinople that Carthage had fallen to the Vandals on 19 October 439, and that the citizen population – but not the slaves – of Italy had been armed for the defence of the peninsula.[59] Sigisvult, the master of the soldiers, was organizing a watch on the Italian coasts. Aetius was on his way from Gaul (p. 76 above). A proclamation was issued by Valentinian's government on 24 June 440 to reassure the people of Rome and to inform them that assistance from the Eastern Empire was already on the way.

Was it necessary for Theodosius to send help to the West? In view of the danger which his northern policy invited, should his armed forces show any weakness, ought he not to have left the West to fend for itself? Such a course would have been impossible, for the defence of North Africa was as vital to Constantinople as to Italy. A hostile fleet based on Carthage could ruin New Rome almost as easily as Old. Already, it would seem, Vandal raiders had made a descent on Rhodes, aiming at the interruption of the grain route from Egypt,[60] and not many years later a panic was caused in Constantinople by the rumour that Geiseric proposed to assail Egypt itself.[61] In the spring of 440 then, a huge naval expedition, said to consist of 1,100 ships and commanded by five generals,[62] all with Germanic names, sailed from Constantinople to rescue Carthage from the Vandals.[63] Its setting forth was not a sign of criminal rashness on the part of Theodosius and his ministers. It was one of many indications that the political history of the fifth century, in the East and in the West alike, was dominated by the loss of North Africa. Before this crowning disaster all other military considerations had to take a secondary place.

By coincidence, a further misfortune occurred at approximately the same time. A Persian army under Yezdegerd II (438–53) launched an invasion of Roman Armenia for reasons which cannot now be recovered. Although the Persian forces soon had to retire because they were menaced in the rear by an attack of the Ephthalites or 'White Huns', a considerable Roman army must have been deployed to meet their threat. The northern frontier was thus still further stripped of its defenders.[64] Attila's chance had come, and he made full use of it.

The first indication Theodosius received that trouble was at hand was the news that a Roman fort lying north of the Danube had been surprised and captured by the Huns. This fort was one where the Huns had trading rights under the

Treaty of Rua.[65] The enemy descended upon it at market-time, outmanoeuvred whatever Roman troops were at hand, and slew many people.[66] The Roman government at once protested against the capture of the fort and the breach of the Treaty of Margus, in which it had been stipulated that the markets should be conducted on fair terms for both sides and without danger to either. But the Huns only revealed some additional grievances. They stated that the bishop of the city of Margus – the city outside which Plintha had signed the treaty of 435 – had crossed the Danube into Hun territory, had robbed the royal Hun graves on the opposite bank, and stolen the treasure buried there with their kings. This was a charge which the Roman ambassadors do not appear to have been able to deny: the bishop had in fact provided the nomads with an excellent pretext. The Huns went on to allege that the Romans had retained possession of a considerable number of fugitives from the Hun empire contrary to the terms of Plintha's treaty. Here again the Huns had the right upon their side. They therefore demanded the immediate surrender both of the bishop of Margus and of the fugitives. The Roman envoys could do no more than feebly and falsely deny the truth of both charges,[67] and the Huns continued their military operations. Crossing the Danube at an unspecified point they devastated a considerable number of towns and fortresses lying on the river's southern bank, and gained their first major success when the great city of Viminacium fell into their hands. The fate of Viminacium (the modern Kostolacz) warned the Romans of what was in store for their frontier cities. It was razed to the ground, and when Procopius had occasion a century later to mention the site, he says simply that 'the old city of Viminacium stood there, but long ago it was destroyed from the very bottom of its foundations'.[68] For a hundred years the site was desolate, until Justinian rebuilt it. When the catastrophe was imminent the local magistrates found time to bury the city exchequer, but they never returned to recover the money, and a find of no less than 100,000 coins has rewarded archaeologists.[69] Those citizens who survived the storm of the city were led away into captivity, and later in our story we shall meet a Greek merchant of Viminacium who was marched away among the prisoners (pp. 205ff below).

The morale of the frontier towns was shaken by this calamity. Men began to protest that the bishop of Margus should be handed over: why should entire provinces be endangered for the sake of a single man? The force of their plea was not lost on the prelate. He suspected that he would be given up, and, as Hodgkin (p. 49) puts it, 'determined to be beforehand with Fate'. He therefore slipped out of Margus, deserted to the Huns, and ensured his safety by promising Attila to hand over to him his city and his flock. Attila accepted the offer. A force of Huns was posted outside the town by night, the bishop managed to have the gates opened, and Margus fell into the hands of the enemy. It met the same fate as Viminacium: but it was never rebuilt, and Procopius knows nothing of it. The fate of its bishop is unknown.[70]

We have no detailed record of the rest of this campaign, but the main successes of the Huns can be discovered in our shattered authorities. At the same time as they took Margus the fortress of Constantia, directly across the Danube, fell into their hands.[71] The major disasters of the year, however, were still to come. Singidunum (Belgrade) was razed to the ground, and, like Viminacium, was left desolate until the days of Justinian.[72] The worst calamity of all was the loss of the vitally important city of Sirmium, the hinge upon which the defence of the whole Danube frontier turned. Sirmium was destroyed and its inhabitants enslaved.[73]

With the capture of Sirmium the campaign of 441 came to an end. In the midst of walled cities and fortresses the manoeuvres of the Hun cavalry were cramped and restricted, and no deep penetration had been made into Roman territory. Nevertheless, the season's achievement had been immense. An enormous gap had been broken in the fortifications of the Danube frontier, and the Balkans lay at the mercy of the Hun squadrons the following year.

Yet, surprisingly enough, there were no military operations in 442. In circumstances of which we know nothing whatever, Aspar, the master of the soldiers, managed to arrange a truce for one year at the beginning of the campaigning season of 442.[74] As soon as they learnt that a major Hun attack had developed, Theodosius and his ministers recalled the fleet from Sicily, where, owing to the subtle diplomacy of Geiseric, it had achieved nothing against the Vandals and had served only to oppress the Sicilians.[75] The fleet was unable to reach East Rome in time to allow the soldiers on board to take part in the operations of 441. Consequently the government had been unable to organize any defence whatever against the attacks on the frontier towns. We are assured explicitly that throughout the campaign Attila had met with no opposition from the Roman field army.[76] The reason was, of course, that he had chosen his time so well, when the campaigns in Persia and the central Mediterranean had absorbed all the available Roman forces. Whatever hope may have existed – and it must have been very slight – was ruined by a highly obscure incident which occurred in Thrace, the area which should have served as a base for a counter-attack on the Huns. A chronicler tells us, in his laconic style, that 'John, the Master of the Soldiers, a Vandal by race, was killed in Thrace by the treachery of Arnegisclus'.[77] Arnegisclus was a member of that clique of Germans which controlled the East Roman armies in these years; and after the murder he succeeded to John's office of master of the soldiers. What personal or even nationalist rivalry lay behind this murder we have no means of saying. Only one thing is clear: when the commanding officer was liable to be murdered and his place filled by the murderer, no organized Roman defence was possible.

Whatever the terms of the truce – they certainly included demands for the fugitives and for the arrears of tribute[78] – Theodosius made the utmost use of the year's respite. His efforts to finance the preparations for a renewal of the war and to provide for the pay of his men have left an interesting memorial in an issue of golden *solidi* dating from the first nine months of 442.[79] The coins, which were issued in considerable numbers and in great haste, show the bust of Theodosius wearing his helmet and his cuirass and holding a lance and shield. On the reverse Constantinople is shown also helmeted, with her left foot on the prow of a vessel: she holds the world in her right hand, and in her left the cross. Behind her a shield lies upon the ground. A small number of the coins show, instead of Theodosius, his wife Eudocia and his sister Pulcheria. It would seem that they made personal contributions of valuables to enable the new issue to be brought out.[80] Now, while many of Theodosius' coins are inscribed with boastful inscriptions, 'glory of the circle of the earth' (*gloria orbis terrarum*), 'the power of the army of the Romans' (*virtus exercitus Romanorum*), 'victory of the emperors' (*victoria Augustorum*), and the like, this issue carries the date alone. The crisis was too acute for idle words.[81]

As a result of his hasty preparations and the return of the fleet from Sicily, Theodosius felt himself able to show a bolder front to Attila when the campaigning season of 443 came round. Attila assembled his army and demanded the fugitives and the tribute money. He added that if there were any delay, or if the Romans carried out any offensive strategical moves, he would no longer hold back the Huns. Theodosius' ministers refused to hand over the fugitives, whom they had enrolled among the imperial forces; but they undertook to send envoys who would attempt to reach an agreement satisfactory to both sides. It seems clear that, in spite of the events of 441, they had not yet realized what war with the nomads meant. They were soon to discover.[82]

When Attila heard the emperor's reply he began in anger to devastate the Roman territory opposite him, and, driving eastwards along the Danube, captured a few forts of minor importance and then took the great and populous city of Ratiaria on the right bank of the Danube in Upper Moesia.[83]

This large city, the capital of the province of Dacia Ripensis, was a base of the Danube fleet and contained one of the state arms factories. It was utterly destroyed and the inhabitants carried off as slaves into the dominions of the Huns.[84]

Their rear was now secure. No Roman attack could be launched on their communications when they turned to the interior of the imperial provinces. Riding up the valley of the river Margus (Morava) they came to the city of Naissus (Nish), the strategic importance of which was as great in antiquity as it is today. It lay on the right bank of the river Nischava in Dacia Mediterranea,[85] and it too was the seat of an imperial arms factory and was thickly populated.[86] As the Huns rode away from it, the birthplace of Constantine lay desolate like Singidunum and Viminacium until Justinian restored it in the following century.[87] It would seem that an encounter outside the walls had sufficed to seal the city's fate.[88]

The Huns now turned southeast up the valley of the river Nischava and devastated another great Balkan city, Sardica, the modern Sophia, and we need not doubt that it too was left almost uninhabited.[89] The road to the capital was now largely cleared, and they galloped down the military highway which ran along the valley of the Hebrus (Maritza). When Philippopolis fell into their hands, the defence of the European provinces was rendered impossible, for at this ancient city the great north–south road from Oescus on the Danube to the Aegean Sea crossed the age-old highway running from the Bosphorus to the West. And, although Adrianople and Heraclea either beat off their attacks or were by-passed, Arcadiopolis was taken also. The booty was enormous and the number of prisoners beyond counting.[90]

At last they met the new army of Theodosius. It was commanded by Aspar, the Alan who had negotiated the truce of the previous year, and by the Germans Areobindus and Arnegisclus, the murderer of the Vandal John. They were beyond doubt the foremost generals in the East Roman service at that time, but they were no match for Attila. They engaged him in a succession of battles outside the capital, but suffered heavy defeats in them all,[91] and, as a result of a rapid manoeuvre by the Huns, were cut off from Constantinople and forced back into the Chersonesus. The Huns now reached the sea at three points, at Callipolis and Sestus south of the capital, and at an unspecified place north of it. Athyras, a fortress dangerously close to the city walls, was also occupied.[92] It was hopeless for the ill-equipped nomad squadrons to attack the new fortifications of Constantinople and no move seems to have been made against the capital itself. Instead, Attila turned upon the remnants of Aspar's army in the Chersonesus, and in a final battle there shattered the last remaining forces of the Romans.[93]

Only one success had been won by the empire, and this had not been due to the regular army. A large squadron of Huns, under some of their most brilliant commanders, had been detached from the main body of the army to invade Lower Moesia. This force collected a large quantity of booty and a considerable number of captives before it approached the small but powerful town of Asemus, which lay on the frontier between Oescus and Ad Novas, where the little river Asemus (modern Osma) flows into the Danube at a point nine miles east of the Utus (Vid). The citizens boldly undertook their own defence, and resolved not to rely on the strength of their moat and walls. Accurately informed by spies of the movements of the enemy, now gravely handicapped by the weight of their booty and the number of their captives, the men of Asemus fell upon them when the Huns believed themselves secure. Although outnumbered, the citizens succeeded in killing a considerable number of the enemy with slight loss to themselves, and rescued the Roman prisoners.[94]

This was a purely local success, and, after the defeat in the Chersonesus, Theodosius had no option but to beg for terms. The negotiations were entrusted to Anatolius, who had successfully closed the recent war with Persia and had been

master of the soldiers in the East since 438. The terms
granted by Attila, who had little to gain by prolonging the
war, were harsh. The fugitives were to be handed over at
once. The arrears of tribute were calculated at 6,000 lb of
gold, and this sum was to be paid without delay. In addition,
the annual tribute paid to the Huns under the treaty of 435
was to be trebled, and Attila was now to receive 2,100 lb of
gold per annum. Further, every Roman prisoner who escaped
from the Huns was to be ransomed at 12 *solidi* a head in
place of the 8 *solidi* stipulated in 435. No fugitive from the
Hun empire was in future to be received by the Romans.[95]
This treaty was provisionally signed before 27 August 443,
for on that date Theodosius returned from Asia Minor to
Constantinople, which he would scarcely have done if
hostilities had still been in progress in the neighbourhood
of the capital.[96]

When the terms of the treaty had been arranged, Scotta,
one of the most eminent lieutenants of Attila,[97] came to the
Eastern capital to receive the gold and the fugitives. He was
given the gold, but the Romans had massacred all the
fugitives who had expressed unwillingness to return north of
the Danube. Scotta appears to have shown no resentment at
this, although some relatives of Attila, who refused to
recognize his overlordship, had been among the slain. Scotta
announced, however, that he had been instructed to add one
to the number of articles in the treaty: the men of Asemus
were to be surrendered together with all their prisoners,
whether Roman or barbarian.[98] Otherwise, the Hun army
would not be withdrawn and the treaty would not be
ratified. Anatolius, who was being assisted in the conduct of
these negotiations by Theodulus, the master of the soldiers in
Thrace, did not feel himself in a position to refuse this
request. The two Romans did indeed attempt to persuade
Scotta to forgo the demand, but their efforts only revealed
the complete willingness of Attila to continue the war. They
therefore wrote to the citizens of Asemus, instructing them
either to hand over the Roman prisoners whom they had

rescued or to pay 12 *solidi* for each of them, for Attila was willing to accept ransom money at the new rate. They also instructed them to set free any Huns whom they had captured. To this letter the men of Asemus replied that the rescued Romans had now dispersed to their homes and could not be reassembled, and, further, that they had already massacred the Huns whom they had captured, with the exception of two. They had retained these two with the intention of exchanging them for some children whom the Huns had captured outside the walls of their town. Attila, when he heard of this, made a search for the children in question, but could find no trace of them. The men of Asemus accepted his assurance that they were genuinely missing, and returned the two Huns whom they had spared. The first Peace of Anatolius was thereupon ratified in the autumn of 443.[99]

V

No real tranquillity descended upon the Eastern Empire. Attila sent another embassy to Constantinople raising some difficulty about the return of the fugitives. This embassy was followed by a second and a third and a fourth. On each occasion Theodosius' ministers presented the envoys with the handsome gifts which it was customary to bestow on ambassadors,[100] but insisted that none of the fugitives now remained on Roman soil. This was probably the truth, for Attila merely sent the embassies so that those of his followers who served on them might reap the rich harvest of costly presents which the Roman government found it expedient to supply. One pretext after another brought fresh ambassadors to the capital. Innumerable minor complaints of the Hun were examined by Roman officials, and Attila's lieutenants amassed greater and greater riches.

At precisely this time the East Roman frontiers were disturbed along their entire circuit. The Persians, although they had withdrawn from Armenia in 442, still kept their forces massed on the frontier, and since Anatolius had only succeeded in arranging a single year's truce with them, hostilities might well break out anew. To make matters worse, the defences of the frontier of Armenia had been weakened by the action of the local landlords, who had usurped some imperial estates in the neighbourhood, so that bodies of men who had formerly garrisoned the frontier were now constrained to work the landowners' newly acquired estates.[101] Somewhat to the west of Armenia lived the nation of the Tzanni, ideally placed to overrun the Roman territory around Trapezus. Their land was barren, and, we are told, they lived only upon what they could steal. They were now raiding.[102] The Isaurians had also broken out of their inaccessible mountains in the south of Asia Minor and were plundering the surrounding countryside. Saracen tribes from the desert were menacing some of the Eastern provinces, and trouble was expected even from the Ethiopian kingdom of Axum.[103] Apart from the Persians' failure to demobilize their troops, none of these incidents formed a serious threat to Theodosius' security. But most of them demanded the presence of troops on the respective parts of the Roman frontier. And throughout 444, while Attila's ambassadors came swarming to Constantinople, Roman forces were being dispersed to every corner of the empire, and the government's capacity to adopt a firm attitude towards the Huns was correspondingly weakened.[104]

In these difficult circumstances, Theodosius took what measures he could to ensure the future safety of the northern frontier. On 12 September 443, within a month of the end of the fighting, stringent orders were given to Nomus, the master of the offices and one of the most trusted ministers of the emperor, to fortify the exposed frontier along the Danube where Attila had won his initial successes in 441, to repair the fortresses there, and to bring all military detachments posted in that area up to their full strength.[105] That these tasks were carried out during the year 444 to the satisfaction of the emperor would seem to be indicated by the fact that Nomus was appointed to the consulship for 445. But while his work was still in progress, the government could do nothing save receive the unending stream of Attila's ambassadors, reward them with handsome gifts, and deal with each irritating complaint as best they could.

After the conclusion of the Peace of Anatolius the plans and movements of the Huns are exceedingly obscure, for the relevant portion of Priscus' work has not survived. That internal dissensions of a most far-reaching character had broken out among their leaders is proved by the murder of Bleda, who fell by his brother's hand sometime in this period. Our various authorities date the event to 444, 445, and 446, but there can be little doubt that Attila murdered his elder brother in the year 445.[106] Of the origin of the dispute we know nothing. Its result was that the peoples formerly governed and exploited by Bleda now came under the direct control of Attila.[107] From 445 until his death he had no rival among the Huns. He seems to have found it expedient, however, to base his supremacy on the solid foundations of his followers' superstition,[108] and for this purpose he had recourse to an old sword which had recently been discovered by one of his followers. A herdsman noticed one day that one of his cattle was lame and that its foot had been cut. Following the trail of blood to its source, the herdsman found an ancient sword buried in the grass. He pulled it up and brought it to Attila, who was not slow to observe its uses. It was the sword of the war-god, he declared; it was honoured by former leaders of the Huns, but had been lost long ago; now it would bring him success in his wars and make him triumphant over all his foes.[109] Anyone who questioned his right to unite the position of Bleda with his own would have to fight, not only himself, but the divine powers as well.

Otherwise the Huns remained at peace in these years, and one of their Roman prisoners could tell Priscus a short while later of the idle, carefree life of the Huns in peace-time, 'with each man enjoying his present blessings and neither causing trouble nor suffering it', a very different life, he thought, from that of the Romans at peace.[110]

A random fragment of Priscus preserves some information about one of the Roman embassies which were sent out to Attila in these years.[111] Theodosius, we are told, sent out to the Huns the ex-consul Senator, one of his closest advisers, who appears as a patrician when he attended the Council of Chalcedon in 451.[112] Nothing is said as to the purpose of his embassy, but Priscus tells us with some scorn that he was afraid to go to the Huns by land. Instead, he sailed up the Black Sea to Odessus (Varna), where he found Theodulus, whom we have already met assisting Anatolius in the negotiations of 443, and who was probably master of the soldiers in Thrace.[113] The fragment there breaks off, so that we hear no more of Senator's travels, but the fact that he was journeying northwards by sea suggests that he, like the historian Olympiodorus before him (pp. 39–40 above), was making for a Hun encampment north or north-west of the Black Sea. Attila, then, seems to have moved into the interior of his dominions at this time.

VI

The Huns invaded the East Roman Empire for the second time in 447. Our sources tell us not a word as to why they did so or what pretext they used. That a continuous intake of plunder was a social necessity for them, as they were organized under Attila, will become apparent later. Of only one other thing can we be certain: the peace was broken through no fault of the Roman government. If it had been, Priscus would beyond doubt have drawn attention to the government's error at considerable length, and some indication of his indictment of Theodosius would surely have reached us in the narratives derived from his. The East Romans had trouble in plenty without inviting an invasion by the nomads. The winter following the ratification of the Peace of Anatolius had been exceptionally severe. Snow lay on the ground, we are told, for almost six months, and thousands of men and cattle died from the cold. In the following year tremendous rain-storms devastated Bithynia, and entire towns and estates were washed away by floods and overflowing rivers. In 445 riots in the Circus at Constantinople resulted in many deaths, and large numbers of the citizens perished in a plague. The calamities continued through 446. In that year the food-supplies of the capital failed and their failure was followed immediately by another plague.[114] Theodosius' ministers were in no position to take risks on the northern frontier.

Whatever the pretexts and preliminaries, Attila, who was now at the height of his career, launched his second invasion in the spring of 447. The attack was planned on an even bigger scale than that of 441 – 'a huge attack, greater than the previous one', says a chronicler.[115] It was carried out, not only by the Huns themselves, but also by contingents of the subject races. The Gepids were led by their king Ardaric and the Goths by Valamer, and there were others whose names have not been recorded.[116] The assault was directed through the provinces of Lower Scythia and Moesia, that is, farther to the east than in 441, so that the new fortifications built under Nomus' direction were by-passed. Furthermore, it seems to have been the first and only occasion on which the Huns attacked the undivided forces of the Eastern Empire, for we have no report that trouble on any other front distracted the armies of Theodosius.

As the Hun squadrons prepared to move, a disaster of the first magnitude befell the Romans. The series of earthquakes which shattered the Eastern Empire for four months beginning on 26 January 447 were, in the belief of Evagrius, the worst in its history. Entire villages were swallowed up and countless disasters occurred both on land and sea. Thrace, the Hellespont, and the Cyclades all suffered. For three or four days after the earthquakes began, the rain poured from the sky, we are told, in rivers of water. Hillocks were levelled with the ground. Countless buildings were thrown down in Constantinople, and, worst of all, a stretch of the massive walls of Anthemius, including no less than fifty-seven towers, fell to the ground.[117] It seemed as though nothing could now save the great city. To crown all, so many of the inhabitants were buried under the ruins of the numerous buildings which collapsed inside the city that plague soon made its appearance again, and thousands of the citizens died. Yet, after a momentary panic, the men of Constantinople showed themselves equal to the crisis. Led by the Circus parties and directed by the praetorian prefect Flavius Constantinus, they managed to restore the walls in their entirety within sixty days of the calamity, when Attila's forces were already swarming forward. Constantinus was not content merely to restore the wall of Anthemius: he also built a second wall in front of it, so that the city was now defended by a triple line of defence. 'The fortifications', writes a modern inquirer, 'rose tier above tier, and combined to form a barricade 190–207 feet thick, and over 100 feet high.'[118] A bilingual inscription commemorates the achievement of Constantinus in verses scarcely worthy of the occasion:

Triumphantly Constantinus set up this firm wall. Pallas scarcely built her walls with such speed and such strength.

In sixty days, Constantinus, promoted Prefect by the sceptred Emperor, built this wall.

These two couplets can still be read on the wall of Theodosius. A third has survived in the *Anthology*:

Theodosius the Emperor and Constantinus Prefect of the East built this wall in sixty days.[119]

The defence of the capital was entrusted to Flavius Zeno, an Isaurian, at the head of a large body of his countrymen. How these Isaurians came to be entrusted with so vital a charge is unknown, for throughout the fifth century they had hitherto appeared consistently among the bitterest foes of the empire.[120] Zeno's defence did not inspire the plague-stricken population with complete confidence. We are told, indeed, that 'the majority' of the inhabitants fled as the Huns drew nearer, and doubtless many did so; but, when another authority tells us that Theodosius himself made preparations for flight, we may suspect him of some prejudice, for Attila's attack had not caught the emperor unprepared.[121]

Near the river Utus (Vid) in Dacia Ripensis Attila was engaged by the imperial army which had marched out of Marcianople to meet him. The Romans were commanded by the German Arnegisclus. He had distinguished himself in 441 by the murder of the Vandal John, whose post of master of the soldiers in Thrace he still occupied. Whatever his faults – and he had been among the commanders so soundly beaten in the campaign of 443[122] – he now seems to have provided a more obstinate resistance to the Huns than they had yet encountered from the Romans. He staked everything on one pitched battle, and he lost. His horse was killed beneath him, and our authorities unite in emphasizing the courage with which he was fighting when he himself fell. Although the victory lay with Attila, his losses had been severe.[123] Indeed, had a detailed account of the engagement survived, we might well find that the battle of the river Utus caused irreparable damage to the strength of the Huns. The fact remains that this was the last of Attila's victories over the Romans.

An immediate result of the battle was the fall of Marcianople, Arnegisclus' base, the capital of Moesia Secunda and the largest city of Thrace. It lay desolate until Justinian restored it a hundred years later.[124] The Huns do not appear to have struck out now for the capital: the walls had been fully restored, and against them the arrows of the nomads were helpless. But they devastated the Balkan provinces with terrible ferocity, and Jordanes[125] lists Illyricum, Thrace, and both provinces of Dacia, together with Moesia and Scythia, as having suffered grievously. The invaders then sought out new areas of plunder: like Zabergan a hundred years later they drove straight down southwards into Greece and were only held at Thermopylae.[126] Nothing is known of the further course of this invasion, about which we are even less well informed than about that of 441/3.

The terrors of the war, however, have been in some measure recorded for us by Callinicus in his life of St Hypatius, who was still living in Thrace at the time.[127] 'The barbarian nation of the Huns', he writes,

which was in Thrace, became so great that more than a hundred cities were captured and Constantinople almost came into danger and most men fled from it . . . And there were so many murders and blood-lettings [αἱματεκχυσίαι] that the dead could not be numbered. Ay, for they took captive the churches and monasteries and slew the monks and maidens in great numbers.

Perhaps the holy writer has exaggerated somewhat in saying that a hundred towns were captured; at any rate, the writer of the Gallic Chronicle of AD 452 is content to put the figure at 'not less than seventy'. But his words contain a phrase of such interest that they may be quoted in full: 'nova iterum Orienti consurgit ruina, qua septuaginta non minus civitates Chunnorum depraedatione vastatae, cum nulla ab Occidentalibus ferrentur auxilia ('a new catastrophe raised itself up against the East, in which not less than seventy cities were devastated by the attacks of the Huns, while no help was brought from the West').[128] What is the meaning of these last words? We can only conclude that there were men in the West who believed that Aetius should not have stood idle when the East was being ruined. East Rome often came to the assistance of West Rome – though not for altruistic reasons – even when such help was almost beyond her strength. This is our only hint that some men believed that the debt should be repaid, and that the Old Rome should carry aid to the New.

Finally, we may notice the words of Count Marcellinus, who lived in the East many years later, for in his entry under the year 447 he writes with a vigour which he rarely displays elsewhere: 'paene totam Europam excisis invasisque civitatibus atque castellis [Attila] conrasit' – 'Attila ground almost the whole of Europe into the dust.'

5

Peace on the Danube Frontier

The three years following the great invasion of 447 were filled by diplomatic encounters between the Huns and the Romans, for the latter, having no military resources left, could now rely only on the skill of their diplomats. Even so, their subtlety and patience brought them greater successes than they probably expected. The story of the diplomatic history of these years is better known to us than that of any other similar period in ancient history and forms a striking contrast to the obscurity of the war itself. Our good fortune is due solely to the fact that Priscus himself served on the chief Roman mission of the year 449, and devoted a quite disproportionate amount of his book to a narrative of what he saw and did. But before we consider this narrative we must recount another campaign of Attila, the last which he fought in eastern Europe.

I

No nation as predatory as the Huns could remain at peace for long, and in the season following that of 447 we find them engaged in a new struggle. Their victims on this occasion were an obscure but valiant people called the

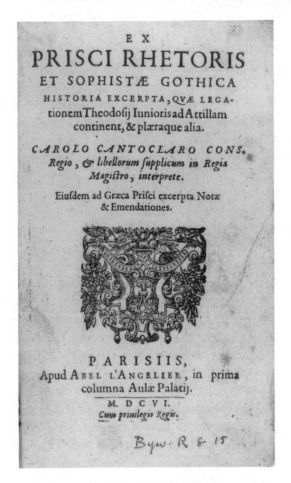

E X
PRISCI RHETORIS
ET SOPHISTÆ GOTHICA
HISTORIA EXCERPTA, QVÆ LEGA-
tionem Theodofij Iunioris ad Attillam
continent, & plæraque alia.

CAROLO CANTOCLARO CONS.
Regio, & libellorum fupplicum in Regia
Magiſtro, interprete.

Eiufdem ad Græca Prifci excerpta Notæ
& Emendationes.

PARISIIS,
Apud ABEL L'ANGELIER, in prima
columna Aulæ Palatij.

M. DC VI.
Cum priuilegio Regis.

Byw. R & 15

*Plate 9   The title page from the 1606 Latin translation of the
surviving fragments of Priscus' History – already the main point
of interest was Priscus' mission to Attila.
Reproduced by courtesy of The Bodleian Library,
Oxford (Byw R.8 15).*

Acatziri.[1] Who precisely they were we do not know for
certain, although several conjectures have been offered: they
were the Agathyrsi of Herodotus, or the Khazars, or the
Magyars, and so on.[2] These conjectures should be rejected:

Priscus tells us that they were a tribe of Huns, and we have no reason to doubt him (p. 14 above). The area in which they lived can only be fixed very approximately. Jordanes tells us that the Vidivarii lived at the mouth of the Vistula: to the east of them on the Baltic coast dwelt the Aesti, and to the south of these, *quibus in austrum*, was settled the nation of the Acatziri. Consequently Marquart locates them around the site of the modern city of Korosten.[3] But Priscus says that the Acatziri inhabited ['Scythia near the Pontus [= Black Sea]' (τὴν πρὸς τῷ Πόντῳ Σκυθικήν), which would seem to indicate an area nearer the Black Sea than Korosten.[4] Many years later, when certain Asiatic peoples were driven into Europe, the Acatziri were the first tribe to endure their onslaught, and a further passage of Priscus gives us reason to believe that they were not entirely remote from the approaches to the Persian empire.[5] All this suggests that a people who may have lived on the Baltic coast in the days of Jordanes' authority – though his statement as to their position should perhaps be rejected outright – had emigrated there from the far south-east after 448 and in that year were living near the eastern shore of the Black Sea or the Sea of Azov. On only one point do scholars show unanimity: Tomaschek, Marquart, and Kiessling agree that the name is Old Turkish and means 'Forest-people' (*Waldleute*),[6] but whether the philologists of the future will show the same harmony remains to be seen.

Jordanes, or his authority, was impressed by the valour of the Acatziri, for they are described as 'a most powerful people' (*gens fortissima*). They knew nothing of agriculture, he tells us, and were nomads, living off their flocks and herds and by hunting. We learn further that they were organized in clans and tribes, each tribe and clan being led by its own chieftain.[7] It is fairly clear then that, like the Huns of Attila, they belonged in point of material civilization to the lower stage of pastoralism. How they had survived the expansion of the Huns under Bleda and Attila in the thirties of the fifth century and had retained their independence we do not know, but it seems probable that the conquerors had not come so far east.

However that may be, the Acatziri were living on friendly terms with the Huns until somewhat after the time of Bleda's murder. Theodosius realized their strategic importance as an independent power lying on Attila's rear, and it was – or soon became – a tradition of East Roman diplomacy that such powers should be bound as closely as possible to the empire, so as to threaten the rear of the hostile nations who lay immediately beyond the Roman frontier. The emperor therefore sent gifts to the chieftains of the Acatzirian tribes and suggested that they should renounce their alliance with Attila and enter upon a treaty with himself.[8] Unhappily for him, the envoy sent to bring about this change in the political relationships of the Acatziri was not adequately acquainted with the social organization of the people with whom he had come to deal. One of their chiefs, Curidachus by name, ranked higher than the chiefs of the other tribes, a fact which seems to have been unknown to the East Roman envoy. Curidachus should have been the first to receive Theodosius' gifts, but in fact he received them second. He felt himself slighted and deprived of his prerogative, and turned in anger to Attila, calling upon him to attack his fellow chieftains among the Acatziri who had usurped his position.[9] Attila did not delay in sending the required forces, and after a succession of battles[10] he reduced the whole race to subjection. He then summoned Curidachus to his presence, but Curidachus was somewhat suspicious of his benefactor's intentions, and sent back a message saying: 'It is difficult for a man to gaze upon a god; for if it be impossible to look full upon the orb of the sun, how could one behold the greatest of the gods without injury?' His caution brought its reward: he was left to rule his particular tribe, but Attila sent his own eldest son Ellac to govern the rest of the Acatziri.[11] Theodosius' hopes of winning a friend in the rear of the Huns thus came to nothing, and we hear of no further attempts by the East Roman government to regain its influence among the Pontic peoples.

II

In 448 peace was restored on the northern frontier.[12] We
have no information as to the precise course of the
negotiations by which this peace was brought about. We
know, however, that the chief negotiator on the Roman side
was that same Anatolius to whom it had fallen to conclude
the war of 443.[13] The most important of the terms of this
second Peace of Anatolius was one which shows that the
treaty as a whole was much harsher than that of 443. Attila
demanded that a wide belt of country south of the Danube
should be completely evacuated by the Romans. This strip of
land was to stretch from Singidunum on the frontier of
Pannonia to Novae, a distance of some 300 miles, and was to
be five days' journey in depth, that is, about 100 or 120 miles.
In other words, all Dacia Ripensis and parts of three other
provinces were to be abandoned and the new frontier was to
run through Naissus. The Danube, with all its fortifications
and great frontier cities, which now lay in ruins, was no
longer to be the boundary of the Eastern Empire.[14] We know
none of the other terms of the treaty save one: the tribute was
to be continued, but at what rate we have no means of
saying.[15] For the next two years Roman diplomacy was
directed towards the aim of securing some mitigation of
these terms.

In the spring of 449 one of Attila's most powerful
lieutenants, Edeco by name, arrived in Constantinople. He
had apparently been there in the preceding year also, in
connection with the negotiations which had resulted in the
signature of the second Peace of Anatolius. Himself a Hun
(p. 15 above), he now came attended by another of Attila's
'picked men' (λογάδες), Orestes, who, surprisingly enough,
was a Roman, having been born in Pannonia. Orestes had
married the daughter of a certain Romulus, after whom he
was to name his son, the last Emperor of the West.[16] On
being introduced into the palace Edeco delivered a letter

from Attila, and made some verbal announcements, which were translated to the emperor and his ministers by Bigilas,[17] an interpreter attached to the office of the master of the offices.[18] This Bigilas, who was to play a major part in the events which followed, had already acted as Anatolius' interpreter in the negotiations of 448.[19] That a man so unsuited to the niceties of diplomacy was so often employed by the Eastern government in their dealings with the Huns is to be explained by the extreme difficulty of finding suitable persons with a knowledge of the Hun language. In all the pages of Priscus we meet with only one other man – in addition no doubt to Aetius – who could speak it. This was Rusticius, a native of Upper Moesia, who had lived among the Huns as a war prisoner since the campaign of 441.[20] At any rate, Bigilas had no doubt experienced to the full the contempt in which the later Romans held their interpreters,[21] and his constant intercourse with such dignitaries as Anatolius and Maximinus seems to have lent an aggressive and tactless character to his behaviour.

The letter which Edeco delivered suggests that the Romans had been as tardy in carrying out the terms of the second Peace of Anatolius as they had been in 435. Attila accused them of withholding some fugitives from his dominions and of failing to evacuate the belt of land south of the Danube. If these two conditions of the peace were not promptly carried out, he threatened an immediate renewal of the war. He further demanded that the Roman government should send him ambassadors to discuss all outstanding points of difference between himself and the Eastern Empire, and insisted that these ambassadors should be no minor officials but ex-consuls of the highest rank. He concluded by declaring that, if such men were sent to him, he would cross the Danube and go as far as Sardica (Sophia) to meet them.[22] It is clear from this letter that he was repeating the policy of blackmail which he had pursued with such persistence after the peace of 443 (pp. 95–6 above). But now the Roman government had decided on a drastic plan by which to free themselves.

When Edeco had delivered his letter to the emperor and had added some verbal explanations through Bigilas, he left the palace accompanied by the interpreter and was brought to another mansion, where he met Theodosius' most powerful minister, the eunuch Chrysaphius, surnamed Tzumas or Ztommas.[23] He appears to have had complete control over Theodosius' government since the fall of the prefect Cyrus (p. 82 above) and the Empress Eudocia, that is, since about the time of the first Peace of Anatolius in 443/4: in fact, it was he who had ruined Cyrus.[24] He was now at the height of his power, although his entanglement in the ecclesiastical policies of his godfather, the heretic Eutyches, was soon to weaken his position. It was whispered that he employed his vast influence with the emperor to increase his personal wealth by unscrupulous means;[25] but the charge was one levelled at all the prominent statesmen of the later empire, and we may believe that in this respect he was better than his reputation, but considerably less than innocent. There could be no difference of opinion as to the skill with which he maintained his position, but his foreign policy, which will occupy us in a later chapter, was the subject of bitter controversy and led to his outright condemnation in the historical tradition.

When Edeco had been introduced to him, the Hun expressed his astonishment at the splendour of the imperial palaces in the capital. Bigilas translated his words. The eunuch replied that Edeco, too, could be the master of great riches and of mansions with gilded ceilings if he would abandon the Scythians and attach himself to the service of the Romans. Edeco naively replied that he could not do this without his master's permission. Chrysaphius asked him if he had free access to Attila's person and whether he possessed any real authority among the Huns. Edeco replied that he did: as one of Attila's lieutenants, λογάδες, it was his duty to guard his master's person in arms for a specified part of each day. The eunuch thereupon told him that, if given an oath of secrecy, he would make him a proposal which would be very much to his interest, but that he must have time to think it over. He suggested therefore that Edeco should return alone to dine with him, without the company of Orestes and the others who had come to Constantinople with him. To this Edeco agreed.[26]

He returned later to Chrysaphius' mansion and dined alone with the eunuch and Bigilas, who again acted as interpreter. Chrysaphius declared on oath that the proposal, which he was about to make, would bring no harm to his guest, but rather the very greatest of blessings. Edeco swore that, whatever it was, he would keep it secret. Then at last Chrysaphius made his proposition: if Edeco would return north of the Danube, murder Attila, and make his way safely back to Constantinople, he would live a life of ease and of great riches for the rest of his days. Edeco accepted the proposal – perhaps a little too readily – but said that he would require money, about 50 lb of gold, in order to ensure the loyalty of the Huns whom he governed. Without hesitation Chrysaphius offered to supply him with the money at once, but the Hun objected. He suggested that he himself should be sent away immediately to tell Attila the result of his mission, and that Bigilas should be sent with him to hear Attila's answer on the problem of the fugitives, about whom he had been complaining. Edeco would be informed by Bigilas as to how the money was to be sent out. He could not bring it himself, he explained, for Attila always made a point of inquiring very closely into the amounts of money which his emissaries received at Constantinople, and it would be impossible to conceal such a sum as 50 lb of gold from him – or, indeed, from Orestes and the others who would be travelling with him. Chrysaphius approved of this amendment, and they finished their dinner.[27]

The eunuch hurried at once to the emperor, who summoned Martialis, the master of the offices (a sort of foreign secretary), and all three discussed the agreement made with Edeco. They made one alteration of the suggestions put forward by the Hun. It would be advisable to deflect Attila's attention from Bigilas. In addition to him, therefore, they would send out Maximinus on a sham embassy to interview Attila, and Bigilas should travel with him unsuspected, in the guise of nothing more than a mere interpreter. Maximinus should know nothing of the plot to murder Attila, but should merely deliver the emperor's reply to Attila's letter, which Edeco had just brought. The terms of the emperor's letter were also agreed upon at this meeting. It should begin by stating that Bigilas was only an interpreter, whereas Maximinus was a man of high rank and noble birth, and was very close to the emperor. The letter would go on to state that the Romans had given Attila no reason to invade their territories, for, in addition to the fugitives restored earlier, the emperor had now sent back the last seventeen in his possession. Theodosius and his two ministers further agreed that Maximinus should tell Attila orally that he ought not to ask for the presence of ambassadors of the highest rank; this had not been customary in his earlier dealings with the Romans nor had other rulers of Scythia made any such request – they had been content with any random soldier or secret-service agent who had happened to be at hand.[28]

Why was this last matter not included in the letter? Why was it merely to be pointed out orally by Maximinus? The fact was that this argument contained an obvious falsehood. Men of the highest rank, that is, *viri illustres*, had, in fact, conducted negotiations with Attila before this: we have already met the master of the soldiers Anatolius and the ex-consul Senator. Theodosius' reluctance to send a *vir illustris* again was doubtless due to his fear that, if the attempt on Attila's life miscarried, no important Roman personage would ever return safely from Hun territory in the future. In these unflattering circumstances the emperor sent Maximinus.

III

The company that set out from the Eastern capital on

horseback[29] sometime in the early summer of 449 was led by the ambassador himself. This Maximinus, a man of considerable distinction although not a *vir illustris*, first appears in history with the rank of *Comes* in the month of December 435, when he was a member of the commission appointed to draw up the Theodosian Code.[30] He evidently won speedy promotion, for when the commission is mentioned three years later he is no longer a member of it,[31] being presumably engaged on higher duties. We do not know why his name suggested itself to Theodosius and his two advisers when they decided to send him to Attila in the dangerous company of Bigilas. They probably considered him to be an able, if uninspired, civil servant, who would not be likely to lose his head in a crisis. However that may be, we have good reason to congratulate ourselves on their choice and on Maximinus' willingness to accept the commission; for as soon as he heard of his appointment, he approached his friend Priscus, the historian, and earnestly requested him to accompany him on his long journey.[32]

We know nothing of Priscus before he received this invitation of Maximinus. On the way he seems to have occupied a position which placed him in a personal rather than an official relationship with the ambassador,[33] and it has been plausibly suggested that the historian had served in one of the *scrinia* (offices) directed by the master of the offices.[34] In this position he will have become known to Maximinus, who then made him his *de facto*, if not *de jure*, adviser and counsellor. Now, it was a frequent custom in the later empire to attach a philosopher or sophist to an embassy so as to furnish the ambassadors with a ready and eloquent speaker.[35] It may be then that Priscus was asked to accompany Maximinus because he had already made a considerable reputation in the schools: perhaps he had published some of those rhetorical exercises which Suidas ascribes to him and of which we otherwise know nothing.

The news that the party was to travel into Hun territory happened to come to the ears of Rusticius, who had a matter of personal business to transact with one of Attila's Roman secretaries, and who obtained permission to travel in the ambassador's company. He was a useful member of it, for, apart from Bigilas, he was the only Roman present who understood the Hun language: he was a native of Moesia who had lived among the Huns as a war prisoner for many years (p. 109 above).[36] The rest of the party comprised the interpreter Bigilas, the Hun Edeco – these two alone knew of the plot to murder Attila – Orestes, who had come to Constantinople with Edeco, and some unspecified Huns of minor importance who had also accompanied Edeco.[37] Priscus scarcely deigns to mention the servants who waited on the principals, and the drivers who looked after the pack-animals.[38] These animals carried, not merely presents to be distributed when the party reached the Huns' encampment, but also food, for Roman ambassadors, travelling abroad, were provisioned by their own government, not by that through whose territory they passed.[39]

Thirteen days' journey brought the travellers to Sardica, which had been ruined in the war of 441. Here Maximinus decided to entertain Edeco and the more prominent Huns to dinner. The inhabitants – for a few were still living on the site – sold him some sheep and cattle, which his servants slew and cooked. But an unfortunate incident marred the humour of the party as they sat drinking after the meal. When the barbarians toasted Attila and Maximinus proposed the name of Theodosius, Bigilas, with his customary tactlessness, protested that a god (he meant Theodosius) should not be mentioned in the same breath as a mere man (that is, Attila). The remark was so indiscreet that, in Hodgkin's opinion (p. 62), it 'can only be accounted for by supposing that he had plied the wine-cup too freely'. At any rate, the Huns showed signs of warm displeasure, and Maximinus and Priscus hurriedly diverted the conversation and passed the bottle round.[40] After the dinner Maximinus found it expedient to present Edeco and Orestes with a gift of Indian pearls[41] and some pieces of silk. But the evening contained a further perplexing moment. After receiving his gifts, Orestes waited behind until Edeco had left, and, approaching the Roman ambassador, paid a tribute to his cleverness: he declared that Maximinus had not been guilty of the same error as some of the imperial officials, who had invited Edeco alone to a dinner and had presented him with gifts. Maximinus was mystified by his words, and asked him in what way he considered that he had been slighted and Edeco unduly honoured. But Orestes merely turned on his heel and left without a word. The ambassador and Priscus were at a loss to explain his behaviour, and, when they resumed their journey on the following day, they mentioned the incident to Bigilas and told him of the dark words of Orestes. Bigilas suspected nothing. He said at once that Orestes had no business to feel angry if he was not shown the same honour as Edeco: he was merely a servant and a secretary of Attila, while Edeco was a Hun and one of his greatest warriors. Having said this, he went straight over to Edeco, who was riding a little way off, and spoke to him for a few moments in an undertone. Returning to the ambassador, he said that he had told Edeco of what Orestes had said and had scarcely been able to calm the Hun's anger. Did the truth not occur to the interpreter? Was it not clear that Orestes had at least suspected something? In fact, the position was worse than anything Bigilas can have imagined: Edeco had revealed the entire plot to his companions, and Orestes had intended to compliment Maximinus on his show of knowing nothing about it.[42]

Many years later, after Theodosius, Attila, and Maximinus were dead, Priscus gave it as his opinion that Edeco had revealed the secret either because he had never seriously intended to murder Attila or because he was frightened by the suspicions of Orestes: he was afraid that Orestes would inform Attila of his solitary dinner with Chrysaphius. At any rate, at the earliest possible opportunity, he had found means to let his master know of the plot to take his life and of the amount of money which he himself was to receive from the eunuch. He had also discovered the contents of the imperial letter which Maximinus was carrying to Attila, but the manner in which he had done this must remain a mystery.[43]

When the company arrived at Naissus, the Roman officials had an opportunity of seeing for themselves the results of nomadic warfare. The city was desolated. The buildings, with which Constantine had once adorned his birthplace,[44] had been wrecked and lay in masses of rubble on the ground. The population had disappeared, save for a few sick persons who lingered on in the Christian hostels[45] of the town. Six years had passed since the Huns had captured Naissus, but no effort had yet been made to bring back life to the ruins. The ambassador and his party did not even try to pitch their tents inside the wall, and, since the river bank immediately outside it was covered with the bones of those who had been slain in the fighting, they went upstream a short distance until they found a clear space where they might encamp.[46] On the following day they fell in with Agintheus, the master of the soldiers in Illyricum, and instructed him to hand over five of the seventeen fugitives of whose retention Attila had complained and whom the master had in his possession. Agintheus handed them over with a few kind words to them on parting.

The next day the party reached the Danube and were ferried across in boats hewn out of tree-trunks, in company with a number of Huns whom they had encountered earlier in the day. These had been making preparations for Attila to cross the river and hunt in the territories which he had newly acquired on the southern bank. On a plain seventy stades beyond the great river the Romans were ordered to halt until some of the Huns, who were in attendance on Edeco, could go on ahead and announce the ambassador's arrival to Attila. Late that same evening, as they sat eating their dinner, they heard the sound of horses approaching, and two Huns galloped up and told them to prepare to meet Attila. The Romans invited them to share their meal, and the two Huns dismounted and did so. The next day they guided them towards Attila's encampment, and the Romans, standing on a hill, saw a cloud of Hun tents pitched on a plain below. But when they prepared to encamp where they were, for it was already the ninth hour of the day, the two Huns checked them: they could not pitch their tents on a hill, they said, when the tents of Attila lay on the plain beneath. The Romans therefore went down to the plain, but before they could encamp they were met by Edeco, Orestes, Scotta, and others of the great lieutenants of Attila, who asked them roughly what they hoped to achieve by their mission. The Romans were astonished at the blunt question and looked at each other in silence.[47] The Huns became insistent and pressed their question with an angry clamour. Maximinus answered that the emperor had instructed him to speak to Attila and to no one else. Scotta angrily shouted that Attila himself had ordered them to ask the question: otherwise they would not have troubled to come at all. Maximinus replied that this was no way to treat an official envoy: no ambassador could be expected to answer questions about the purpose of his mission if he never even saw the man with whom he had come to negotiate. The Huns themselves were very well aware of this, he said, for they had often come on embassies to the emperor and so were familiar with diplomatic usages. He insisted on fair treatment and declared that on no other terms would he mention the purpose of his mission.[48]

His firm words silenced the Huns, who mounted their horses and rode back to their master. Shortly afterwards they returned and Bigilas may have been momentarily disturbed to notice that Edeco was no longer with them. To the amazement of Maximinus and Priscus, the Huns now proceeded to recite to them the precise instructions which the government had given to Maximinus and the exact contents of Theodosius' letter, and then roughly ordered them to go back to the Roman frontier unless they had something further to say. The ambassador and his friend were quite unable to understand how the Huns had been able to find out the secret decisions of the emperor. They decided, however, that they must persist in refusing to discuss the purpose of their mission, and Maximinus therefore replied that, whether his reasons for coming were such as they had described or not, he would speak of them to no one save Attila. The Huns curtly ordered him and his party to be gone.[49]

There was nothing for it but to prepare for the return, and while Maximinus gave instructions to his servants, Bigilas turned on him and abused him for making such a reply to the Huns; it would have been far better to tell them a lie than to return with his mission unachieved. 'If I had a chance of speaking to Attila,' said he, 'I could easily have persuaded him to abandon his dispute with the Romans. I became a friend of his,' he added, little knowing the truth, 'when I was serving on Anatolius' embassy.' Evidently it had not yet occurred to him that Edeco might have betrayed him.[50] The packs were now strapped to the horses, for, although night was falling, Maximinus thought it best to go at once. But before a start could be made, some Huns whom they had not seen before rode up and, saying that Attila would allow them to remain until morning, produced an ox and some fish which, they said, were gifts from their master. The Romans consequently expected better treatment on the morrow, but they were disappointed. The same Huns returned and declared that unless they had something to say beyond what Attila already knew, they must depart. The Romans made no answer and prepared for the journey. Bigilas protested again. He insisted that Maximinus should say that in fact he *had* other things to speak of; but this the ambassador, who was in great dejection, refused to do.[51]

Priscus noticed his friend's melancholy and decided to act on his own initiative in an effort to break the deadlock. Taking aside Rusticius, who knew the Hun language (p. 109 above), he approached Scotta and promised him very considerable gifts from Maximinus' store if he would arrange an interview between his master and the Roman ambassador. He insisted on the advantages which a peace settlement would bring to Scotta, and ended by saying that he had heard a report to the effect that Scotta had great influence with Attila, but that he could not fully persuade himself of the truth of this report unless he saw him exercise his influence in practice. Scotta resented the slur on his authority, and, interrupting Priscus angrily, declared that no one in the camp had greater influence with Attila than he, and, to prove his words, mounted his horse and galloped off. Priscus hurried back to Maximinus, whom he found lying disconsolately on the grass and talking to Bigilas. As soon as he heard what Priscus had done, the ambassador jumped up with a word of gratitude for his initiative and shouted to his servants, who were already setting off with the pack-horses, to come back. Shortly afterwards Scotta returned and told them to come to Attila's tent.[52]

A throng of guards stood outside their master's tent, but Maximinus and his friend were admitted at once, and found Attila sitting on a wooden chair. When Maximinus strode forward with Bigilas, Priscus and one or two others who had come with him stood at a respectful distance, and the historian had his first opportunity of studying the Hun leader. He observed the short, squat body and the huge face, with its small, deep-set eyes, and found little to admire in the flat nose and the few straggling hairs which took the place of a beard.[53] As he watched, Maximinus greeted the barbarian, handing him the emperor's letter and declaring that Theodosius prayed for the well-being of the king and his men. Attila darkly replied that the Romans would have the same fate as they wished him to have; but Maximinus missed the point of this salutation, for he still knew nothing of the murder plot. Before he could say more, Attila turned in anger towards Bigilas, and, calling him a shameless beast, asked him why he had come when he knew that it had been agreed in Anatolius' treaty that no Roman ambassadors should be sent out until all the fugitives had been handed back to the Huns. Bigilas replied that there were no more fugitives in the hands of the Romans: they had all been surrendered now. Attila's anger grew visibly. With the utmost abuse of Bigilas, he shouted that he would have had him impaled and flung out as food for the birds, were it not that he was protected by the rank of ambassador. He insisted that there were still many Hun fugitives in the Roman Empire, and he called to his secretaries to read out their names. When this had been done, he ordered Bigilas to leave, and said that he would send Esla, Rua's old ambassador, to Constantinople with him in order to negotiate a final settlement on all the Huns who had deserted since the time when Aetius' son Carpilio had been a hostage among the Huns. He could not allow his slaves, as he called them,[54] to enlist in the Roman army and fight against him – though, he added grimly, it was not likely that they would be of much service to the Romans if he went to war again, as he most certainly would do if the deserters were not restored. He then dismissed his audience, telling Maximinus not to leave his dominions until he had received an answer to the emperor's letter. So ended the first interview with Attila: apart from his unfortunate greeting at the beginning, the ambassador had said nothing whatever.[55]

Back in their tent, the Romans reviewed the conversation. Bigilas confessed himself quite unable to understand why Attila had abused him so bitterly, for he had been exceedingly mild and calm when they had met in Anatolius' company. Priscus suggested that Attila must have heard of his unfortunate remark at the dinner at Sardica, when he had called Theodosius a god and the Hun a mere man. Maximinus also thought this a likely explanation, but Bigilas remained unsatisfied. As they talked, Edeco appeared in the doorway of the tent and called Bigilas outside. Still pretending to have kept the secret, he told the interpreter to bring out from Constantinople the 50 lb of gold which it had been agreed that he should distribute to his followers. He then went away, and Bigilas, going back into the tent, said that Edeco had told him that he, too, had been the victim of Attila's rage in the matter of the fugitives. Some

Huns arrived from Attila at this moment and said that the Romans were to buy nothing when in Hun territory except food – it will be remembered that Roman ambassadors had to buy their own food (p. 114 above) – until all points of difference had been settled between their government and Attila. This was a trap for Bigilas. If, before going back to Constantinople with Esla, he knew that he could buy nothing when in Hun territory, how would he be able to explain away the 50 lb of gold which he was to bring out to Edeco? The Huns further said that Maximinus was to wait in Attila's dominions until Onegesius returned to camp.[56] This Onegesius, a brother of Scotta,[57] was the chief lieutenant of Attila, and, after him, the most powerful man in the empire of the Huns.[58] He was at present absent from the camp, having gone away to install Attila's eldest son Ellac as governor of the Acatziri, who had been subjected the year before. While Maximinus waited for his return, Bigilas set off for Constantinople, still convinced that the plot to murder Attila would succeed if only he could bring back the 50 lb of gold.[59]

On the following day the Huns struck camp and moved northward. The Roman ambassadors did not travel with the main body of their hosts, but were guided by a different route, for Attila wished to visit a certain village where he intended marrying the daughter of one Eskam, of whom we know nothing.[60] The Romans accordingly travelled on over a great plain and crossed several navigable rivers which cannot now be identified.[61] They came to many villages on their journey, passed a lake, where they almost lost all their possessions in a violent storm which broke over them at night, and were entertained in a village ruled over by a woman – one of the wives of Bleda – who offered them, not only food, but also comely women; the latter they refused. In return for her hospitality they presented the lady with gifts of three silver goblets, some furs, a quantity of pepper from India,[62] dates, and other edibles which the Huns prized. Seven days later they were instructed by their guides to halt at a village so as to allow Attila's cavalcade to pass on to the road ahead of them. In this village they fell in with some West Roman ambassadors, who were also trying to secure an interview with the Hun leader. In a later chapter we shall consider the purpose of this Western embassy; but here we must note that the envoys included Romulus, the father-in-law of Attila's lieutenant Orestes, who, as we saw, was a Roman of Pannonia and was later to become the father of Romulus Augustulus. They also included Promotus, governor of the province of Noricum, for, despite the storms of the early years of the century, Noricum was still part of the Western Empire, as it long continued to be.[63] They had with them an army officer called Romanus, and Tatulus, Orestes' father, who was making the journey in order to see his son, and finally a certain Constantius, whom Aetius had sent to Attila to act as his secretary.[64]

The East and West Romans joined company, and, when Attila had passed on to the road ahead of them, travelled on together, crossing many rivers, and at last reaching the headquarters of the nomads. This was a village larger than any through which they had yet travelled. It stood in the midst of a wide, treeless, and stoneless plain where cavalry could manoeuvre freely and where no one could hope to surprise it. Inside the village, Attila's houses were more elaborately constructed than the rest, and were built of planed and polished boards. They stood on a natural mound and were enclosed in a wooden palisade ornamented with wooden towers. This palisade, despite its towers, was not intended as a military defence – in fact, it would merely hinder the movements of the nomads' cavalry – but was designed only for ornament. At some distance from Attila's houses, but still inside the village, stood another palisade, also of wood, but without the decorative towers. This second palisade encircled the buildings of Onegesius, the most powerful of the λογάδες (picked men). His buildings included one which immediately struck the eye of the Romans, for it was built of stone and was, in fact, a bath-

Plate 10   Attila in his camp, Hollywood style
(with Jack Palance as Attila in The Sign of the Pagan*).*

house. The stone had been brought with immense trouble from the Roman province of Pannonia, for there was none to be found in the immediate neighbourhood of the village, and the bath-house had been erected by an architect who had been among the prisoners taken when the great city of Sirmium had fallen in the campaign of 443. He had hoped to gain his freedom by constructing this building for Onegesius, but, in fact, he had only succeeded in ensuring his continued slavery among the barbarians, for Onegesius, highly pleased with his craftsmanship, had now made him his bath-man, and the architect still waited upon him and his friends as they enjoyed their baths. The road which led into the village ran straight through Onegesius' palisade, which therefore had two entries, and continued through the village for a

considerable distance before it reached the huts of Attila.
The huts of the more humble members of the community
were probably made, as Gibbon (iii, p. 437) suggested, of
mud or straw, since there was no timber or stone in the
vicinity.[65]

The Romans were present when Attila entered this village.
He rode into it between several lines of barbarian girls
standing beneath canopies of fine, white linen, held over their
heads by other Hun women. The girls walked beside Attila's
horse singing songs in the Hun language. When Attila was in
the midst of Onegesius' buildings on the road to his own
enclosure, Onegesius' wife came forward with her handmaids and offered him dainties to eat and a silver goblet of
wine. To honour the wife of his lieutenant, Attila accepted
the gifts, and tasted the food and wine while still sitting on
his horse, and then rode on towards his own palisade. The
Romans watched him depart, but themselves remained
among the houses of Onegesius, who had now returned
from his mission among the Acatziri. He had, in fact, failed
to install Ellac as their king, for on the journey to their
territory the young man had chanced to slip and break his
right wrist. Onegesius was at present making his report to
his master, and it was his wife who entertained the Roman
ambassador and his party. After they had been refreshed the
Romans pitched their tents not far outside Attila's palisade,
so as to be close at hand in case he should call for them.[66]

The next day Maximinus sent Priscus to Onegesius to give
him the gifts which the emperor had sent for him, and to
learn when he might be interviewed. Priscus found the gates
of Onegesius' palisade closed, and, as he waited outside, he
was surprised to be greeted in Greek by a stranger whose
appearance suggested that he was a Hun. Priscus had already
noticed that Hunnic and Gothic were the usual languages in
the camp, although those of the barbarians who had had
dealings with the West Romans had picked up some Latin.[67]
Greek, on the other hand, was heard only from the lips of the
prisoners whom the Huns had carried away from Thrace and

Illyricum. Yet this man, who had just said '$\chi\alpha\tilde{\iota}\rho\varepsilon$' to him, did not look like one of the prisoners, who were easily recognizable from their tattered clothing and squalid appearance. The man before him, on the contrary, appeared to be one of the ruling Huns, with his neat dress and his peculiarly Hunnic hairstyle.[68] It was with some curiosity then that Priscus asked him who he was and how he had come to the dominions of the Huns and adopted their way of life. The man asked him why he wanted to know. Priscus confessed that his curiosity had been aroused by hearing the Greek language in such an unexpected place. The stranger laughed. He admitted that he came from Greece;[69] but the conversation which ensued was of such extreme interest, and the report of it in the pages of Priscus throws so much light on so many relevant issues, that we must reserve it for separate discussion later on.[70]

When at last the gates of Onegesius' palisade were opened, Priscus hurried in, and, after a slight delay, was introduced to Onegesius himself. The Hun accepted the gifts and promised to come to Maximinus at once. When he entered the Roman ambassador's tent he thanked him immediately for the presents and asked him of what service he could be. In the name of Theodosius, Maximinus invited him to come to Constantinople to discuss all outstanding questions with officials of the Roman government. If he could arrange a settlement, said the ambassador, he would bring great blessings on himself and his family, and he and his children for ever would be the friends of the Roman Emperor. Onegesius asked if Maximinus were suggesting that he should betray his master Attila and abandon his life among the Huns, and his wives and children. If so, he declared in advance that he would not do so, for it was better to be a slave with Attila than a rich man among the Romans. With these words he withdrew. He was even less corruptible than Edeco.[71]

The following day Priscus was sent to bring gifts to Attila's wife Hereca,[72] the mother of Ellac, and thus had an opportunity of inspecting the buildings inside Attila's palisade. He made his way through a throng of Huns into Hereca's tent, and found her reclining on a soft rug laid on the felt with which the floor was covered. Her handmaids sat on the ground in front of her, embroidering linen with threads of many colours to serve as clothing for some of the Huns. Priscus' interview was brief. He merely approached, greeted Hereca, presented his gifts, and withdrew. Outside, he continued his inspection of the buildings, hoping that he might see Onegesius, who was again in conference with Attila, and find out if it was worth Maximinus' while to stay in the camp any longer.[73] He wandered about as he pleased, for Attila's guards now knew him by sight and did not interfere with him. At last he saw a great throng of Huns all running towards one point with a confused clamour: Attila himself had walked out of his hut, and Priscus had another opportunity of studying him. He noticed his arrogant walk and his insolent glance from side to side, as he listened to the complaints and disputes of his followers who were crowding around him, and he gave them his rough justice on the spur of the moment as he stood among them at the door of his hut. But he soon went inside again, and Priscus learnt that he was about to hear an embassy from some barbarian people which had recently arrived in the village.[74]

Priscus still waited for Onegesius, and whiled away his time chatting to the West Roman envoys, who approached him as he lingered. They asked him whether Maximinus had been dismissed from the village or was compelled to stay longer. Priscus replied that this was precisely what he hoped to find out from Onegesius. The conversation turned to the violent temperament of Attila. Romulus, the leader of the West Romans and a man for whose judgement Priscus clearly had the utmost respect, declared that Attila would no longer listen to any plea, however just, unless he considered that it would conduce to his own profit. No one, he said, who had ever ruled Scythia – or indeed anywhere else – had achieved so much in so short a time, and it was likely that, in order to increase his power, he would now attack Persia. Someone interrupted to ask how he would be able to reach Persia, and Romulus recalled the history of Basich and Cursich to show that that country was by no means inaccessible to the Huns (p. 35 above). Attila, he thought, would have very little trouble in passing over the same route and would easily succeed in reducing Persia to a tributary state. Priscus and one or two others expressed the hope that Attila would, in fact, turn against the Persians and thereby give the Romans some respite, but Constantiolus, another of the West Romans, declared that, if Persia were to collapse, the outlook for the Roman Empire would be very black, for he doubted if Attila would allow them to maintain an independent existence once Persia had fallen. Moreover, the recent discovery of the sword of the war-god seemed to portend an immediate increase of his power.[75]

At last Onegesius came out. The Romans approached him and tried to tell him their business, but he merely spoke to some of the Huns around him. Then, turning to Priscus, he reopened the question of the East Romans sending an ambassador of consular rank: he told Priscus to go to Maximinus and find out which consul would be likely to be sent. Priscus went and brought back the message that the Roman government would like Onegesius to visit Constantinople, but, if that were impossible, they would send any ambassador the Huns might choose. Onegesius evidently considered this concession to be of the utmost importance. He at once had Maximinus summoned and brought him to Attila. Priscus was not invited to accompany them, but when Maximinus returned he said that Attila had requested the presence of Nomus or Anatolius or Senator, all of whom had negotiated with him earlier, as we have seen. He had declared with some emphasis that he would be prepared to receive no others than these three, and that war would be the answer to any quibbling. Maximinus gave this account of the interview to Priscus as they walked back to their tent. When they arrived there, Tatulus, the father of Orestes, joined them with the news that Attila required their presence at a banquet that evening.[76]

The two Romans, with their companions from the Western Empire, stood upon the threshold of the banqueting-hall inside Attila's palisade at the appointed time, the ninth hour. According to the Hun custom, they were given a drink before they sat down, and, when they were seated, Priscus had an opportunity of studying the banqueting-hall. Along both sides stood the chairs upon which the Huns and their guests sat, and out in the middle of the room was the couch of Attila, facing the door through which they had entered. Behind him was another couch, but this was unoccupied, and Priscus does not appear to have been able to discover its purpose. Behind this again were a few steps leading up to a bed on a raised dais, and this bed was screened off with embroidered linen curtains from the rest of the room. The truth is, despite the doubts of some scholars, that the Hun lord slept in his dining-room.[77]

The chair next to Attila was the seat of honour, and this was occupied by Onegesius. We are explicitly told, indeed, that, after Attila, he was the most powerful man in the camp.[78] On the left of Attila was Berichus, in the place of second honour, with the Romans next to him. Two of Attila's sons sat immediately in front of him with their eyes fixed on the ground in fear of their father. When all were seated, a wine-bearer entered and handed a goblet of wine to Attila. He took it and toasted Berichus, who at once rose to his feet, for it was the custom that the person toasted thus by Attila should not resume his seat until he had either tasted the wine or drunk it outright and handed the goblet back to the wine-bearer. When Berichus had sat down again, each of the other guests, including the Romans, honoured Attila likewise: the Hun saluted them, they took the goblet, and tasted the wine. When this ceremony had been completed, tables were brought in – one to every three or four of the guests, in the Roman fashion – loaded with meat, bread, and dainties, ὄψα, served on silver platters, the plunder of some

Roman city. It seemed a very worthy banquet to the Romans, but they noticed that Attila himself was served off wooden plates and ate only meat. His drinking-cup was of wood, though his followers drank from looted silver and gold. He alone had no sword girt to his side, and his shoes were not studded with gold or precious stones like those of his followers.[79] When the food was finished, further quantities were brought in, and the salutations of Attila were repeated. What followed may be described in Priscus' own words:

When evening began to draw in, torches were lighted, and two barbarians came forward in front of Attila and sang songs which they had composed, hymning his victories and his great deeds in war. And the banqueters gazed at them, and some were rejoiced at the songs, others became excited at heart when they remembered the wars, but others broke into tears – those whose bodies were weakened by time and whose spirit was compelled to be at rest.[80]

The tension was broken. When the singers had ended, a madman was brought in, speaking wild, unintelligible words that drew shouts of laughter from the feasters.[81] Then came Bleda's buffoon Zerco. Bleda had given him the wife he had so much desired, but, after Bleda's murder, Attila had presented the dwarf to Aetius, who had in turn given him to Aspar. He had now come back to the Huns, for he had been forced to leave his wife behind when he had gone to the West. At Edeco's suggestion he had approached Attila directly: the lord had angrily rejected his plea. But Zerco hoped that he would change his mind, if only he could amuse him. He succeeded in raising loud shouts of applause from the other Huns by means of his curious dress and his quaint mixture of the Latin, Gothic, and Hunnic languages. The hall re-echoed with peals of laughter; but throughout it all Attila remained indifferent. His face was sullen and unsmiling. He neither moved nor spoke, until suddenly the door of the hall was opened and Ernac, the youngest of his sons, stood on the threshold. The young man walked forward and stood beside his father. With the shouts and laughter of the banqueters ringing in his ears, Priscus watched the scene intently. He saw Attila's hard eyes soften, as he turned to his son and stroked his cheek.

The Roman was astonished at this hint of tenderness, for Attila had treated his other sons with unmistakable contempt. His curiosity induced him to turn to the Hun sitting beside him, who, he had discovered, understood Latin. He asked him the meaning of what they had just witnessed. The barbarian first swore him to secrecy, and then explained that soothsayers had informed Attila that his family would fall from its greatness, but would be restored by this young man, Ernac, the youngest of his sons.[82]

The banquet continued all night, but the Romans withdrew long before it was over, because, according to Priscus, they did not wish to persist with the drinking for long.[83]

The following morning they went to Onegesius and told him frankly that they felt themselves to be wasting their time and wished to be allowed to depart. Permission to go was granted at once, for the Romans had given way on the question of the personnel of their next embassy, and Onegesius, after conferring with the other λογάδες (picked men), composed a letter to Theodosius, which was written down by Rusticius. That day the Romans were entertained by Attila's wife Hereca in company with some of the λογάδες, and at the end of the entertainment each of the Huns present handed a goblet of wine to the Romans, and as they drank it embraced and kissed them. On the following evening Attila entertained them again at a banquet similar to the first one. It passed off without incident, but it was noticed that the place of honour at Attila's right hand was now occupied by Attila's paternal uncle Oëbarsius. We do not know why Oëbarsius had not reigned with his brothers Rua and Octar, but his survival until 449 suggests that he was considerably younger than they. At any rate, on this occasion Attila spoke to Maximinus throughout the meal and pressed the claims of his Roman secretary Constantius to the hand of a wealthy woman of Constantinople, the daughter of one Saturninus. The conversation was a long and intricate one, and cannot but have been of extreme tedium to Maximinus.[84]

Three days later the Romans were presented with gifts and set out on the long journey to Constantinople. Attila had appointed Berichus to travel with them in order to confer with the emperor's officials and to collect the customary gifts. The journey was not uninstructive. In one village they came to they found that a 'Scythian' spy, sent out from Roman territory to secure information about the Huns, had just been captured and on Attila's orders was about to be impaled. On the following day they passed through other villages and saw two slaves of the Huns with their hands tied behind their backs, charged with having killed their masters, who had taken them prisoner in war. These two were crucified. While the Romans were still in Hun territory, they found Berichus a quiet but sociable companion. But when they crossed the Danube his behaviour changed after a dispute about their servants. When they had departed from the Hun encampment Attila had instructed each of his λογάδες to present the Roman ambassador with a horse, and Berichus had done so with the others. But he now demanded the return of his horse, and refused to ride beside his companions or to share their meals. When they arrived at Adrianople the Romans taxed him with his change of attitude, told him that they had done him no wrong, and invited him to eat with them. But it was only at Constantinople that he explained the reason for his anger. It appears that Maximinus had told him that the Germanic commanders of the East Roman army were in disgrace and that Aspar and Areobindus had no longer any influence with the emperor. What reason Berichus found in this for his anger we do not know.[85] At any rate, the party returned safely by a different route from that by which they had gone out, and reached the capital after passing through Philippopolis and Adrianople.[86] They had conducted their impossibly difficult mission with tact, firmness, and dignity.

IV

As Maximinus and Priscus rode along the highway from Philippopolis to Adrianople they met Bigilas the interpreter, who was now returning to Attila's chief village with the 50 lb of gold by means of which he hoped to induce Edeco's men to murder Attila. After a few questions as to what had happened after he had left the encampment, the interpreter passed on, still without an inkling that the plot had long ago been betrayed and that he was entering the trap which had been laid for him.

In company with the 50 lb of gold he eventually reached Attila and was arrested at once. The money was discovered and taken from him, and he was led to Attila, who asked him why he was carrying so large a sum. He had his answer ready. He was bringing this money, he said, so as to buy food for himself and his servants, and to purchase replacements if any of his horses or pack-animals should be worn out by the long journey. Furthermore, he declared that many persons in the empire, whose relatives had been captured in the recent war, had given him money with the request that he should ransom their friends if he could. 'You foul beast,' roared Attila, 'no quibbles will save you from justice; you have no excuse for escaping your punishment, for your money is far too much for your expenses and for the horses and pack-animals that you propose to buy, and for the ransoming of prisoners which I forbade when you came here with Maximinus' (p. 121 above). Bigilas had made the mistake of bringing his young son with him on this second journey to the Huns. When Attila had finished speaking he ordered this son to be stabbed with a sword if his father would not say to whom he was bringing the money and for what purpose. The boy was brought forward, and Bigilas broke down. With tears and lamentations he shouted out that they should direct the sword towards himself, and not at the young lad who had done them no harm. Then, without hesitation, he told the whole story of the plot hatched between Edeco, Chrysaphius, and the emperor, and begged insistently that he himself should be slain and the boy set free. Attila knew from what Edeco had already told him that Bigilas was telling the truth at last. He ordered him to be kept in chains until his son should go back to Constantinople accompanied by Orestes and Esla, and bring out an additional 50 lb of gold as his ransom.[87] He instructed Orestes to carry around his neck the purse, in which Bigilas had brought the original 50 lb of gold, and to show it to the emperor and Chrysaphius and ask them if they recognized it. Esla was to tell Theodosius that Arcadius, the emperor's father, had been a noble man, and that Mundiuch, Attila's father, had been noble also: but whereas Attila had preserved the generous qualities of his father, Theodosius had fallen away and had become Attila's slave and paid him a tribute of money. He did not act justly towards his master, but attacked him secretly, like a wicked slave. He would only be forgiven, the message concluded, if Chrysaphius were delivered over to the Huns for punishment.[88]

This last demand was particularly embarrassing in that another of Chrysaphius' enemies was demanding his life as the price of peace at this very time. We have seen that Zeno the Isaurian had defended Constantinople in the crisis of 447 (pp. 100–1 above). Zeno was rewarded for the defence of the capital with the consulship for 448, and in 449 we find him holding the powerful office of master of the soldiers in the East. He now felt himself strong enough to challenge his most powerful opponent under the emperor, the eunuch Chrysaphius. It will be recalled that throughout his second banquet Attila had insisted to Maximinus that his Roman secretary Constantius must obtain in marriage the wealthy daughter of a Roman called Saturninus. This Constantius had come to Constantinople in the spring of 449 with Edeco and Orestes, and Theodosius had agreed to give him Saturninus' daughter. But before the bargain could be carried into effect Zeno had stepped in, carried the lady away from the fortress in which she was confined, and married her off to one of his henchmen called Rufus. Constantius had complained bitterly to Attila of the abduction of his bride and demanded that the emperor should be compelled to give him another, who would bring him as great a dowry as that of Saturninus' daughter.[89] Attila accordingly had insisted to Maximinus during the banquet that Constantius must be provided with a wife. He went on to say that, if the emperor was not strong enough to rescue Saturninus' daughter from Zeno, he would himself be willing to make an alliance with Theodosius aimed at the destruction of Zeno. It is calamitous that we know so little of this extraordinary proposal, which, if Theodosius had been so rash as to accept it, might have led to Attila's conducting a campaign *inside* the Eastern Empire against the forces of the master of the soldiers in the east.[90]

Zeno's wanton interference in Chrysaphius' negotiations with Attila – which were difficult and dangerous already – seems to have been due to nothing else than a desire to embarrass the eunuch. At any rate, Theodosius angrily blighted the happiness of Rufus by confiscating the property of his newly won bride. Zeno concluded, doubtless correctly, that the hand of Chrysaphius was behind this move, and he therefore followed the example of his enemy Attila by demanding the death of the eunuch, against whom all his machinations appear to have been directed.[91]

Faced with this double threat, from the Huns without and the Isaurians within, Chrysaphius decided to settle with the stronger of his enemies first. Attila had made it clear to Maximinus (p. 127 above) that in future he would only be prepared to negotiate with either Anatolius or Nomus or Senator, a choice of which we shall examine the significance in a later chapter. The Roman government had conceded the point, and Chrysaphius now decided to send him Anatolius and Nomus. His instructions to them were that they should calm Attila's anger and induce him to keep the peace on the conditions negotiated in 448; in return they were to promise that Constantius should receive a wife no less noble and wealthy than the daughter of Saturninus. In connection with this last matter they were instructed to draw Attila's attention to the fact that among the Romans it was not lawful to marry a woman against her will – presumably the point required explanation because the contrary was the case among the Huns. Further, Chrysaphius personally sent a sum of gold to Attila to induce him to forget his demand for his life.[92]

In the spring of 450 Anatolius and Nomus set out accompanied by the son of Bigilas, who was bringing the extra 50 lb of gold necessary to redeem his father. They crossed the Danube into Hun territory, and to spare them the fatigue of the long journey Attila came southwards as far as the unknown river Dreccon to meet them; he was evidently pleased that these two men had been chosen to come to him. True, he spoke to them arrogantly enough when they first met, but soon their rich gifts and soft words so calmed him that the ambassadors were able to win such a resounding diplomatic success as was rarely obtained by a Roman government. They induced Attila to swear an oath to maintain the peace on the conditions laid down in the treaty of 448. This alone meant that they had achieved what Chrysaphius had ordered them to accomplish. They further induced Attila to swear that he would trouble Theodosius no more with the charge of receiving fugitives from the Hunnic empire, unless the Roman government should admit any in the future. But their greatest success lay in persuading Attila to retire from the whole strip of territory south of the Danube which in 448 he had ordered the Romans to evacuate completely. Not content with these major successes, Anatolius and Nomus also saw to it that Bigilas was released. The demand for Chrysaphius' life was withdrawn, and with rare tact neither side appears to have mentioned the late murder plot. Finally, as a special and personal favour to the two Romans, Attila agreed to set free the majority of his Roman prisoners without any ransom whatever. Before the ambassadors left him he presented them with some horses and a quantity of the skins and furs which the Hun rulers liked to wear. Constantius accompanied them on their homeward journey in order to receive his bride, and Theodosius selected for him a rich and nobly born lady, the widow of a son of that Plintha who had signed the Treaty of Margus with the Huns in 435. Her husband had died after a successful campaign in Cyrene, and she did not see fit to reject the emperor's persuasions that she should marry Constantius.[93]

The third treaty negotiated by Anatolius was a brilliant success for the East Roman government, although, as we shall see, circumstances were more favourable to them than they probably knew. Many an inhabitant of the Eastern Empire must have been convinced in the early summer months of 450 that peace on the northern frontier was now assured, and such convictions must have been confirmed when Attila's new plans were announced in June. But on 26 July, when hunting near the river Lycus not far from his capital, the Emperor Theodosius fell from his horse and injured his spine. Two days later, on 28 July, he was dead.[94]

6

The Defeats of Attila

Our narrative has now carried us through the major fragments of Priscus, and little remains of the rest of his work to illuminate the subsequent movements of the Huns. But the last episodes in Attila's life were also the most striking, and it is calamitous that, in proportion as our curiosity grows, so his career is more and more closely enfolded in the gloom of the Dark Ages. It may be, as we have suggested (p. 69 above), that Priscus knew little about the far West; yet nowhere in our study shall we have more cause than here to deplore the loss of his *Byzantine History*. For the student of the mid-fifth century there can be no substitute for Priscus.

I

Attila's relations with the West during the years which followed the defeat of Litorius at Toulouse in 439 are a subject of the utmost obscurity. It is certain, however, that after the massacre of Litorius' Huns he supplied Aetius with no further army; and the cause of the landlords in Gaul therefore suffered several reverses. In the thirties of the century the Burgundians, the Visigoths, and the Bagaudae of the *tractus Armoricanus* had been their chief foes, and all three continued to occupy Aetius' attention in the forties. He settled the remnants of the Burgundians in Savoy in 443, but we know nothing of the political and social significance of that action. The roles played by the Visigoths and the Bagaudae, although desperately obscure, must occupy us here, for both figured in the calculations of Attila on the eve of his march westwards. The scantiness of our information prevents us from analysing their relations with the Huns in any detail: what must be said must perforce be said briefly.

It will be remembered that in 433 Aetius had fled to the Huns because of the attacks made on his life by the Empress Placidia and by Sebastian, the son-in-law and successor of his old enemy Boniface (p. 71 above). This Sebastian had had a chequered career in the meantime, but, although he was now exiled from Rome and from Constantinople alike, his hostility towards Aetius had never relented. When we find the Visigothic king Theodoric entertaining him at his court towards the year 440 and putting him in a position to capture Barcelona, we cannot doubt that Theodoric's enmity towards the patrician was fully maintained even after the treaty of 439.[1] Nor can we doubt that this enmity still continued in 446, when we hear of a body of Goths assisting the Suevi in plundering Spain: they could hardly have come there without Theodoric's permission – and in 449 the Suevian king Rechiarius married Theodoric's daughter.[2] The devastation of considerable areas of Spain up to that date must have been at least approved by Theodoric. It is essential to bear in mind the continued, though perhaps not overt, hostility of Aetius and the Visigoths as late as 449 and even after.

The defeat of the Bagaudae by Litorius' Huns in 437, as we have already pointed out, did not alter the fundamental economic facts of the later empire: the Bagaudae continued to be as active as ever. Spain was racked by the struggles of the central government against the peasants of that province throughout many of these years, and we soon hear again of their comrades in Gaul. In 442 Aetius had settled a body of Alans near Orleans so as to keep an eye on the neighbouring territory of the *tractus Armoricanus*, and almost at once, 'offended by the insolent pride of the region' (*offensus superbae insolentia regionis*) – it may have been now that they threatened Tours[3] – he gave permission to these Alans under their king Goar to attack the Bagaudae, but the attack was called off on the intervention of Germanus, bishop of Auxerre. Their leader on this occasion was none other than that same Tibatto who had commanded them in 435–7: apparently he had escaped from his captivity in the meantime.[4] We do not know how the rising ended, although the result was certainly disastrous for Tibatto personally.[5] The most interesting piece of information about the Bagaudae at this time, however, comes from that same Gallic chronicle which told us of Tibatto's earlier revolt. Its entry runs thus: 'Eudoxius, by profession a doctor, evil despite his education, fled from the Bagaudae to the Huns at this time after his denunciation.'[6] The name is Greek – perhaps Eudoxius was the son of one of those Syrian traders who were to be found in every city of Gaul at the time. He was certainly no slave, for physicians were an exceptionally privileged class in the urban life of Gaul in the fifth century.[7] The fact that such a man is found assisting the Bagaudae recalls Salvian's statement that some of those who fled to the 'rebels' were 'of high station, not obscure birth, and liberally educated'.[8] But somebody betrayed him and he fled. Now comes the surprise: in his peril he fled to the Huns.

Two of Aetius' earlier enemies, then, the Visigoths and the Bagaudae, are his enemies still towards the close of the forties. But the friendly relations which had existed for so long between him and Attila seemed on the surface to have suffered no interruption until the affair of Eudoxius. Somewhat before Maximinus' embassy in 449, Aetius had sent an Italian called Constantius to the Hun to act as his Latin secretary.[9] This was not the first secretary he had sent him – as well as being tokens of friendship, such men were

doubtless useful in keeping him informed of the intentions of
the barbarians.[10] It was during his Gallic campaigns of the
thirties that Aetius had sent Attila the first of these
secretaries whose name has survived. He was a Gaul and,
curiously enough, was also called Constantius; but he had
fallen into trouble in circumstances which we shall discuss in
a moment, and had been crucified while Bleda was still alive,
that is, sometime before the year 445.[11] After the murder of
Bleda, Aetius and Attila were still on friendly terms: Aetius
had sent out the second Constantius and had been presented
with Bleda's dwarf Zerco.[12] This friendship had its more
practical side. Attila was given the rank of master of the
soldiers in the Western Empire. He did not intend, of course,
to assume command of Roman troops, nor did Aetius
suppose that he would. But this office brought with it a high
rate of pay, and the master received large quantities of grain
for the maintenance of his soldiers. Consequently the title
was often conferred honorarily on foreign rulers.[13]

    In 449, however, the friendship was no longer running on
a smooth course, and the West Roman envoys, whom Priscus
met in Attila's headquarters, had come in order to restore
good relations and to calm Attila's anger.[14] The Hun had
found a pretext for a dispute in an incident which had taken
place long before. When the great city of Sirmium had been
threatened in the campaign of 441, the Gallic secretary
Constantius had struck a bargain with the bishop of the
place before it actually fell. The bishop entrusted him with
some gold plate, the property of his church, on the
understanding that, if Sirmium were taken and he himself
led away captive, Constantius should use the plate to ransom
him; but if the bishop were killed, then Constantius should
ransom as many of the townsfolk as the plate would buy. In
fact, when the city had been stormed and the citizens
enslaved, Constantius had done neither. He had gone to
Rome on a business matter shortly after, and had pawned the
gold vessels with a banker called Silvanus. On his return to
Hun territory, Bleda and Attila suspected him of treacherous

activities in other directions and crucified him. Subsequently, after Bleda's death, Attila had found out the fate of the gold vessels, and had demanded that Silvanus should be handed over to him on a charge of possessing stolen property which by right belonged to himself. It was with a reply to this demand that Romulus and the other West Roman ambassadors were travelling to the Huns when Priscus and Maximinus met them in the summer of 449. They had been sent by Aetius and Valentinian III – Priscus significantly names the patrician before the emperor – and they had been instructed to tell Attila that Silvanus had merely lent money to Constantius and had received the plate as a pledge, not knowing that it had been stolen. In fact, he had sold the plate to certain Roman priests, for it was considered impious to use for one's own service vessels which had been dedicated to the service of God. The ambassadors were to add that, if Attila would not abandon his claim, Silvanus would be persuaded to send him the equivalent of the plate in cash: but the Roman government would certainly not hand over a man who had done no wrong.[15]

The affair had not been settled when Priscus left the headquarters of the Huns. In his conversation with Romulus and the others (pp. 126–7 above) the historian had been careful to ask how their negotiations were going, and was told that Attila was holding fast to his original position: war would ensue if Silvanus were not handed over.[16] We do not know what was the final outcome of the matter, for, as Hodgkin (p. 100) says, 'after wearying us with the details of this paltry affair, History forgets to tell us how it ended'. It is clear at any rate that there was now an additional cloud on Aetius' horizon. The friction caused by the gold vessels of Sirmium might be a trifling affair designed merely to lead to the recovery of the gold and no more. But students of the diplomatic methods of the Huns could see that it might be much more: it might be the beginning of a series of pin-pricking complaints such as the Eastern government had had to endure in the years following the first Treaty of Anatolius (pp. 95ff above).

Plate 11   Coin portrait of Valentinian III (AD 424–455).
Ancient Art and Architecture Collection.

In so far as we can reconstruct it then the position in the
spring of 450 was this. Attila had secured his rear by the
third Treaty of Anatolius; so long as Theodosius lived – and
he was not yet fifty – there was no reason to expect any
hostile movement on the Danubian frontier of the Hun
empire. With regard to the West, Aetius was as hostile both
to Theodoric and to the Bagaudae as ever he had been, but
Attila had had no relations, known to us, either friendly or
unfriendly, with the Visigoths since the foundation of the
kingdom at Toulouse. His attitude towards Aetius and the
Western government was complex. He had been their
consistent friend since 434, but now he had produced some
cause for displeasure. This cause, however, was such as
could easily be removed, provided that it was not a mere
pretext for further demands. A symptom of hostility, which
must have been considerably more disagreeable to Aetius
than the demand for the surrender of Silvanus, was the
readiness with which Eudoxius had fled for refuge to the
Huns. If Attila proposed to support the Bagaudae, the
senatorial estates in Gaul would experience a speedy change
of ownership; but the patrician's reflections on this
possibility are hidden from us.

In all, a contemporary observer, if he had had at his

disposal no more information than is available to us now, could scarcely have foretold in the spring of 450 what Attila's objective would be twelve months later. But how much information was in fact at the disposal of contemporaries? It is very possible that in the spring of 450 no mystery whatever enveloped the plans of the Huns.

II

In the light of what happened subsequently – the invasion of Gaul in 451 and of Italy in 452 – it is easy now to see why Attila had been so lenient to Anatolius and Nomus in their negotiations with him. He had already made up his mind to launch an attack in Gaul, and he wished to safeguard his rear when he was engaged in the West. Anatolius had negotiated in very favourable circumstances, and the Eastern government must have been well pleased when, in the early months of 450, Attila gave out that he was about to attack the Visigothic kingdom centred on Toulouse and that he intended to do so as Valentinian's ally.[17]

If we can accept Attila's word, if in fact he did intend to march as the ally of the Western court (as distinct from Aetius), it does not follow that Romulus and his companions had brought their negotiations concerning Silvanus to a successful conclusion. If this demand were still outstanding, Aetius and Valentinian would be somewhat less likely to interfere with anything distasteful that might be done in Gaul. A more immediate problem is, when had Attila taken the decision to turn westwards? We only know that shortly before the spring of 450 Geiseric in Vandal Africa had been instigating him to undertake a campaign against the Visigoths. But the idea had already occurred to him even before Geiseric suggested it to him: in fact, it would seem that a plan to fight in the West had long been in his mind.[18] What had put it there? We must confess bluntly that we do not know: our authorities give us no hint, and nothing that we hear of the politics of the time seems to have called for such a surprising step. There was certainly plenty of wealth in the Eastern Empire which Attila could have continued to extort in the years that followed. It may indeed be that the Balkan provinces were drained of plunder, but plunder was of less importance to the Huns than tribute, and Marcian was able to leave 100,000 lb of gold in the treasury at his death six years later.[19] How was Attila to know that Theodosius would die a few months after he had taken his decision to turn westwards?

Nothing in our authorities permits us to believe that in the early months of 450 Attila had already planned an eventual campaign against the Western Empire as a whole. The Visigoths of Toulouse were his sole military objective at this time, and their destruction could bring nothing but profit to the Western landowners.[20] When Attila stated that he was marching as Valentinian's ally – 'as guardian of the Romans' friendship', as a contemporary puts it[21] – we have little reason to doubt his word. But if he were still the friend of Valentinian, it by no means followed that he was still the friend of Aetius. We are told that his plans could not be realized unless Aetius were first removed.[22] His original intention may have been to remove Aetius as the champion of the West, and to make a reality of the office of master of the soldiers which had already been bestowed upon him (p. 140 above). If the Western government were to recognize Attila, in place of Aetius, as their champion in Gaul, the Hun could control the Western Empire *from the inside*. But it must be emphasized again that we simply have not sufficient materials to enable us to understand Attila's motives.

We cannot believe, at any rate, that the Huns' attack on the Visigothic kingdom was intended as nothing more than a mere service to Valentinian or Geiseric. It was not the manner of the Huns to endanger their entire position in Europe merely to please a foreigner. Their real reason for marching can only be conjectural. Furthermore, even before they set out on their long journey, their relations with the

Western court had undergone a dramatic change. Having formed his plan to attack the kingdom of Toulouse and having received encouragement from Geiseric to carry it out, Attila, at about the time when he was negotiating with Anatolius and Nomus, sent a message to Valentinian III assuring him that he had no quarrel with the Western Romans (of Aetius he said nothing) and that his forthcoming campaign was aimed at the Visigoths alone. At the same time, he directed Theodoric to denounce the insecure treaty with West Rome which Avitus had negotiated in 439.[23] At this point came the celebrated affair of Justa Grata Honoria.

Honoria, the sister of Valentinian III, had a residence of her own at Ravenna, probably inside the palace, and this establishment was managed by a steward called Eugenius.[24] In the year 449 Honoria allowed herself to be seduced by Eugenius – indeed it was said in Constantinople that she had become pregnant[25] – but her intrigue was discovered and Eugenius put to death. The princess was forcibly engaged to a respectable and wealthy senator named Herculanus, who could not possibly be suspected of rebellious tendencies or of designs upon the throne.[26] Honoria, enraged beyond measure at her dismal fate, resolved upon a drastic plan to escape it. In the spring of 450 she sent one of her eunuchs, Hyacinth by name, to Attila, to beg him, in return for a sum of money, to rescue her from her intolerable marriage. She gave her ring to Hyacinth to hand to Attila, so that the barbarian might be assured of the authenticity of the message. Honoria's motives had been political from the first. Her plan was to make Eugenius emperor and to reign as his empress.[27] There is no reason to doubt that her offer to Attila resulted from similar motives and was intended to result in her reigning in Gaul, if not in Ravenna, as Attila's consort.

The news of what Honoria had done came very soon to Valentinian's ears. Hyacinth was arrested as soon as he returned, and, put to the torture, he revealed the whole story before he was beheaded. Theodosius wrote at once from the East advising Valentinian to hand over Honoria to the Hun and so give no pretext for further demands on his realm. But Valentinian decided otherwise. Honoria's mother Placidia – who had herself married a barbarian chieftain, the Goth Athaulf, thirty-five years before – begged that the princess should be handed over to her keeping. Valentinian consented, and the subsequent fortunes of Honoria remain unknown.[28] Whatever the princess's fate, Attila welcomed the opening which she had given him; he at once claimed Honoria as his wife. His position, on any interpretation of the evidence, was strengthened immeasurably by her invitation.

His position grew more complicated as the summer of 450 wore on. Hyacinth had come to him in the spring bearing Honoria's message and her ring. The Hun then heard that Theodosius had died on 28 July, and that on 25 August Marcian had been crowned Emperor of the East. He heard further that Marcian had not hesitated to announce a radical change in the foreign policy of the Eastern Empire. One of the first acts of the reign was the execution of Chrysaphius, the minister who, more than any other, had been responsible for the policy of concessions and tribute to Attila. Marcian lost no time in announcing that the payment of tribute had now come to a stop: no more gold would be sent out from New Rome to the Huns.

Faced with this altered situation on the Danube, Attila dispatched two embassies, one to Ravenna and one to Constantinople. The Western government was instructed to do no harm to Honoria: she was Attila's bride, and he would avenge her if she suffered wrong and if he did not receive half of the Western Empire as her inheritance.[29] But the embassy was fruitless. Valentinian's ministers replied that Honoria could not be given to him in marriage, for she was already pledged to another man. Further, the government of half the Western Empire did not belong to Honoria: inheritance of the throne was through the male, and not the female, line in the Roman Empire.[30]

The purpose of Attila's second embassy was to direct

Marcian to resume payment of the tribute to which Theodosius had agreed. The Eastern government adopted an even stronger attitude than the Western. It would on no account resume Theodosius' tribute. If the Huns remained at peace, Marcian would give them 'gifts', but if they threatened war, he would meet them with a force quite equal to their own.[31]

Towards the end of the year yet another complication arose. This was a dispute with the Western government concerning the succession to the leadership of the Ripuarian Franks. The Frankish king had recently died and a quarrel had broken out among his sons. The elder had appealed to Attila for an alliance, while the younger had had recourse to Aetius. Priscus, who was at Rome towards the end of 450, saw the young man there and noted the long, golden hair which streamed down over his shoulders.[32] Aetius adopted the prince as his son and joined with Valentinian in heaping gifts upon him, and the alliance which the young man sought was readily granted. It is clear that Aetius and the Western government were now – about November 450 – resigned to a complete and open breach with the Huns, and were seeking allies wherever they could find them.[33] Valentinian showed no sign of jettisoning Aetius. Yet, although their relations with Attila had reached breaking-point, it did not follow that war was inevitable or that it was regarded as such by either side.

The immediate question to be decided by Attila was whether he should start his operations by accepting Marcian's challenge and smashing the East Romans. The Hun, as we have seen, had determined on a Western campaign before Marcian came to the throne; but the new emperor's blunt refusal of the tribute and his tactless pronouncements on the military preparedness of his government invited Attila's attention. We are told that he had great difficulty in making up his mind as to the direction in which he should launch his attack, but that he eventually decided to undertake the more exacting campaign first when his forces were unimpaired.[34] It is difficult to avoid the impression that Marcian's display of audacity was to the last degree untimely. Within a few months of his accession he had brought the East Romans to the edge of the abyss, and all but lost what Theodosius had won by eleven years of patient, exacting, and costly effort. Attila did not forget his effrontery.[35]

Having reached the decision to continue with his original plan of attacking the Visigoths in Gaul, Attila surveyed the position at the end of the year 450. What had at first been planned as a campaign against the Visigoths at Toulouse now involved the Franks also, for it would seem that the late king's elder son, who had appealed for help to the Huns, possessed few followers among his nation. The Ripuarian Franks as a whole had therefore to be counted as enemies.[36] On the other hand, it was not even yet certain that a fight with the West Romans was unavoidable, and when he was actually entering Gaul Attila seems still to have been proclaiming that he had come 'as guardian of the Romans' friendship'.[37] Yet he cannot but have reckoned on the possibility of meeting with opposition from the government at Ravenna. Finally, Geiseric in Africa, the subtlest states- man of the century, would certainly be more than glad to see a blow dealt to the Visigoths,[38] but he gave no practical support in dealing it. Apart from the aid given voluntarily or otherwise by the subject nations, then, Attila set out from his log huts on the Hungarian plain without foreign allies.

III

It must have been soon after the new year that the Huns left Pannonia[39] and started on their journey to the West. Terrified contemporaries put the number of the army, which Attila gathered as he went, at half a million men, a figure which testifies to their panic.[40] This panic is clearly reflected in the description of the army which is given us by the Gallic landlord Sidonius Apollinaris, who assuredly had nothing to gain and a vast amount of property to lose if the invasion were not repelled. His lines run thus:

when suddenly the barbarian world, rent by a mighty upheaval, poured the whole north into Gaul. After the warlike Rugian comes the fierce Gepid, with the Gelonian close by; the Burgundian urges on the Scirian; forward rush the Hun, the Bellonotian, the Neurian, the Bastarnian, the Thuringian, the Burcteran, and the Frank, whose land is washed by the sedgy waters of the Nicer.[41]

In terrified recollection of the event Sidonius even conjures up half-forgotten tribes to fight among the squadrons of Attila. The Bastarnae, Bructeri, Geloni, and Neuri had disappeared hundreds of years before the times of the Huns, while the Bellonoti had never existed at all: presumably the learned poet was thinking of the Balloniti, a people invented by Valerius Flaccus nearly four centuries earlier. But when Sidonius names the Burgundians as being among the host of Attila he perhaps preserves, more by accident than by design, a fact of some interest. We have seen that some of the Burgundians had remained east of the Rhine when the bulk of the nation had fled into Gaul, and that this remnant had defeated the troops of Attila's uncle Octar (or Uptar). It would seem then that in the meantime the Huns had taken their revenge and had brought these eastern Burgundians at last under their sway. There is certainly no reason to doubt that Sidonius is correct in his references to the other peoples whom he catalogues in his poem: the Rugi, Gepids, Sciri, and Thuringi will beyond doubt have marched with their masters. The Ostrogoths, although unmentioned by the poet, were there too, led by their king Valamer and his younger brothers Theodimer and Vidimer.[42] What are we to say of the Franks, that is, the Ripuarians? Before he started the campaign Attila had certainly looked upon them as enemies:[43] presumably Aetius had won a diplomatic success among them and had established as their king the young man who had appealed to him. Now, although Sidonius' mention of the Neckar does not by itself indicate that Attila's route lay in the neighbourhood of that river, the Hun is exceedingly unlikely to have disregarded an ally of Aetius lying on his flank. We may take it then that his first objective in the campaign was the Ripuarian Franks, and that, after conquering these, he compelled some of their warriors to march in his ranks side by side with the other subject nations.[44] It may well be, then, as has sometimes been suggested, that the host crossed the Rhine in the neighbourhood of Neuwied, north of Coblentz, after cutting down the trees on the river's bank so as to build rafts.[45]

While already on the march Attila had taken a step which was to cost him dear.[46] The West Romans, as we have seen, had refused to hand over Honoria and had explained that, even if they had been willing to do so, her husband, in Roman law, would not inherit half of the Western Empire (p. 146 above). Attila was not satisfied with this reply, and now, when his army was actually marching on the Visigoths of Toulouse, he sent another embassy to the court at Ravenna. The envoys stated bluntly that Honoria was engaged to marry Attila and as proof of their words they produced the ring, which Attila had given them for the purpose. They also insisted on the curious legal claim: Valentinian was to retire from one half of his kingdom, for Honoria, they said, had inherited the sovereignty of half the West from her father, but had been robbed of her inheritance by Valentinian. These demands were rejected outright by the Western government, and Attila therefore continued on his march, collecting his forces as he went.[47] The West Romans still did nothing: they hoped even yet that the Hunnic attack might be restricted to the Visigoths. They found it necessary to abandon this hope when Attila sent them his final message.

In the pages of John Malalas, who is faithfully and even verbally echoed by the author of the *Chronicon Paschale*, we read the following story:

In the reign of Valentinian III and Theodosius II Attila with an army of many tens of thousands of men made a campaign against Rome and Constantinople. A Gothic ambassador, sent by him to Valentinian, declared, 'Attila, my master and thy master, hath ordered thee through me that thou shouldst make ready for him thy palace.' At the same time Attila sent a similar message by a Gothic ambassador to Theodosius at Constantinople. But Aetius, the foremost senator at Rome, when he heard the surpassing audacity of this insane demand, went to Alaric in Gaul, who was an enemy of the Romans, and induced him to help repel Attila.[48]

Now, this story as it stands makes nonsense; but if, ignoring one or two minor points, we substitute the names of Marcian and Theodoric for those of Theodosius and Alaric, it becomes coherent at once. There can be little doubt that we should make this substitution. The author of the story, as Gibbon (iii, p. 446, n. 2) says, 'may have anticipated the date; but the dull annalist was incapable of inventing the original and genuine style of Attila'. If then the Hun had sent his previous message *while actually on the march*, as an impeccable authority tells us,[49] this final and forthright command must have been dispatched as the army was in the neighbourhood of the Rhine or actually engaged in crossing it. In any event, it is clear that Attila sent an abrupt message which induced Valentinian and Aetius, almost at the eleventh hour, to take the momentous decision to resist the impending invasion of Gaul, and, with that end in view, to seek an alliance with the Visigoths, Aetius' lifelong enemies. The consequences of Attila's acceptance of Honoria's ring had become clear at last: his campaign was now directed against all the organized armies of Western Europe.

While all this had been happening, the Visigoths had been quite resigned to shouldering the burden of the war alone. Aetius' hostility towards them for the previous twenty years had left them with no hope of assistance from him, and indeed with no desire for it. Theodoric received the news of Attila's approach with fortitude: 'although he is puffed up by his victories over various races', he is reported as saying, 'yet the Goths know how to fight with pride'.[50] Aetius then was faced with no mean task when he sought an alliance with the king. The problem, which perplexed him gravely, was two-fold. First, he had to induce Theodoric to forget the politics of the last two decades and to join forces with the Western Romans. Secondly, he had to persuade him to extend the field of his operations. The Goths were confidently awaiting Attila's onset in their own country: their purpose was to defend their kingdom centred on Toulouse. But it was Aetius' business to save Gaul as a whole. He had therefore to induce Theodoric to march northwards and fight Attila as near as possible to the frontier. In view of his past record it would be hopeless for him to ask personally for any such agreement; but in 439 Theodoric had been induced by Avitus to sign a peace, and perhaps Avitus could persuade him again (p. 76 above). The future emperor set off carrying a letter from Valentinian and accomplished his difficult task successfully: Theodoric undertook to join forces with the man whom he had spent his life in fighting, and Aetius prepared to repulse Attila, his lifelong friend.[51]

It was now almost too late. The Gallic cities were already going up in flames when Aetius set out from Italy: 'and now Attila with his fearsome squadrons has spread himself in raids upon the plains of the Belgian. Aetius had scarce left the Alps, leading a thin, meagre force of auxiliaries without legionaries.'[52] His position had been weakened by the famine which was ravaging Italy in these very months.[53] A famine, of course, could not have stopped him from going ahead with his diplomatic arrangements, but it prevented him from mustering a considerable army when at last he set out. In fact, he could do no more than bring a few auxiliary troops with him, and when he finally joined Theodoric and the Visigoths – perhaps towards the end of April or the beginning of May – he set out northwards to meet the enemy at the head of a very motley host. Jordanes has preserved a curious list of the peoples whose warriors comprised it.[54] The Liticiani and Olibriones are quite unknown. The Burgundians, whom Aetius had settled in

Savoy in 443 after his Huns had crushed them a few years
earlier (p. 72 above), now fought for their conqueror,
although their fellow tribesmen from beyond the Rhine were
marching with Attila (p. 149 above). The Ripuarian Franks
were also present – presumably many of them had escaped
after Attila had fallen upon them in the early stages of the
campaign. They were joined by some Salian Franks, a people
who had been settled inside the Roman frontier for the best
part of a century. By *Sarmatae* Jordanes may mean us to
understand the Alans who had refrained from striking at the
Armorican Bagaudae a few years previously, and now, as we
shall see, their behaviour was more than ambiguous. The list
contains two other names. The Saxons may already have
established some settlements north of the Loire and received
recognition from the Roman government:[55] contingents of
them now came to Aetius' help. The last name is surprising:
it is that of the Armoricans. How had they come to fight for
their old foe against the man to whom Eudoxius had fled for
refuge in 448? We do not know, and cannot even guess. Our
only information is Sidonius' none too trustworthy remark
that it was his father-in-law Avitus who roused them to
battle.[56] No problem connected with this famous campaign
is more baffling than that concerning the attitude of the
Armoricans.

Many cities fell to Attila when he crossed the Rhine, and it
is not impossible that some opened their gates to him in the
belief that he came as a friend.[57] On 7 April Metz fell, and
Attila then made for Orleans. This move was incited by
Sangibanus, Goar's successor as king of those Alans who had
been settled in Gaul in the expectation that they would act as
a check on the Bagaudae of Armorica (p. 139 above).
Sangibanus had entered into a secret correspondence with the
Huns and had promised to betray Orleans to them if they
approached it.[58] A report of this agreement had come to the
ears of Aetius and Theodoric, and it now became their first
object to seize Orleans before Attila could reach it. They
were almost too late. The Huns besieged the place with

vigour and actually entered it before the approach of the allies forced them to withdraw.[59] The citizens were greatly heartened by St Aignan during their ordeal, but how exactly the Huns were compelled to retire we do not know. Whatever happened, it can scarcely be doubted that Attila suffered a major reverse before the city, and he fell back to what were then called the Catalaunian Plains, a term which probably denoted almost the whole of Champagne.[60] The precise spot where the two armies met cannot now be decided, although the question, despite its unimportance, has been endlessly discussed. On any supposition it is clear that the engagement took place on ground admirably suited to the manoeuvres of the Hun cavalry at an unknown place called Maurica (or the like) which was said to lie five miles from Troyes.[61] The date of the battle is as obscure as its site, but if, as the author of the *Vita S. Aniani* implies, Attila was repulsed from Orleans on 14 June, Bury may be right in suggesting 20 June as the approximate date of the engagement.[62]

The battle opened at about the ninth hour of the day with an effort by both sides to occupy a hill which dominated the battle-field. This struggle was indecisive. Each army succeeded in posting a force on part of the hill, but the summit was left unoccupied. On the plain below, the Goths, with the aged Theodoric at their head, were assigned to the right of the allied line, while Aetius and the Romans held the left. Between them they placed Sangibanus and the Alans whose loyalty was so dubious, for, as a Gothic historian puts it, one readily admits the necessity of fighting when it is difficult to run away.[63] Attila took the centre of his own line, facing the wavering Sangibanus, and the various nations of his subjects stood on either flank, the Gepids and Ostrogoths facing their kinsmen the Visigoths. The Huns started the battle by losing the entire hill of which they had earlier occupied a part.[64] There followed, says Jordanes, a 'fierce, unyielding, and long-drawn-out battle' but of the precise course of the fighting we know nothing. The Gothic king

Theodoric was among the slain, and his body was only found on the following day. In the end, after fighting into the night, Attila retreated into the circle of wagons which he had drawn up behind him. Jordanes asks us to believe that 165,000 men fell on either side, but historians have declined to do so. Nor is his information made any more credible when he adds that this figure excludes 15,000 men who fell in an engagement between the Gepids and Aetius' Frankish allies on the night before the main engagement.[65] Not many years later it was believed in the East that the fighting was so severe 'that no one survived except only the leaders on either side and a few followers: but the ghosts of those who fell continued the struggle for three whole days and nights as violently as if they had been alive; the clash of their arms was clearly audible'.[66]

In fact, however, a less impressive incident took place in Aetius' camp on the day after the battle. The Goths, enraged by the death of their king, were eager to resume the struggle and to blockade Attila in his wagon-camp with a view to starving him out. Now it seems that their chances of success were bright, and Aetius concluded that the Huns might in fact be utterly destroyed. Indeed, the Goths afterwards said that Attila had prepared a funeral pyre from his followers' saddles and had made up his mind to throw himself upon it if the enemy succeeded in breaking in among his wagons. This was precisely what Aetius wanted to avoid. The Huns had been his lifelong friends, and it was by means of a mercenary force supplied by them that he had been able to keep the Visigoths in check. He still hoped, amazing as it may seem, that the Huns might be induced to serve him similarly in future. At any rate, if they were wiped out now, the Western Empire would be hard put to it to defend itself against the kingdom of Toulouse. He therefore suggested to the late king's son, Thorismud, that he should at once return to Toulouse so as to prevent his brothers from seizing the throne in his absence. Thorismud took the advice given him, and led his men away.[67] The patrician then turned his attention to the young Frankish king whom he had befriended. He pointed out to him that Attila's homeward route would take him close to the land of the Franks: if the main Frankish army were away from home, the Hun would have no difficulty in maintaining as king the elder brother who had appealed to Attila the previous year. He therefore advised the young prince to return home without delay. This advice too was accepted,[68] and Aetius accordingly allowed Attila to retreat from Gaul at his leisure. Of the patrician we can say this at least: when once he had decided to support a social order of which the economic foundations had long since passed away, honest political methods were no longer adequate. The wisdom of his duplicity was revealed the following year.

IV

In 451 the Danube frontier was not as quiet as Attila had hoped it would be, when he concluded his treaty with Anatolius and Nomus in the spring of the previous year. Despite the Hun's threatening embassy (p. 147 above) Marcian had persisted in his resolution not to pay Theodosius' tribute. In reply to Attila's threat of war he sent him as ambassador a certain Apollonius, a follower of the Zeno who had so nearly ruined Chrysaphius' negotiations a year or two previously (pp. 133–4 above): in fact, Apollonius was a brother of that very Rufus who had eventually married Saturninus' daughter. Despite the high office he held – he was *Magister militum praesentalis* – he crossed the Danube to no purpose: Attila refused even to grant him an interview. The Hun, who was now about to set out for Gaul, was in great anger when he heard that Apollonius had brought no tribute, but had merely come to negotiate, and the refusal to interview him was intended as a public slight on Marcian. Attila sent an abrupt message to the ambassador ordering him to hand over whatever 'gifts' he had brought from the emperor, and threatening him with death if he refused. Apollonius was not dismayed. He said proudly that he would hand over the gifts if he were received as an ambassador ought to be; if he were killed, the Huns would have them, but they would no longer be gifts – they would then be spoils stripped from a dead man. Attila allowed him to go without ever having seen him.[69] East Roman relations with the Huns had deteriorated drastically since Anatolius had received presents from Attila only a year before.

In September 451 Attila gave a foretaste of what his answer was to be. A small band of Huns was launched on a plundering raid upon eastern Illyricum: its purpose was merely to remind Marcian of what lay in store for him when the campaigning season came round. The new emperor's anxiety as to his northern frontier prevented him from holding his great Council at Nicaea, as he had originally planned, and the bishops had therefore to assemble at Chalcedon instead.[70] Even then Marcian was unable to give them his undivided attention, for, although the plundering band sent across the frontier by Attila cannot have been a large one, Marcian decided to take the field against it in person. Whether or not he succeeded in intercepting it we do not know: but he certainly was pleased with the result of his excursion.[71]

Yet, when the summer of 452 arrived, Attila once more delayed his projected assault on the dominions of Marcian. He intended to postpone it only for a year, but in fact he postponed it for ever.

His precise motives in undertaking the campaign in northern Italy in 452 are not at all clear. We can only be certain that he felt himself under no obligation to Aetius for allowing him to escape from Gaul the previous year. Indeed, he began the campaign in Italy in bitter anger against the Western Romans upon whom he actually laid the blame for his disaster in Gaul.[72] It is also known that he welcomed the separation of the Roman and Visigothic armies, and felt that

*Plate 12   Thirteenth-century book painting of Attila
besieging Aquileia. Sachsische Wettkvonik.
Photograph: Mary Evans Picture Library.*

he could easily defeat them piecemeal.[73] Whatever his
motives, he assembled as large an army as that which he
had led in 451, marched through the Pannonian provinces,
and crossed the Alps into Italy at the opening of the
campaigning season of 452.[74]

Rarely in history has a statesman been caught so
completely off his guard as was Aetius in the spring of
452. There can be little doubt that he was convinced of the
success of his ambiguous conduct in Gaul on the morrow of
the Catalaunian Plains: he expected that he had merely to
open negotiations with Attila and the Huns would readmit
him to their friendship. Consequently no garrisons had been
posted in the passes of the Julian Alps, although the Hunnic
cavalry could easily have been checked in mountain warfare,
as indeed a contemporary writer points out. Attila crossed

entirely without opposition, and the news of his arrival in Italy must have struck the patrician with the violence of a thunderbolt. When he recovered from his astonishment he could form only one plan: he decided to take Valentinian with him and abandon Italy altogether.[75]

Attila's first operation, when he descended into the plains, was one of the most difficult he had ever undertaken. It was often said that, in all the years of its long history, the city of Aquileia, though often besieged, had never been stormed and never forced into capitulation.[76] The first assaults of the Huns were beaten back from its walls despite the vigour with which they had been pressed home, and so little progress was made that murmurs soon began to be heard in the camp that the attack should be called off. It would seem, however, that Attila sent back for those of his subject nations who were more skilled in siegecraft than were his own horsemen, and that these constructed the siege-engines before which the city eventually fell. But, to explain the pause in the attacking operations and the renewal of the assaults, a pretty story was invented of the kind which we have learned to associate with the history of Priscus when he had no genuine information to retail. It was said that, as Attila rode round the great walls one day, doubtful as to whether he should strike camp or press on with the siege, he saw a flock of white storks, which had built their nests in the roofs, rise up with their young into the sky above Aquileia and fly away from the doomed city. He accepted the omen gladly, and continued his attacks with eventual success. However that may be, Aquileia was cruelly plundered and razed to the ground. The destruction of this great city was long remembered among men, and in the sixth century it was a difficult task even to trace out the site where once it had stood.[77]

After their first victory the Huns galloped on, and city after city opened its gates in terror at their approach.[78] As they rode southwards Concordia and Altinum fell before them. A change had come over the relations of the Romans with the barbarians since Martial had written these lines:

'Altinum's beaches that vie with the villas of Baiae, and the woodland that knew Phathon's pyre, . . . and you Aquileia, happy in Ledean Timavus, when Cyllarus drank sevenfold waters: you shall be the repose and haven of my old age, if my retirement shall be at its own disposal' (4. 25). The next of their conquests was Patavium, where Livy had been born half a millennium before. All these cities were burnt and razed to the ground, and their inhabitants led away into slavery: they had been too terrified to resist. 'The Huns revelled their way through the cities of Venetia.' Turning westwards they stormed Vicetia, Verona the city of Catullus, Brixia, and Bergomum, and so arrived at Milan. Both Milan and Ticinum were taken, but for some reason were not plundered nor were the citizens massacred.[79] In connection with the capture of Milan another of those stories is told which smack of the historical methods of Priscus. In the palace there, it is said, Attila saw a picture representing the emperors of the East and of the West seated on their golden thrones, and, lying before them on the ground, the bodies of some slain Scythians. The Hun compelled a local painter to draw a picture of Attila himself sitting upon a throne and before him the two Roman Emperors holding a sack and pouring out gold from it at his feet.[80]

Yet a third of these tales has come down to us, and this one is explicitly ascribed to Priscus. To an inhabitant of the empire it must have seemed strange beyond measure that Attila, after devastating the plains of northern Italy, did not cross the Apennines and plunder Rome itself as Alaric had done before him. According to this third story, he did in fact propose at first to march on the ancient capital, but his followers dissuaded him by reminding him of that same Alaric and how he had died almost immediately after sacking the great city. They warned Attila that his fate might well be similar.[81] But, as it happens, we know why the Hun retreated from Italy without ever crossing the Apennines, and sentiment did not enter his calculations.

Aetius had abandoned his scheme of deserting Italy and

leaving her to her fate. The plan, it seems, was not merely disgraceful; it was also dangerous.[82] The patrician therefore decided to beg for peace from the Huns without further ado.[83] It was a curious embassy that met Attila on the banks of the Mincius, and unfortunately no eyewitness's account survives to tell us how it was received. The embassy was headed by none other than Pope Leo himself. Why the Pope should have been sent is not clear, for, as Bury puts it,[84] 'it is unreasonable to suppose that this heathen king would have cared for the thunders or persuasions of the Church'. None the less, Leo went, and was accompanied by the ex-prefect Trygetius, who had already had experience of diplomatic encounters with a barbarian chief: in 435 he had signed away a considerable tract of Africa to the Vandals.[85] The third member of this 'most gentle of embassies' was Gennadius Avienus, the consul of 450, a man of vast wealth, whose energy in promoting the interests of his immediate relatives aroused unfavourable comment among contemporaries. His opinions, which he was always painfully ready to advance, were, in the judgement of those who knew him, singularly worthless.[86]

Attila concluded peace with this trio. That it was they who induced him to leave Italy was the pious belief of Prosper, but we know from another source, also contemporary, the real reasons which compelled the Huns to withdraw north of the Alps. It will be recalled that, at the time when Aetius was setting out for Gaul the previous year, Italy was being devastated by a famine (p. 152 above). The crops were no better now, and the devastations of the Hun invasion did not improve the harvest. Consequently the lands through which the invaders rode in the summer of 452 were lands ravaged by famine and its inseparable companion, pestilence. It was idle for Attila to endanger his men in such a country. Whatever the figures of the slain at the Catalaunian Plains, the Huns had lost cruelly; and their man-power was always weak. If the plague once laid hold of the forces in Italy, their position in Europe would soon become

*Plate 13   Relief from St Peter's Basilica, Rome, depicting the
meeting of Attila and Pope Leo.
The Mansell Collection, London/Alinari.*

desperate – and the first cases of sickness had already been reported. It would have been folly in these circumstances to cross the Apennines, even if the Danube frontier had remained at peace. But in fact Marcian had seen and grasped his opportunity. After the public affront shown to his ambassador Apollonius (pp. 156–7 above), he must have been waiting for some such chance as now presented itself. North of the Danube the Germanic nations groaned under the ruthless exploitation of their masters; but the flower of the Hunnic army, in so far as it had survived the Catalaunian Plains, was now far away. In these circumstances, an East Roman force crossed the Danube under the command of an officer who, curiously enough, bore the name of Aetius.[87] He had taken part in the Council of Chalcedon the previous year as count of the domestics, and for his services in 452 was appointed Eastern consul for the year 454. This Aetius was successful in his enterprise. He routed the Hun force which had been left behind to safeguard their territories, and Attila, hard pressed by both human and natural forces, retired from Italy without ever setting foot south of the Po. His empire had been shaken to its foundations.[88]

V

It must have seemed that nothing could save Marcian when the campaigning season of 453 came round. For two years Attila had delayed his destruction in vain attempts to settle his own affairs in the West. His first act when he regained his log huts on the Hungarian plain was to send Marcian a message of which the terms were not ambiguous: he stated bluntly that, since the tribute agreed upon with Theodosius had not been sent out, he proposed to make war upon the Eastern Empire and to enslave its inhabitants.[89] But the blow that he longed to deal was never delivered.

Before the campaigning season began he decided to add yet another to the long series of his wives.[90] On this occasion his

bride was Ildico. Her name, if it has not been corrupted in
the tradition, would seem to betray her Germanic origin, and
we are told that she was a girl of great beauty. Beyond that
we know nothing of her, and cannot say whether the
marriage had any political implications. After the wedding
Attila drank far into the night, and, when much of the
following day had passed and he did not reappear, his
servants shouted loudly outside the door of his room and
eventually forced an entry. They found their master dead and
his bride weeping beside him, her face covered with her veil.
Attila had bled heavily through the nose during the night (as,
indeed, he had often done before), and being heavily drunk
had been suffocated in his sleep. His body bore no trace of a
wound.[91] The Huns were dumbfounded. They cut off their
hair and slashed their faces with their swords, so that 'the
greatest of all warriors should be mourned with no feminine
lamentations and with no tears, but with the blood of
men'.[92]

Attila's body was laid in a silken tent pitched on the plains
over which he had so often led his men to war. While the
mass of his followers gazed on him in wonder, horsemen
chosen for their extreme skill from the whole nation galloped
wildly around him, 'in the fashion of a circus', so as to
gladden the heart of the dead chieftain.[93] The song that was
sung over the body has been preserved by Jordanes. He
found it in the Greek of Priscus and translated it after his
fashion. Priscus doubtless had it from a Goth, who rendered
the words of the original Hunnic. Yet, though the song has
survived at least three translations, it retains a rhythmical
beauty in the humble prose of Jordanes:

> Praecipuus Hunnorum rex Attila,
> patre genitus Mundzuco,
> fortissimarum gentium dominus,
> qui inaudita ante se potentia
> solus Scythica et Germanica regna possedit
> nec non utraque Romani urbis[94] imperia
> captis civitatibus terruit, et

ne praedae reliqua subderentur,
placatus praecibus annuum vectigal accepit:
cumque haec omnia proventu felicitatis egerit,
non vulnere hostium, non fraude quorum,
sed gente incolume
inter gaudia laetus
sine sensu doloris
occubuit.
quis ergo hunc exitum putet,
quem nullus aestimat vindicandum?[95]

(The chief of the Huns, king Attila, born of his father Mundiuch, lord of the bravest tribes, sole possessor of the Scythian and German kingdoms, something unheard of before, captured cities and terrified both empires of the Roman world, and, appeased by their prayers, took an annual tribute to save their remnants from plunder. And when he had accomplished all this by the favour of provenance, he fell not by an enemy's blow, nor by treachery of his own people, but in the midst of his people at peace, happy in his joy and without sense of pain. Who can rate this as death, when none considers that it calls for vengeance?)

In the meantime, his barrow had been heaped up, and, when the lamentations were over, the Huns celebrated his burial with wild revelry, mixing their grief with joy in a manner that amazed the Gothic monk.[96] When night fell the body was removed from the tent and laid in the barrow. They covered it first with gold and silver, then with iron. It was said afterwards that the precious metals indicated that he had received the tribute of both empires, and the iron that he had conquered all the nations. The arms which he had stripped from his enemies, along with gems and other treasures, were placed in the barrow; and those who laid him to rest were slain over his body and rested beside him.[97]

No part of these rites can be claimed as Germanic. The similarities between them and those described in *Beowulf* are striking, but scarcely more so than the differences. Some writers have supposed a common origin for both sets of ceremonies, and one student has been so bold as to suggest that both the Anglo-Saxons and the Huns derived them from Homer, the Huns having studied Homer, no doubt, in the intervals of tending their flocks outside Olbia. We shall rather agree with that great scholar who pointed out that the similarities must be explained in terms of the uniform social background of the Heroic Age.[98] A further point in Jordanes' account of the burial has some interest. Of the entire Hun language, of all that vocabulary in which they called to their herds, planned their campaigns, and sought to placate the angry spirits of the steppe region, only a solitary word has survived: *strava*, 'funeral'. How Jordanes came to know it we cannot tell. All that can be said is that a single word does not enable us to classify the language of the Huns, and *strava* has been variously claimed as Germanic, Slavic, and Turkish.[99]

It was not long before it began to be whispered that Attila had not died a natural death, but had been struck down as he slept by his new bride Ildico. The circumstances of his death were such that these reports were inevitable, and the chronicler Count Marcellinus, writing a century later, quotes the view that the great conqueror was murdered by a woman, no doubt the bride whom he had married a few hours before his death.[100] In some Nordic saga we read that Attila was slain by his wife in revenge for her two brothers whom he had treacherously murdered. The rumour, though it may have begun to circulate within a few days of the chieftain's death, was none the less false:

> Loke, Attila, the grete conquerour,
> Deyde in his sleep, with shame and dishonour,
> Bledinge ay at the nose in dronkenesse;
> A capitayn shoulde live in sobrenesse.[101]

We can readily imagine that the news of the chieftain's death spread with great rapidity to every corner of Europe, bringing delight to all nations alike and not least to the Romans.[102] The news, we are told, actually came to Marcian before the event itself had occurred. On the very night of the Hun's death – and Priscus swore in his *History* that he was reporting the mere truth – on that very night a divine figure had stood beside the emperor as he slept and had shown him the bow of Attila broken apart.[103] Perhaps the blame for the tale lies upon Marcian rather than the historian: some exuberance was justifiable when the almost incredible news was brought to him that the bow of Attila was broken asunder. Certainly it was not the only legend about himself that he found it politic to invent.[104]

VI

After Attila's death his sons divided up the subject nations equally among themselves, so that, as a shocked Goth puts it, 'warlike kings with their peoples should be divided among them like a family estate'.[105] We do not know how many sons there were: we only have Jordanes' statement that 'through the boundlessness of [Attila's] lust, they were almost a people in themselves'. At any rate, this was the only occasion in Hun history, so far as we know, when a father's kingdom was thus shared out by his sons. It will be noted too that they did not parcel out the land over which Attila had ruled but the peoples who occupied that land: land without men was of no interest to the Hun now. Beyond doubt, the sons did not intend to cut themselves off completely from each other: Attila and Bleda before them seem never to have undertaken separate campaigns. But the experience of Octar pointed to what was to come: when the new rulers retired each to his own domains, each with his own followers, concerted military action at short notice by the united Hun forces became impossible.

It was not many months after their father's death that they began to quarrel. As to the cause of their quarrel, it would seem that one or more tried to dispossess the others from their share of the inheritance,[106] and that several great battles were fought between them as a result.[107] At any rate, it is clear that their military strength was impaired and the way prepared for a rebellion of the subject nations. Poor as our sources have been for the history of the last few years, they are poorer still now. The embers of the historical tradition flicker once or twice before going out, and by their light we catch dim glimpses of tremendous struggles on the steppe and movements of peoples, but the details are utterly lost.

The rebellion was started, it seems, by a number of the Ostrogoths in the Theiss valley, whither they had been moved by their masters long before.[108] But this was only a preliminary: the great revolt of the Germanic peoples was led and inspired by Ardaric, the king of the Gepids, who had been a confidant of Attila. It was he above all others who raised the hearts of the Germans 'with the uplifting desire for freedom'.[109] After a succession of bloody battles, the decision was reached, probably in 455, in a great conflict at the unknown river Nedao in Pannonia.[110] The Ostrogoths, who seem already to have been free, took no part in the battle – a fact by which they later won the hostility of the Gepids – and some of the subject nations still thought fit to support their masters.[111] But the Gepids were joined by the bulk of the subjects, including most of the Sciri, Rugi, Suebi, and Heruls. Their victory was as complete as it was unexpected, and in their jubilation they claimed to have slain the impossible figure of 30,000 Huns and allies, among them Attila's eldest son Ellac, whom we have met as the governor of the Acatziri.[112] His surviving brothers with the remnants of their followers fled across the Carpathians to the shores of the Black Sea, where, eighty years before, the Huns had signalized their arrival in European history by crushing the Ostrogoths.

But they were not content to remain there: they, or some of them, soon began to filter back again across the Carpathians to their old homes in the Theiss valley.[113] Their hatred of the Ostrogoths, who had started the series of campaigns which culminated at the Nedao, must have been boundless, and we soon find them seeking to restore their

Plate 14   The Roman Empire triumphant in a coin of Valentinian III and Marcian (c. AD 450–455). The serpent beneath the emperor's feet is believed to symbolize Attila and the Huns.

fortunes by falling upon Valamer (p. 149 above) and his followers. The Ostrogoths had been isolated politically: there was marked tension between them and the Gepids, and, as they had not supported the Gepids at the Nedao, so now they had to stand alone.[114] The Huns attacked them 'as deserters from their rule, and sought them as fugitive slaves', and managed to surprise Valamer before his brothers could come to his aid. But the result was another shattering defeat for the Huns, only a fraction of whom escaped from the battlefield under Ernac, Attila's favoured younger son, to take refuge with Marcian's permission at the confluence of the Danube and the Theiss.[115]

For the rest, we hear of nothing save occasional raids by isolated Hun bands and of the settlement of Huns on the soil of the Eastern Empire by Marcian. Some Huns, for instance, were settled in company with a body of other barbarians in the neighbourhood of Castra Martis, which had fallen to Uldin long ago.[116] Emnetzur and Ultzindur, two otherwise unknown *consanguinei* (relatives) of Attila's sons, were settled in Dacia Ripensis and controlled the fortresses of Utus, Oescus, and Almus.[117] The dates of these settlements are quite unknown, and we have no chronological information as to Jordanes' statement that, besides these, 'many of the Huns rushed into *Romania* everywhere and gave themselves up; of these some are even now called Sacromontisi and Fossatisii'. Not all of them came peacefully. In the middle of the sixties Anthemius, the son-in-law of Marcian and future Emperor of the West, won distinction against one of their bands. The leader of this 'roaming multitude from the lands of Scythia' (*Scythicae vaga turba plagae*), as Sidonius, our sole authority, calls it 'teeming with savagery, frightful, ravening, violent, barbarous even in the eyes of the barbarian peoples around them', was called Hormidac, whose previous and subsequent career is unknown.[118] They had launched so unexpected a raid that the city of Sardica (Sophia) had been unable to close its gates in time and had fallen into their hands. Anthemius besieged them there in circumstances of considerable hardship, for it appears that his troops were continually short of food and drink – the devastation of the surrounding countryside must have been very severe. But Hormidac's position was equally grave, for he eventually came out and offered battle in the hope of breaking up the siege. At the first onset the Roman officer commanding Anthemius' cavalry deserted to the enemy. His name is not recorded, but, being a cavalry officer, it is not impossible that he was himself a Hun. At any rate, Anthemius fought on with the infantry and in the end scored a victory. He made peace with Hormidac on condition that the traitor was handed over to him.[119]

In the wild confusion of the generation which followed Attila's death we catch an occasional glimpse of one or two of the λογάδες. Indeed, the fortunes of one of them are well known. There is little need, however, to recount here the story of Orestes and how he returned to the Western Empire, where he eventually rebelled against the Emperor Julius Nepos and set upon the throne his own son Romulus, named after the Romulus with whom Priscus had spoken in Attila's encampment a quarter of a century before. But when the young Romulus had sat dimly upon the throne for only a year or so, he and his father were overthrown by Odoacer. Now, by a strange irony, Odoacer, the first barbarian king of Italy, appears to have been the son of that very Edeco who had travelled to Constantinople with Orestes in 449 and had undertaken to murder Attila. At any rate, we hear that Odoacer was the son of a certain 'Idico', as John of Antioch calls him, or 'Aedico', as the Anonymous Valesianus has it,[120] and from the days of Valesius and Tillemont scholars have agreed to identify this Idico or Aedico with the Edeco of Priscus.[121] Jordanes gives us some information about the activities of Edeco – he calls him Edica – after the death of Attila.[122] He and one of his sons – not Odoacer, but another who is significantly named Hunoulphus – joined in a great confederacy of nations who aimed at the final and definitive destruction of the Ostrogoths. The age-old hatred of the Huns for the Ostrogoths still lived on in Edeco. The Gothic king Valamer was now dead, but his younger brothers Theodimer and Vidimer utterly routed the confederates on the unknown river Bolia in Pannonia. Edeco may have fallen in the rout, for we never hear of him again.

We learn something also of two sons of Attila called Dengizech and Ernac – the latter had been seen by Priscus during the first banquet given to the Roman ambassador in the log hut of Attila.[123] Ernac had settled, with Marcian's permission (p. 169 above), at the confluence of the Danube and Theiss. Dengizech appears to have stayed in the Theiss valley until, hearing that the Ostrogoths were attacking an unknown people called the Sadagi, he assembled the few tribes who still remained under his control and whose names are given as the Ultzinzures, Angisciri, Bittugures, and Bardores. Coming to Bassiana, a city of Pannonia lying to the east of Sirmium, these Huns began to devastate the countryside, but the Ostrogoths fell upon them with such effect 'that those Huns who survived have been in dread of the arms of the Goths from that time down to the present day.'[124] For many years Dengizech drops out of history, but he reappears towards the end of the sixties. We are told that, in the year 468/9, an embassy arrived in Constantinople from 'the children of Attila'. Its purpose was to clear up the differences which existed between the East Roman government and themselves – evidently some fighting had taken place – and to negotiate a peace treaty which would reopen the market towns along the Roman frontier to the Huns (see pp. 198–9 below). But the envoys achieved nothing: the Emperor Leo (457–74) saw no reason why the benefits of Roman trade should be given to men who had done so much harm to the empire. When the children of Attila heard of the failure of the embassy, our source goes on, they disagreed among themselves. Dengizech wished to declare war upon the Romans – and it is clear that he had often done so before – but his brother Ernac refused to join him: he declared that the wars already going on inside his own dominions occupied him sufficiently.[125] Thereupon Dengizech undertook the campaign alone. He appeared upon the bank of the Danube and was met by the master of the soldiers in Thrace, Anagast, the son of that Arnegisclus who had so often fought Attila. Anagast sent some envoys to ask Dengizech what he wanted: the Hun contemptuously sent them back without an answer, and himself sent an embassy direct to Leo declaring that, if the emperor would not give land and money to him and his followers, war would result. Leo listened to the ambassadors and was clearly not unwilling to enlist the barbarians in his army;[126] but the negotiations broke down and Dengizech invaded the Roman provinces. It was his last campaign. He was defeated and killed by Anagast in 469, and his head was brought to the Eastern capital, where it was carried in procession along the street called Mesé, and fixed on a pole at the Xylokerkos Gate. The whole city turned out to look joyfully upon it, and to prove incidentally the terror which a Hun raid could still inspire in Constantinople.[127] The fate of Ernac remains unknown, but the oracle, which foretold that he would restore the fallen fortunes of Attila's descendants, proved wrong after all, and it has been plausibly suggested that he died an obscure mercenary in the service of the Eastern Empire.[128] The last raid carried out by Huns during the fifth century on the lower Danube provinces was launched over an unguarded part of the river in the early days of the Emperor Zeno (474–91), whose generals seem to have beaten it back without much trouble.[129]

The main strength of the Huns, such as it was, remained then on the lower Danube during the reigns of Leo and Zeno, but they did not all play the part of plunderers of the Roman dominions: some, as Ernac may have done, were glad to take service in the imperial armies. At the time of Dengizech's death, or a little earlier, we hear of a certain Chelchal, a junior officer on Aspar's staff serving under Anagast and other Roman generals against an army of Goths supported by yet another company of Huns.[130] Chelchal summoned the Gothic commanders to his presence during a truce, and declared to them that Leo would be willing to grant them land, but that in doing so he intended to benefit only the Huns serving in their ranks. He went on to emphasize the immeasurable hatred which every Goth felt for them: in the days of their ancestors, he said, the Goths had sworn to avoid all treaties with Huns. He finally stated that, although himself a Hun, he had told them of Leo's intentions because of his love of truth. This reason would not have satisfied every Roman, but the Goths believed his words, and suspected the loyalty of their Hun comrades. They therefore gathered them together and tried to massacre them. Anagast was delighted with the trickery of his subordinate, which could not have been bettered by the most skilled East Roman, but the combatants soon saw that their struggle benefited no one except the enemy. They therefore came to terms again with one another and resumed their struggle with the imperial forces. Chelchal's deceit had not been so successful as he and Anagast had hoped.[131]

Companies of Huns are also found in the service of the Western Romans very soon after the battle of the Nedao. In 457 Huns were enlisted in the motley army which Majorian had assembled for his projected campaigns in Gaul and Africa.[132] Majorian had reason to regret hiring his Hun mercenaries, for, as he was about to set out from Italy, they alone of this multinational army mutinied: 'Only one race refused you obedience, a race who had lately, in a mood even more savage than usual, withdrawn their untamed host from the Danube because they had lost their lords in warfare, and Tuldila stirred in that unruly multitude a mad lust of fighting for which they must needs pay dear.' Tuldila bears a Germanic name, so that it would seem that these unruly Huns were incited to mutiny by a Goth. At any rate, we know nothing more about him except the fate of the mutiny which he incited: 'You, however, put off the punishment of the offence; but in sparing them you caused yet greater bloodshed. For a band of your men, more heedful of your prosperity than you yourself, could bear this crime no longer, and for your sake spurned your mildness, and the rebels fell one and all, victims offered at the start of the war.'[133]

Other Huns too were enlisted to take part in Majorian's planned invasion of Africa. Part of Majorian's plan of campaign in 461 was that the famous Marcellinus, count of Dalmatia, should occupy Sicily so as to shield the island from the descents of the Vandals by sea. The army which Marcellinus brought with him included a very considerable band of Huns, but they were as faithless to him as Tuldila had been to the luckless emperor. Ricimer, who was presumed to be the friend of Majorian, bribed these Huns to leave Marcellinus in the lurch, and Marcellinus could do no more than retire from Sicily, and allow Geiseric to devote his undivided attention to Majorian.[134] Treachery and mutual divisions are as strongly marked a characteristic of the Huns in their latest days as in their earliest.

VII

It is not known whether such war-lords as Dengizech and Edeco believed that they could one day restore the great empire which Attila had ruled. Whatever hopes they may have had of uniting the Huns once more into a confederacy and dominating the steppe were ruined by the events of the sixties of the fifth century.

It has been said that the last paragraph of Priscus' thirtieth fragment 'is certainly one of the most important [passages] for the ethnographer to be found in ancient literature, for it is the sole record of one of those great race movements which have been such important factors in rearranging the ethnographic distribution of man'.[135] In it Priscus tells us that in the middle of the sixties ambassadors arrived in Constantinople from the people of the Saraguri,[136] the Uguri, and the Onoguri. These nations had been driven out of their homes by the Sabiri, who had themselves been set in motion by a nation whose name is now mentioned for the first time, the Avars. What had set the Avars on the move? The peoples living beyond them on the shore of the Ocean, says Priscus, had themselves been driven from their homes by an inroad of the sea, and, so the reports said, by a ferocious brood of griffins who were only destined to stop devouring the human race when not a man was left alive. So as one nation set its neighbour in motion, the Saraguri had at last been thrown on the Acatziri, whom Attila had subjected in 448 (pp. 104ff above) and who had since regained their freedom. They were now conquered again after a succession of battles and their conquerors had come to Constantinople to win the friendship of the Eastern Romans. This in fact they secured. But they were only the forerunners of the nations pressing westwards behind them. A dozen years after Attila's death the steppe was drenched by floods of new and warlike nomadic barbarians.[137] So Dengizech, Ernac, and the others were compelled to stay in the Roman Empire or on its immediate borders: for them there was no retreat into the open steppe.

Priscus' reference to the 'ocean' has been taken to mean that this vast movement of peoples originated in the regions lying north and north-east of the Altai in eastern Siberia.[138] On this we may reserve our opinion: perhaps the movement started no farther away than the shores of the Aral Sea. In any case, the steppe was now crowded with military nations among whom the pitiful remnants of the Huns played nothing more than the role of minor robbers and cattle-raiders.

7

Hun Society under Attila

The isolated bands of nomads whom we sought to describe in chapter 3 could never have reared up that vast empire which covered central Europe in the middle of the fifth century if their society had remained always as it had been at the end of the fourth. But their society, like all others, did not remain stationary. We have seen how, as wealth grew, kingship made its appearance among them. We have now to inquire into what happened when wealth began to accumulate on the steppe in even larger masses.

I

About the year 430 Rua made a treaty with the Romans of the East by the terms of which the emperor undertook to pay him a tribute of 350 lb of gold per annum.[1] In 435, under Bleda and Attila, this tribute was doubled and thenceforth the Huns received 700 lb of gold a year.[2] After the battle in the Chersonesus in 443 Anatolius signed his first treaty with the Huns. By its terms 6,000 lb of gold were to be paid in a lump sum as arrears of tribute, and the annual payment trebled, that is, the Huns now received 2,100 lb of gold every year.[3] As early as the days of Uldin we find the Huns selling off their prisoners at 1 *solidus* a head (p. 38 above). In 435 they had the right of disposing of their Roman prisoners at 8 *solidi* a head, and this was raised to 12 *solidi* in 443. An occasional windfall would bring them far larger sums. For instance, the wife of one Sulla who had been captured in Ratiaria in 443 brought in no less than 500 *solidi*.[4] Stringent precautions were taken to ensure that no prisoners escaped without payment of the ransom money. The money was to go to those who captured the prisoner, but the tribute was paid directly 'to the kings of the Scythians', that is, to Bleda and Attila, and after 445 to Attila alone.[5] Also, when a city was captured the booty was not distributed evenly to all the Huns: the most powerful of them received a disproportionately large share.[6] In addition to all this, the Huns obtained enormous quantities of plunder during their many raids on the Roman provinces and especially during the two great invasions of 441/3 and 447. What was the effect on Hun society of this influx of huge sums of money and limitless quantities of plunder, and how was the money spent?

Bleda and Attila ruled jointly. They were the sons of Mundiuch,[7] the brother of Rua and Octar, the latter two of the three having held the leadership of the confederacy simultaneously. Attila handed down the sovereignty of his empire to his numerous sons 'like a family estate'. It is evident then that one family had succeeded in making of the military leadership an hereditary office held by successive generations of brothers, and a Roman can refer to Attila's 'progeny' as ruling the Huns.[8] This is an entire innovation in Hun society and implies that an hereditary nobility has made its appearance. The leaders differ now from the *primates* of Ammianus' day in that they derive their authority, not from military prowess, which cannot be inherited, but from wealth, which can.

Attila is shown in the pages of Priscus to have been an entirely autocratic khan even in peace-time. He appears among his people amid the shouts of their applause;[9] but their respect is based on fear, and we are assured by Priscus that the entire multitude of the Huns was pervaded by terror of him.[10] There is no hint in any of our authorities that he felt the slightest limitation on his power either in war or in peace. He plans and conducts campaigns and negotiations apparently without any consultation with, or advice from, his followers. In peace-time he administers justice: standing at the door of his log hut, a crowd of disputants hears and accepts his judgements without protest and, it seems, with complete submission. The judgements are delivered by Attila on the spur of the moment after hearing the contending parties, without reference even to Onegesius, who is standing beside him.[11] He has the power of life and death over all his followers.[12] Nothing could be farther removed from the *primates* of the fourth century. Attila has emancipated himself from tribal obligations and from the limitations which a tribal society imposes upon the excessive growth of any one individual's power. Neither the tribe nor even the entire nation can control him. He can murder members of his kin without retribution;[13] he has slain even his own brother. His followers regard him as a god, and his subjects find it convenient to address him as such (pp. 107, 114 above). This is a state of mind which Attila has reinforced among his rude followers by the use he has made of the sword of the war-god (p. 97 above). In a word, the growth of wealth has revolutionized Hun society.

II

In this autocratically governed community there seems to be no room for the *primates*, who, as we saw, owed their war-time position less to wealth than to military prowess. We hear instead of Attila's λογάδες (picked men) or ἐπιτήδειοι (close associates), as they are sometimes called. Edeco belonged to their number because of his outstanding successes in warfare.[14] On the other hand, Berichus, who was also 'one of the picked men',[15] owed his position to his

Plate 15   The cicada – a Hunnic badge of rank.
Nationalmuseum, Budapest. Copyright © C.M. Dixon.

noble birth,[16] which probably means that his family in the preceding generation had won distinction in the field and, in doing so, had acquired considerable wealth from plunder and the like. At least one of the λογάδες, admittedly a minor one, was not a Hun at all but a Roman: this was Orestes, the father of the last Emperor of the West, Romulus Augustulus.[17]

What were the functions of these λογάδες? They went on diplomatic missions for their master on very numerous occasions, and sometimes they negotiated with foreign ambassadors who came into the steppe to see Attila.[18] The ulterior motive of their frequent visits to Constantinople was the collection of the rich harvest of gifts which every ambassador received there.[19] Again, they were called upon to guard Attila's person, and each of them accompanied his master in arms for a specified part of the day, a fact which gave them ready access to his person and conversation.[20] Although they regarded this task as δουλεία, 'slavery',[21] they were capable of the greatest loyalty in carrying it out.[22] Edeco was perhaps corrupted by Chrysaphius, but he confessed to Attila almost at once, and Priscus suggests that he may never have intended murdering his master at all (pp. 115–16 above).

A far more important duty concerned the government of the rest of the Huns. A portion of the horsemen seems to have been under the direct orders of Edeco, and, when the murder of Attila was suggested to him, his first thought was to assure the co-operation of the men under his immediate command.[23] It is clear that, although each of the λογάδες was assigned a military force of his own, that force was well aware to whom it owed its first loyalty. With this military support the λογάδες ruled over specific portions of the great empire which Attila, Rua, and their predecessors had built up. We are told that Berichus was 'the ruler of many villages in Scythia',[24] and doubtless Onegesius, Edeco, and the others were so too. In this they resembled Attila's own sons: it will be recalled that, when the brave and powerful nation of the

Acatziri was subdued, Attila appointed his eldest son Ellac to rule over it.[25] It seems reasonable to suggest that the λογάδες corresponded to the οἰκεῖοι καὶ λοχαγοί of Uldin (p. 63 above), and that they commanded during a campaign, not only the specific squadrons of the Huns assigned to each of them, but also the contingents of subject warriors provided by the districts which they governed. We know further that a sort of hierarchy existed among them, which was indicated by the seats allotted to them when they sat down to feast with their master: Onegesius sat at Attila's right hand and Berichus at his left, and Attila's paternal uncle was similarly honoured.[26] Again, the Roman Orestes ranked much below Edeco, because the latter was 'the best fighter and a Hun by race'.[27] All this perhaps allows us to conclude that the territories over which they ruled were unequal in area, population, wealth, and strategical importance.

Apart from keeping order among the subject nations, the λογάδες had a further duty: they had to collect tribute and food-stuffs from them. Chelchal, in his solitary appearance in history (pp. 173–4 above), said to certain Goths, in reference to the days of Attila, that the Huns, who themselves despised agriculture, descended upon the Gothic food-supply and snatched it away like wolves, so that the Goths had the status of slaves and laboured for the sustenance of the Huns; to this relationship he assigned the bitter enmity of the two races.[28] Whether the Goths were able to produce a sufficient surplus of food to support both themselves and their parasitic masters may be doubted – and more than doubted. At any rate, it was not the Huns who went short, even though they had to import grain to supplement their supplies. It was certainly this collection of Gothic food which enabled the Huns to concentrate larger armies now than when they had first appeared in Europe and were dependent exclusively on their own products. We have no details as to the manner in which they extorted the grain from their subjects or as to the amount taken. Nor have we any information as to how they enrolled their subjects into their forces. We know, however, that the Huns had compelled their subjects to fight for them as early as 375, when we find the newly conquered Alans heading the attack on the Ostrogoths, and in 408 Uldin had invaded Thrace with a body of Sciri in his army (pp. 27, 33 above). We may take it as certain that Attila rarely went on a campaign without bringing with him considerable numbers of his subjects: they helped to swell his numbers, and it would have been dangerous to leave them behind when the main Hun forces were far away. All this brutal treatment was precisely reflected in the attitude of the Huns towards their subjects. Again and again our sources tell us that the Huns regarded their subjects as nothing more than slaves. The successors of Attila sought out the Goths 'as fugitive slaves', and we have abundant evidence to show that their attitude was merely traditional.[29]

It is clear that the λογάδες were the hinge upon which the entire administration of the Hun empire turned. The Latin secretaries sent to Attila by Aetius (pp. 139–40 above) were of quite minor importance, their chief functions being merely to compose letters which Attila wished to send to one or other of the Roman Emperors, and to keep a few documents and records of various kinds.[30] But without the λογάδες Attila could not have administered his domains at all.

It is to be noticed that Berichus, although 'ruler of many villages in Scythia', was absent from his dominions in 449 and was found by Priscus at Attila's camp; thereafter he was able to serve on an embassy to Constantinople. This would seem to suggest that the military force by means of which he kept his portion of the conquered peoples in subjection was very considerable: he could not have absented himself thus unless he had been absolutely assured of the safety of his garrison troops and of their wives and children from the bitter hostility of the subject population, who with hungry eyes saw their grain carried off year by year to feed their masters. But, as we saw in an earlier chapter, there is no reason to believe that the Huns were very numerous; it was impossible for the λογάδες to garrison the entire enormous empire. Hence some of the subject peoples continued to be ruled directly by their own native kings or chiefs, who were, however, far more the slaves of Attila than were the λογάδες. But the favoured Ardaric, king of the Gepids (who afterwards headed the allies at the river Nedao), and Valamer, the senior king of the Ostrogoths, seem to have been almost on a par with the λογάδες themselves. Of Ardaric Jordanes reports that 'because of his great loyalty to Attila, he shared his plans'.[31] It is difficult to avoid the impression that, although Ardaric incited the great rebellion after Attila's death, he must have welcomed the state of affairs existing in his lord's lifetime. True, he was not entirely independent; but, on the other hand, his position was guaranteed so long as he retained the confidence of the Huns – no enemy, either internal or external, could rise up effectively against him if Attila continued to be his friend. To a considerable extent, in fact, the continued existence of the Hun empire must have been a vested interest in the Germanic world of Ardaric as it certainly was in the Roman world of Aetius (p. 155 above). Not all German kings received the favour which Ardaric enjoyed. Of the mass of minor princes and chieftains Jordanes writes sorrowfully as follows: 'the rest of the crowd of kings, if we may call them so, and leaders of various nations hung upon Attila's nod like slaves, and when he gave a sign even by a glance without a murmur, each stood up in fear and trembling, and without hesitation did as he was ordered'. Even the Gothic kings did not hold a particularly dignified position: 'but nevertheless, as has often been said, they ruled in such a way that they respected the dominion of Attila, king of the Huns . . . ; they would have even had to commit parricide had their lord commanded it'.[32] But, although food might be short, it was not the king who went hungry; and whatever the discontent of his followers, they could do nothing as long as Attila lived.

It seems reasonable to conclude that the Huns in part kept the Goths in subjection by co-operating with the Gothic rulers. Even before the fourth century came to a close, the Huns ruled the Goths, according to Jordanes, 'so that one of their own number always ruled the Gothic people, though subject to Hunnic control'.[33] It may not have been an heroic life, but at least it was a safe one. In the case of the Romans it was the poorer classes who welcomed the invaders; among the Germans it may have been the kings who filled this role.

III

Before considering the factors which led to the downfall of Hun society we must digress – if it is a digression – and consider the position which women held in this community of plunderers. For the period before Priscus we have practically no information. Ammianus merely mentions the women living in the wagons which formed the headquarters of the various groups of nomads: in these wagons, he says, they spent their time in stitching together the crude garments worn by their menfolk and in bearing their children. This picture, such as it is, suggests the desperately hard conditions of life which are the customary lot of women on the steppe,[34] and, if we possessed no further evidence, we might conclude that the Hun women suffered the cruel fate which is usual in primitive nomadic societies. But if so, we should be wrong. Ammianus does not prepare us for the information offered by Priscus.

It will be recalled that, when Attila rode into his chief village, the Hun women ran from all sides to catch sight of him: some of them formed up in a choir about his horse, and sang songs of welcome to him.[35] This action does not suggest the seclusion of the womenfolk which Ammianus' words might have led us to expect. On that same occasion, when Attila had gone a little farther along the road, the wife of Onegesius came out of her hut with a throng of her handmaids and offered food and drink to the chieftain. He accepted the gifts, still sitting on his horse, because, says Priscus, 'he wished to please the wife of his lieutenant'.[36] On this occasion, too, the women appear in public and rub shoulders in the throng, not only with their own menfolk, but with strangers and foreigners, like Priscus, who was himself standing there watching. Again, the historian had no difficulty in entering Hereca's tent, in looking at her handmaids busy with their embroidery, and in speaking to the queen herself.[37] But the most surprising fact of all is still to be recalled. One of the villages through which the ambassador and his party journeyed was actually ruled by a woman, a wife of Bleda.[38] Whether she ruled only this one village, or whether the village was the capital of a considerable area, we have no means of saying. We hear of no other women rulers among the Huns themselves, but the Utiguri, a nation closely akin to the Huns of Attila, knew at least one female tribal leader,[39] while in the time of Justinian the Sabiri, who were also considered to be Huns (p. 175 above), were led by a woman called Boärex, who took command of her tribe on the death of her husband Balach.[40] Considering that the Huns were a race of pastoral nomads, we can only conclude that women held among them a position of unexpected dignity and respect: there is, as Hodgkin (p. 82) points out, no trace of Oriental seclusion about their treatment. It is well worth recalling Fox's words (p. 43) about the early Mongols, particularly when we have the case of Boärex before us:

When a man died leaving his children still in infancy, the widow assumed all the rights of her husband, including even the leadership of the clan or tribe, until such time as her children grew to manhood and married. Among both Mongols and Turks the position of the widow was one of great importance. In some cases she might become the ruler of a great empire.

The little evidence that we possess, and particularly the status of Bleda's widow, seems to indicate that to some extent this holds good of the Huns also.

Onegesius lived in a group of huts enclosed within a

palisade. He did not live alone there with his wife and servants: he also had the company of 'those who were related to him by clan (κατὰ γένος), and the number of slaves and servant girls resident in his huts was very considerable.[41] There seems to be no reason why we should not generalize from what we know about Onegesius, and suppose that this extensive household organization was the rule among the Hun. With this we must closely associate the polygamy practised by them, which, it would seem, was not restricted merely to the rulers.[42] Bearing both these phenomena in mind, we may conclude with some assurance that the Huns were organized in what Lewis Morgan called 'patriarchal families'. Morgan points out that, in this organization of the family,

the chiefs, at least, lived in polygamy; but this was not the material principle of the patriarchal institution. The organization of a number of persons, bond and free, into a family, under paternal power, for the purpose of holding lands [this point would not, of course, apply to the nomads] and for the care of flocks and herds, was the essential characteristic of this family . . . Authority over its members and over its property was the material fact.[43]

A very significant feature of the patriarchal family is the exclusive domination of the male within it, for tending the flocks and herds is essentially the male's work and the female is economically quite dependent. But the women of the Huns have not yet suffered the full degradation which the growth of property in a primitive society usually entails.

IV

The growth of wealth and the influx of money, then, had not yet radically affected the position held by women in Hun society. Let us consider now the position of the military leader in the new conditions.

Attila only had followers because he could reward them

well. In the conditions of pastoralism on the steppe, as Fox (p. 49) says, 'a generous lord had many followers, a weak or unsuccessful one' – such as Uldin had become in 408 – 'soon had none'. Hence the chieftain had continually to bestir himself to keep his rude followers well supplied and to present them with the costliest gifts. He gave them the best share of the booty,[44] and sent them on embassies to Constantinople so that they might enrich themselves at the Emperor's expense.[45] Attila never failed, until the last two years of his life, to supply endless booty and a huge quantity of money. Thus we find the λογάδες owning, or receiving as gifts, silk and Indian pearls,[46] gold and silver platters,[47] silver goblets and trays,[48] bridles studded with gold and precious stones,[49] beds covered with linen and variegated hangings.[50] To eat they have Indian pepper, dates, and other delicacies.[51] At the feast which he gave for his followers and the Romans Attila supplied meat, 'bread', 'delicacies',[52] and other edibles.[53] On the steppe the Huts had only eaten meat 'on festive occasions or as a consequence of a visit of special honour'.[54] It would seem to be quite a customary dish now, at least for the ruling stratum. There was wine to drink at the banquet, although the Huns had now become acquainted with several varieties of Germanic beer as well – both *medus* (mead) and *camum* (beer) are specified.[55] Even an East Roman can refer to the feast as 'a sumptuous dinner'.[56] It began about the ninth hour and went on all night.[57] There were tables,[58] chairs, and couches of the Roman fashion.[59] The Roman influence is very clear in the arrangement of the tables, each of which was set before three or four of the guests.[60] The large huts of Attila and Onegesius illustrate the difference between Attila's Huns and those of Ammianus' day, who lived in horse-drawn wagons and feared to enter a Roman or Gothic dwelling.[61] Most of these possessions and luxuries have one negative quality in common: few of them could have been made or produced by the Huns themselves, so small was their productive power. Further, although they were all in such obvious display at Attila's banquet, it may be doubted whether they were enjoyed by the Huns at large: they were more probably confined to the rulers. At any rate, some minor Huns out on the steppe as late as 449 could provide the Roman ambassador with no bread, but only with 'millet' (κέγχρος).[62] Hun society, in the form which it had attained under Attila, could only continue in existence if supplies of these luxuries continued; but before we consider that point it is necessary to examine a source of supply which we have hitherto overlooked, but which is of fundamental importance.

V

'Gifts', tribute, and plunder were not the only sources from which the luxuries of the λογάδες were derived. It is time now to approach the vitally important question of trade. Scholars are agreed that a nomadic society existing exclusively on its flocks and herds without any contacts with settled agricultural communities is only a theoretical conception: there is no evidence that it has ever existed in practice. Exchange with settled populations is essential for the nomads' existence, and it was above all else the need for exchange that compelled the Huns in the first place to come into contact with the border towns of the Roman Empire.[63] The omission of this fact is the most serious weakness in the accounts of the nomads which have survived from ancient times; both Ammianus and Nestorius (p. 68 above) say nothing of it whatever.

For the period before Attila our sources tell us nothing about trade except for Ammianus' remark that 'they buy and sell when seated on their horses'. Of the Altziagiri somewhat later Jordanes has the following significant statement: 'the Altziagiri are near Cherson, where avaricious traders bring in the goods of Asia', and we have already quoted his words on the skin trade of the Hunuguri.[64] Their internal trade was of little importance, for one Hun community can have had but little to exchange which another wanted, since all alike were restricted to the one productive technique and the same limited material resources. Indeed, it is a common feature of all nomadic peoples of the steppe that they have practically no internal trade, although their external trade is quite brisk.[65] We have indicated above some of the articles which had to be imported into the steppe in the earliest days of the Huns. A clear example is their linen clothing: this continued to be worn by Attila and his grandees in Priscus' time, but the historian speaks of the precious skins which they also liked to wear.[66] Arms too were certainly required on a large scale, not merely because the extremely primitive steppe society has always been deficient in providing itself with weapons, but also because the steppe is treeless – hence the use of horn and bone in the making of bows.[67] Accordingly, even if the conditions of their society had allowed them sufficient time and technique to make their own weapons, the raw materials were lacking. But in fact they had insufficient technique. Even the Mongols of the twelfth century, a military nation if ever there was one, had to import their weapons, chiefly from China and Khorasan. In normal times they could make their own bows and arrows, spears and lances, 'but as soon as they began to make war on a large scale their slender productive resources failed them and they were forced to rely on other countries for their weapons'.[68] This fact is not explicitly mentioned by any ancient authority in the case of the Huns; nevertheless, it was well known in the fifth century and we shall see presently that it had not escaped the vigilant eyes of the East Roman government. It is to be noted, too, that Menander Protector indicates the early Turks' inability to arm themselves, and he stresses their difficulty in obtaining adequate supplies of iron.[69] We know that the Avars suffered likewise, for when their ambassadors reached Constantinople in 562 they made it their business to purchase a supply of weapons from the imperial factories: they were contemplating an immediate campaign against the Romans themselves. But the Romans, after accepting payment for the arms, promptly arrested the envoys and took the weapons from them.[70] The significance of these points must be emphasized and a distinction drawn. Germany imported large quantities of Roman weapons: 'there is scarcely a single deposit of antiquities dating from the first four centuries, not only in the south and west of Germany but even in Denmark and other Baltic lands, which does not contain a large proportion of Roman articles . . . , above all, armour and weapons.'[71] Yet the Germans, with the resources of their forests and mines at their disposal, could have fared reasonably well without such imports. Again, in 337, when the Persian king wished to *increase* his striking power, he sought to import iron from the Roman Empire.[72] But even without imported iron he was strong, as many a Roman had reason to know. Such cases as these must be distinguished from those of the Huns, Avars, Turks, and other steppe peoples. These *could not arm themselves at all* for purposes of large-scale offensive operations without the assistance of imported weapons.

To linen and weapons we may confidently add grain. That the Huns ate grain even in their earliest days is shown by Honorius' importation of it from Dalmatia into Italy for their use in 409 (p. 52 above). Claudian, however, says that they did not eat it, and since Peisker (p. 340) observes that bread is a luxury for the nomad horsemen, we may conclude that in general the poet is speaking of the masses of the population and that the grain was mostly consumed by the *primates*.[73] Indeed, bearing in mind that the trading was carried on mostly by the chiefs,[74] we may believe with some assurance that the purchased or bartered goods – the iron swords, the linen clothing, the grain, and some miscellaneous luxuries of a primitive kind – were pretty nearly restricted to the *primates*, at any rate in the early days when even the necessities of life were only obtained with difficulty. In return for their imports the Huns will have given what the steppe nomads have always been able to supply to settled agricultural societies – horses, meat, furs, and slaves. Even in Attila's day, when the Huns had found other means of paying for their imports, they expected the Roman ambassadors to be anxious to purchase slaves, horses, and furs when they visited their dominions.[75]

By the time of Attila the trade in luxuries had grown out of all recognition and had become a basic factor in the maintenance of his empire. The reader who fails to grasp the importance of this luxury trade will not understand the social organization of the Huns. It is known that, when essentials have spread more or less universally within a steppe society, there succeeds an imperative demand for luxuries from outside the range of steppe production as an altogether necessary method of distinguishing between the greater and the lesser people, between the λογάδες and the humbler horsemen.[76] Hence Attila's endless demands that Hun ambassadors should be received with 'gifts' at Constantinople is not merely to be ascribed to a *politique de prestige* on his part, as Alföldi believes;[77] it was a vital support of the social order then prevailing among the nomads. The λογάδες owed their allegiance to Attila alone, but they gave it to him solely because he could provide such gifts on a larger scale than anyone else. The Huns have now travelled a long way from the days when there was no leisured class among them and they were ruled 'not subject to the authority of any king'. The growth of wealth has split their ranks.

We shall see presently that the East Roman government was very well aware that its bitterest foes were not only militarily dependent on the produce of the empire, but also economically and socially. For the Huns carried on their trade almost exclusively with East Roman merchants and market towns. Indeed, it seems to have become unnecessary for large areas of Danubian country to maintain their long-established trade with the Western Empire. A survey of Roman coins found in Rumania yields an interesting result. Coins of all Aurelian's successors down to Theodosius I have been found there, a fact which shows that trade with the

West was as lively in that period as trade with the East. But after the reign of Theodosius I a peculiar phenomenon is noticeable: a great number of gold pieces have been found in Rumania which were struck by Arcadius, Theodosius II, Marcian, and Leo I, but those of contemporary Western Emperors are extremely rare.[78] It is reasonable to conclude that the Huns traded exclusively with the East Romans, or, to put it in other words, the East Romans had obtained a monopoly of trade with the Huns. Doubtless the same state of affairs prevailed in the more western Danubian lands, although perhaps to a lesser degree. When the time came, the East Romans knew how to make the most of the advantages of their economic position.

Unhappily, it is impossible to say what role this trade between the Huns and the Eastern Empire played in the rise of the earlier confederate kings, Uldin, Donatus, and the rest, or in the process by which the *primates* developed into the λογάδες of Attila. Lattimore (pp. 519ff, et al) is emphatic in believing that the very existence of trade flowing between nomads and non-nomadic communities 'must repeatedly have suggested the use of nomad military power first to govern the profits of trade with non-nomads and then to exact tribute'. Our Greco-Roman authorities allow us to say little on the subject; but it seems legitimate to draw one or two conclusions as to the East Roman point of view. It is certainly likely, for instance, that the more settled conditions in Europe brought about by the domination of the Huns would be welcome to merchants. It is difficult to resist the impression that the huge dimensions of the trade must have been very profitable to the market towns concerned as well as to individual traders who went among the nomads. The renegade Greek with whom Priscus spoke in Attila's encampment had been a merchant in Viminacium, but found himself much better off among the Huns. We do not know whether his increased prosperity was due to increased facilities for trading, but this may have been the case. A more significant figure in this connexion is 'Eustace, a merchant of

Apamea', who, about the year 484, long after Attila was dead, is found accompanying a band of Hun marauders in the role of their chief adviser on a plundering expedition against Persia.[79] If we could accept Hirth's conclusions with safety, we should have evidence for enormous trade relations between the realm of Ernac, Attila's son, and its eastern neighbours as far as the borders of China, and proof of the existence in considerable numbers of merchants and traders in his dominions in the years immediately following Attila's death. But Hirth's conclusions are more than doubtful, and cannot be utilized here.[80] More valuable is Jordanes' statement, quoted above, that the Altziagiri dwell near the Crimea 'where avaricious traders bring in the goods of Asia'.[81] That so few traders are mentioned and so little is said in our sources of the commerce between the Eastern Empire and the Huns is, of course, not in the least surprising: the historical writers are practically all out of sympathy with the trading class. In fact, the wonder is that the merchant of Viminacium, Eustace of Apamea, the skin trade of the Hunuguri, and so on are mentioned at all. Even if their names were not recorded, we could still safely conclude that the trade in question existed on a vast scale: modern study of nomadic societies of the steppe has not been barren. And the fact remains that the great bulk of the coins sent out by Theodosius' government must have come back to the empire by way of trade. Where else could the λογάδες have expended them? Why else should they have needed them at all? It is difficult to resist the impression that the continued existence of the Hun empire must have been recognized by many Roman subjects as essential to their prosperity. The traders in the frontier towns, the wandering merchants – or should we call them pedlars? – like Eustace, and the importers of slaves, furs, and skins, must all have reaped an acceptable profit – and the profit doubtless took the form of those very coins which Theodosius paid over to Attila with so much reluctance and humiliation.

It will have been clear from the narrative in earlier

chapters that this trade left its mark on the politics of the times. As early as Rua's day the Romans had been forced to provide markets for the Huns, and trade figured prominently in Attila's politics. In his first treaty with the Romans, in 435, he insisted that all Roman markets hitherto open to the Huns – the matter had been the subject of negotiation previously – should continue to be so, that the terms prevailing there should be fair, and that access to these markets should be attended with no danger to the Huns.[82] In 448 Attila, who had evidently been reasonably satisfied with the trading arrangements in the meantime – nothing was said of them in the Peace of Anatolius in 443 – again raised the question of his people's facilities for trading with the empire. He now insisted that the chief market town should be moved from Illyria to Naissus (Nish).[83] The primary aim of this was to advance the frontier of the Hun dominions, or at any rate to compel the Romans to evacuate the powerful fortifications of the Danube line, but doubtless also much greater quantities of goods were available at the new site, despite its recent devastation. At any rate, the arrangements now reached must have remained in force for several years, for we do not hear that Attila raised any further question about them. He can hardly have guessed how important the matter would become after his death.

VI

Hun society, then, when Priscus visited it in 449 was a parasitic community of marauders. In view of their acute shortage of man-power, which we shall discuss in a moment, it seems unlikely that they were still nomadic pastoralists. There is no indication in our sources that in the days of Attila the Huns still drove flocks and herds from summer to winter pastures and back again. Instead of herding cattle they had now learned the more profitable business of herding men. Sharp differences of wealth have appeared among them, though not perhaps differences of class. Their society could only be maintained as long as Attila was able to supply the mass of his men with the necessities of life and a few luxuries, and his λογάδες with those additional goods and facilities which served to mark them off from the humbler horsemen. Attila extorted these goods and facilities, which formed the corner-stone of Hun society as it was organized in his time, from the subject peoples and from the Eastern Empire by means of his military strength, and by that means alone. What tie would hold the community together if he or his successors could no longer induce the imperial government to supply them with lordly gifts and revenues, with trading facilities, and even with weapons?

The most immediate source of weakness was the great dispersal of Hun military strength entailed by their vast conquests – Attila's empire stretched from the Caucasus to the confines of France and Denmark. The most striking symptom of his weakness in this respect is the fact that he found it necessary to retain Ardaric and a legion of other kings in their posts. If he could have administered their peoples directly by means of his λογάδες and garrisons of Huns, he would certainly have done so. In the exceedingly great dispersal of the Hun warriors entailed by the collection of food and tribute and by garrison duties we probably have the explanation of Attila's peculiar insistence that the Romans should at once restore all the Hun prisoners and fugitives whom they had taken. He made few treaties and sent few embassies in which this demand was not urged with particular vigour. On one occasion the prisoners numbered seventeen, on another only five: yet he had a list of their names prepared so that none should be kept back without his finding it out.[84] The current view is that he went to such pains so as to keep recruits out of the Roman army. This doubtless is a part of the truth, although Attila had a very low opinion of the value of such troops to the Romans,[85] as he was careful to inform their ambassadors: naturally he did not mention his major reason for the repeated demands.

The Huns had to garrison, not only the peoples whom they found in the steppe as their conquests developed, but also the new-comers whom they themselves introduced there. Jorga (pp. 61, 62) was the first, I think, to suggest that among those demanded back were many Roman subjects brought forcibly by Attila to his territories so as to serve as agricultural workers. There is no direct evidence in our authorities to show that this is so,[86] but it is all but certain that Jorga is right in believing that the Huns imported agricultural workers into their dominions. Such has always been the custom of the steppe nomads when they have sufficient power to carry it out, not merely because the imported agricultural workers were more skilful than they themselves could possibly be, but also because the exploitation of foreigners left the fabric of the steppe society itself as far as possible intact. 'When nomad chiefs patronize agriculture', writes Lattimore, 'it is a subject agriculture that they prefer, exploited under their military protection and practised by imported peasants, between whom and the dominant nomads there is an emphatic social distinction.'[87] We have already seen that as early as 395, when considerable areas of Syria were devastated, troops of captives were led off north of the Caucasus and large districts were left depopulated.[88] Since the majority of those carried away must have been poor peasants, who could provide no hope of ransom, they were presumably destined for the most part to be put to work on the land. Again and again we hear that the inhabitants of the Balkan cities were similarly carried off during the great invasions of 441/3 and 447. They too can scarcely have had much value as potential sources of ransom. Their fate was almost certainly to be put to work on the land. However that may be, the ever-repeated demand that all Hun prisoners of war should be returned by the Romans would seem to indicate that Attila himself was not completely unaware of the insecurity of his position.

Despite his victory on the river Utus in 447, Attila suffered bloody losses in the battle there. He was heavily defeated in

Gaul in 451, and in 452 he was repulsed from Italy by plague and famine. The following year he died, and his empire was divided among his sons. They at once quarrelled among themselves. After internal struggles they engaged in a series of costly battles with their subjects, and were routed in the struggle on the river Nedao. Our authority exaggerates greatly when he puts the number of the Hun dead at 30,000; none the less, a very considerable number of them must have been wiped out. Since the rulers could no longer provide the λογάδες with their social needs, the latter separated with all their dependants and retainers and sought each to build his own fortunes.

What part did Marcian's government take in this final chapter of Hun history? It may well be that it instigated and supported the uprising of the subject peoples after Attila's death. We have no direct evidence to this effect, but it is very unlikely that the emperor made no move whatever to follow up the raid carried out by his general Aetius in 452 (p. 163 above): indeed, the primary object of that raid must have been to stimulate the Germanic peoples to act for themselves. Certainly, in the period of confusion and defeat which followed, the East Roman government struck two blows at the Huns which showed clearly how well they understood the economic weaknesses of the nomads' society. The first of these blows is revealed to us by an invaluable fragment of Priscus which relates an incident in the careers of two of Attila's sons.[89] We are told that in 468/9 the children of Attila sent an embassy to Leo to demand from the Roman government that the old markets should be restored along the Danube so that the Huns and Romans could mutually trade their surplus goods; Leo saw no reason why a people who had done so much damage to his territories should have the benefit of Roman exports, and the embassy was a failure. The demand that the markets *should be restored* gives us information which we learn from no other source: at some date before 468 the East Roman government had felt itself strong enough to shut the market towns to the Huns, and had thereby dealt a deadly blow at the continuance of Hun society in the form which it had reached under Attila. The necessities of life could no longer be supplied to the Huns at large, and the λογάδες – so far as they survived – could no longer retain the outward marks of their social superiority. The precise date of this measure cannot be recovered with certainty, but it is not likely to have been entirely unconnected with a second and not dissimilar blow, which was certainly delivered by Marcian. We have seen above that the Huns, once they began to fight on a large scale, were unable to supply themselves with weapons and that they therefore found it necessary to import arms of all kinds (p. 190 above). By a law dating from 455/6 – the morrow of the battle of the Nedao – Marcian forbade the export of all weapons to the barbarians and of all materials for making weapons, and specifically mentioned bows, arrows, and spears.[90] This enactment is addressed to the praetorian prefect of the East, who included in his dominions the countries most exposed to the raids of the Huns: Thrace and Lower Moesia. Although the law was afterwards applied to other nations, there is little reason to doubt – considering its date – that, when first published, it was primarily directed against the Huns. When the result of the battle of the Nedao became known, then, the East Roman government felt itself in a position to make use of its knowledge of the Hun economy. It therefore closed the market towns and cut off the enemy's supply of weapons. With these measures we may date the end of the period of nomadic domination.

Such were the stages of the ruin of the Huns. But it may be asked, in connection with the first of these stages, whether a mere personal quarrel between the sons of Attila would be likely to set in motion the momentous series of events which destroyed an empire covering the whole of central Europe. Unhappily we are unable to trace in the last years of Attila's reign or during the rule of his sons those conflicts between the different groups which made up Hun society and which Lattimore analyses in his brilliant account of the break-up of an imperial nomadic community. Attila, in so far as we can tell, was not at all in doubt whether his real interests lay in war and the conquest of new territories, or in the collection of revenues from the peoples whom he had already subjected; nor did the antithesis between those of his followers who garrisoned the agricultural subject peoples and those who stayed with him as a sort of military reserve become in any way apparent. In the present state of the evidence we must be content with stating the contradictions which were obvious enough in the fabric of Hun society in the time of Attila and perhaps before it. On the one hand, as essential goods and some luxuries became readily available to the mass of the horsemen, it became more and more imperative to provide greater and greater quantities of more costly luxuries for the λογάδες, so as to distinguish them from their humbler comrades. This was a social need of the utmost importance, as we have already seen (p. 196 above). On the other hand, the effort involved in providing these goods became so great, and the conquest of such vast territories became so imperative, that the man-power of the Huns, which was always weak, became extended to its limits, and even then was unequal to the task of policing the vast number of the subject peoples. We have also guessed that the Huns so dispersed their forces in their effort to guard their subjects that they found it necessary to abandon their pastoralism (p. 195 above). In other words, the productive resources of the Huns had been exceedingly primitive when they first appeared in Europe; in the days of Attila, as a result of the manner in which their society had developed, they had no productive resources of their own at all – they depended entirely on their subjects and on the Eastern Romans. The more they tried to satisfy their major social need, the weaker became their military strength, on which their continued existence as a nation depended. But this social need could of its very nature never be satisfied completely, so that when their strength finally became so dispersed that their subjects were able to throw off their yoke, the Huns had no longer any sources of food-supply at all, and Dengizech had to beg on the Roman frontier for land and for money with which to stock it.[91]

When Attila was dead and his sons defeated, the old turmoil and insecurity of nomad life returned to the steppe, bringing greater chaos than ever before. Each petty chief sought to attract as many followers as he could, so as to subdue others and make them his vassals. As among the Mongols before the rise of Chinghis Khan, 'the old society had been destroyed, life was a series of wild forays, of continual desertions' (cf. Chelchal), 'of the splitting up of groupings' (cf. Dengizech and Ernac), 'a constant struggle'.[92] We have a vivid picture of the fate of a descendant of Attila in the sixth century. Jordanes writes thus in his quaint Latin of a Hun called Mundo:

For this Mundo, who traced his descent from the Attilani of old, had fled from the tribe of the Gepids and was roaming beyond the Danube in waste places where no man tilled the soil. He had gathered around himself many outlaws and ruffians [*scamarisque*][93] and robbers from all sides and had seized a tower called Herta, situated on the bank of the Danube. There he plundered his neighbours wildly out of control and made himself king over his vagabonds. Pitza came upon him when he was nearly reduced to desperation and was already thinking of surrender. So he rescued him from the hands of Sabinian and made him a grateful subject of his king Theodoric.

Mundo was lucky, however. After Theodoric's death he managed to join the Roman military service, and, as master of the soldiers in Illyricum in 530, he drove off a band of Huns and other raiders.[94] Not many of Attila's descendants can have been so fortunate as he.

Clearly the Huns have now reverted to a type of society closely resembling that which Ammianus knew, and the tribal organization based on blood relationship still continues in existence, although higher forms of organization, such as the confederacy, have entirely disappeared. Peisker (p. 334) points out that, even when a confederacy disintegrates and disappears, 'the camp, the clans, and in part the tribes also, retain an organic life', and their deep roots survive among the people: indeed, Peisker even speaks of the 'indestructibility' of the clans and camps. We have explicit mention of them among the followers of Dengizech shortly after his father's death, for his men comprised the tribes called Ultzinzures, Angisciri, Bittugures, and Bardores (p. 172 above). Now, a point of interest arises in connection with the first of these, the Ultzinzures. It will scarcely be denied that this tribe took its name from Ultzindur, the *consanguineus* of Attila whom we have already met (p. 170 above). According to Peisker (l.c.), tribal names arose very frequently on the steppe from the names of celebrated war heroes, real or legendary, a process which can be illustrated from the Ottoman Turks, the Seljuk Turks, the Chatagai Mongols, and the Nogai Tartars, among others.[95] Here we have an example of the process. Ultzindur, as a *consanguineus* of Attila, must have been a distinguished man in the Hun empire, although we happen to hear of him on only one occasion. As soon as Attila is dead, Ultzindur gives his name to a tribe. He has built up a following, and his men are prepared to trust him to restore their fortunes. And although he disappears and his men transfer their allegiance to Dengizech, the name which he gave them lives on.

We may conclude then that successful petty chieftains eventually created new clans and new tribes, so that before long the steppe once again swarmed with such overbearing lords, like Attila's sons and Edeco and Chelchal and Mundo, each as wretched and as quarrelsome as his neighbour, and each struggling with the empire or with other barbarians, or enlisting himself and his men as mercenaries in the Roman or barbarian service, as we see so often in the pages of Procopius. But no new Attila and no new confederacy arose, because of the tremendous influx into eastern Europe of new and powerful nations in the sixties of the fifth century and during succeeding decades (pp. 175–6 above).

8

Roman Foreign Policy and the Huns

On earlier pages we have tried to trace the varying attitudes of various Romans towards the Huns, and we shall gather up our results later. What we cannot do is to trace the reactions of the Roman government in the early days of the Huns. Our sources are too fragmentary to allow us to hazard even a single sentence as to the outlook of the ministers of Theodosius I and Arcadius on the new invaders. It is not until we come to the forties of the fifth century that the surviving extracts of Priscus' work allow us to catch an occasional glimpse of the motives which inspired the policies of the various governments controlling the East. But if we are to form a reasonably accurate estimate of the two emperors, Theodosius II and Marcian, who bore the brunt of the conflict and guided East Rome through the great storms of the mid-fifth century, we must not accept the judgements of Priscus uncritically. The historian undoubtedly provides us with an accurate record of facts; but what of his interpretation of those facts? We have no reason to suppose that he achieved an impartiality and objectivity which were beyond the powers even of Thucydides. Indeed, it would be very surprising if Priscus, alone among ancient historians, were the victim of no prejudices and no partialities. Only an examination of his own words can supply us with an answer

Plate 16   Bust of Theodosius II (AD 401–450).
Ancient Art and Architecture Collection.

to our question, what is the value of his interpretation of the facts which he records?

I

Social and political views were so closely intertwined in the days of the later Roman Empire, as indeed they still remain, that we cannot hope to understand the one without some inquiry into the other. Now, Priscus' social views are clear enough owing to the fortunate survival of his account of a curious incident which took place when he was in Attila's encampment (pp. 124–5 above). One day, as he waited to interview Onegesius, he was accosted by a man who, in spite of his Hun clothing, addressed him in Greek. He was, in fact, a native of Greece who had settled as a merchant in Viminacium. He had prospered there for a considerable time and had married a wealthy wife, but had been ruined when the city fell to the barbarians in 441. It was a Hun custom that their leading men should take the wealthier among the captives who fell into their hands, because these brought in a larger ransom than the poorer ones: and our merchant had been given to Onegesius. He had fought well for his new master in battles against the Romans in 443 and 447 and against the Acatziri in 448, and had purchased his freedom with the booty he took. He had married a Hun wife and was the father of several children by the time Priscus met him. He shared Onegesius' table and lived in greater comfort among the Hun than he had enjoyed as a prosperous merchant in Viminacium. Now, he pointed out to the historian that, were he still living in the empire, his lot would be very different. In war-time, he said, a Roman was bound to perish owing to the incompetence of the army leaders and because the great mass of the inhabitants of the empire were never armed to fight the invaders; hence no resistance was ever shown by the population as a whole. Yet peace was even more wretched and miserable than war owing to the pitiless collection of the taxes and the haplessness of the citizens before wealthy law-breakers: while the latter could easily escape punishment, the poor man was powerless in the law-courts. He had inevitably to endure the full rigours of justice – or injustice. His only hope was to die before a decision was given, for lawsuits dragged on endlessly and vast sums had to be paid out by the litigants as bribes.

The humble merchants and traders of the later empire rarely speak to us. It is charming to find that, when their voices can be heard, their words are so effective. Priscus was faced here by the most crucial problems presented by Roman society in his day – the insecurity of life due to the oppression of the tax-gatherers, the incompetence of the army, and the corruption of the courts. Our estimate of his ability to understand the most fundamental issues of contemporary society must be based on the answer which he made to this renegade merchant. Ammianus and Olympiodorus before him had protested with bitter anger against the social injustices of their times: what is Priscus' attitude? His reply, which Gibbon (iii, p. 429) justly calls 'a feeble and prolix declamation', consists of almost incredibly unreal and pedantic phrases from the philosophical schools. He said that the men who had framed the Roman constitution were wise and good. They had ordained that part of the population should be the guardians of the laws, part should exercise the profession of arms, and part should devote themselves to agriculture so as to feed those who defended them. The law-courts were scrupulously fair, and the protracted nature of lawsuits was due solely to a desire on the part of the judges to avoid a hasty or unfair decision. It was absurd to assert that justice was weighted in favour of the wealthy – even the emperor was subject to the laws. It may be observed that the emperors themselves had pretended to admit this last point, and, only twenty years before the date of Priscus' conversation with the renegade, Theodosius had stated that 'it is a principle worthy of declaration that the majestic rule of the laws applies even to the prince himself: so much does our authority depend upon the authority of the law'.[1] Yet Priscus' contemporary, the bishop Theodoret, takes a more realistic view. 'Children are terrified by the bogy-man,' he writes, 'youths by pedagogues and schoolmasters, but to a man the most terrifying thing in the world is a judge, the law court, the heralds, etc.; and if the man be poor, his terror is doubled.'[2] However, this was not Priscus' opinion. The Romans, he went on, treat their slaves more humanely than the Hun ruler treats his subjects. The Romans, in fact, behave towards their slaves like fathers or teachers, and correct their faults as they would those of their own children. On this point the historian is at one with the bishop. Masters, according to Theodoret, are the 'benefactors' of their slaves, and Nature bids slaves defend their masters as children would their parents.[3]

As Hodgkin (p. 79) says: 'It is easy to see that Priscus felt himself to be talking as sagely as Socrates, upon whose style his reply is evidently modelled; but that reply has the fault so common with rhetoricians and diplomatists, of being quite up in the air, and having no relation to the real facts of the case.' Priscus may have had misgivings about the conditions obtaining in the empire; but, if so, he has not included them in this frigid composition. Speaking to one who had first-hand experience of the upheavals of the fifth century, Priscus is complacent and content with the *status quo*. He is a 'safe' citizen, and would have found favour with Augustus, who is reported to have said, 'whoever wants to keep the established order unchanged, is both a good citizen and a good man'.[4] Whatever the validity of this attitude in the first century of the empire, it was indefensible in Priscus' time. The fact that he held it throws a sinister light on his ability to record with understanding the history of his age.

II

Such being his outlook on social questions, let us try to find out if his political opinions offer any parallel. We must proceed by considering the judgements made by him in the fragments which are certainly authentic. These judgements are not very numerous, and owing to the character of the *Excerpta de Legationibus* of Constantine VII, in which they are mostly preserved, they unfortunately do not deal directly with the internal politics of East Rome. Yet, such as they are, they seem to point clearly enough in one direction.

Senator, consul in 436, is known to have attended the Council of Chalcedon in 451 as a patrician and to have been a correspondent of Theodoret, who professes to rejoice that the Saviour continually heaped high office upon him. The chapel which he built to the archangel Michael in Constantinople, however, was considered by Justinian to be much too small and badly lighted to be suitable for an archangel.[5] Despite his high place in the cubiculum of Theodosius, Priscus shows considerable contempt for him, because, although he had the rank of ambassador, he was not possessed of sufficient courage to visit Attila's camp by land: instead, he went by sea to the military commander at Odessus (Varna), whose name was Theodulus.[6] This Theodulus and his associate Anatolius are clearly condemned for what Priscus considered to be their craven attitude towards Attila when negotiating the treaty of 443.[7] Now Anatolius, the signatory of three major treaties with the Huns, was master of soldiers in the East in 438, and, apart from concluding a peace which terminated a war with Persia, he had built a stoa in Antioch which long continued to bear his name.[8] He went on to win further distinctions as consul in 440, patrician, *Magister militum praesentalis*, and a zealous adherent of orthodoxy at Chalcedon. None the less, Priscus implicitly criticizes the mission of Anatolius and Nomus to Attila in the spring of 450,[9] and here again his reason is the ambassadors' attitude to the Hun, whom they heavily bribed into keeping the peace – or so the historian would like to suggest. This Nomus, consul in 445 after laying down the great post of master of the offices, is described by a nephew of Cyril of Alexandria as having, in 444, 'held in his hands the control of the world'.[10] Of Theodulus nothing is known beyond what Priscus himself tells us; but it is clear that the others had vast influence at Theodosius' court, and wielded only less authority than the eunuch Chrysaphius himself. When the people of Edessa wished to call upon the greatest powers in the Eastern Empire, they shouted the names of Zeno (the enemy of Chrysaphius: pp. 133–4 above), Anatolius, Nomus, Chrysaphius, Urbicius, who is otherwise unknown, Senator, and the emperor.[11] The ambassadors attacked by Priscus were all close associates of the eunuch Chrysaphius and were clearly representatives of a policy of appeasing the foreign enemies of the Eastern Empire – and as such Attila looked upon them.[12] It is precisely for this policy that Priscus blames them; in each case he draws attention to what appeared to him to be their lack of courage in dealing with Attila. He nowhere dwells upon the results of this policy, which, at the end of Theodosius' reign, had issued in a state of affairs far from unsatisfactory to the Romans. The whole administration of Chrysaphius is censured for this 'timidity' in face of the foreign enemies of East Rome in a curious passage where Priscus says that the government 'obeyed every instruction of Attila, and considered what he commanded as the orders of a master'.[13] But here the historian is fair enough to go on to point out the tremendous difficulties under which Theodosius' ministers were carrying on their negotiations with the Huns. The Eastern Empire, he admits, was at this time threatened by the Persians, the Vandals, the Isaurians, the Saracens, and even the Ethiopians (pp. 95–6 above). But the very catalogue of the troubles of the government reads suspiciously like an indictment of the policy which had allowed so many crises to arise simultaneously; and the words in which the historian sums up his description of the state of affairs, 'therefore having been humbled by Attila they paid him court', certainly do not spare the government.[14]

To all this there is a converse. Apollonius, a friend of

Zeno, is praised in warm terms for his courageous answer to Attila's threats during his fruitless embassy in the autumn of 450 (p. 157 above). The historian's admiration for the men of Asemus, who were actually bold enough to attack and defeat a body of Attila's Huns in 443, is testified to by the disproportionately long account of the exploit in his pages.[15] Nor is this attitude confined to those who made a bold stand against the barbarians in the East. Priscus cannot hide his approval of the heated words addressed to Geiseric by a bishop called, curiously enough, Bleda.[16] He also has a proud word to say of Aegidius, whose stubborn defence of the Western Empire against Gothic encroachments won his admiration.[17] But the warmest words of praise in the whole of his extant work are given to Euphemius, the master of the offices under Marcian and perhaps a relative of the emperor. This eulogy can scarcely be ascribed altogether to the fact that Priscus himself had been Euphemius' *assessor* and therefore had close personal ties with him; the panegyric goes beyond what such a relationship would have demanded. The historian says that under Marcian Euphemius had a general supervision of the entire policy of the government, and had personally initiated the many beneficial measures which marked that emperor's reign.[18] It is inconceivable that Priscus was not partly thinking of the new foreign policy initiated at the beginning of the reign, whereby the policy of Chrysaphius, who was himself put to death, was reversed: payments and subsidies to the Huns were stopped and a more warlike attitude was adopted.

Finally it should be noted that the δόλος καὶ ἀπάτη, the trickery and deceit, by which Anagast and Chelchal set the Goths and Huns at each other's throats is greeted with no criticism by our historian.[19] It is even more revealing to find that, throughout the entire narrative of Maximinus' embassy and its antecedents and aftermath, Priscus utters no word of disgust either at the concealment from Maximinus of the ulterior purpose of his mission, or at the immorality of the planned assassination of the man with whom the diplomat was to negotiate. Most striking of all, Priscus all but openly expresses his approval of the view of the men of Asemus, 'that to swear a false oath for the sake of the safety of men of one's own race is not perjury'.[20]

It would seem then, at any rate on a superficial view, that Priscus was a strong patriot. Whoever faced the barbarians, either in the West or in the East, with boldness and courage, and was prepared to answer them in their own coin, won his warmest admiration, while those who adopted the opposite attitude stand condemned in his pages. So strongly did he feel on the subject of resolute behaviour towards the Huns that, like another great historian of the later empire,[21] he was prepared to condone and perhaps even approve practices which Roman authors of a less decadent day would have rejected – at any rate on paper – as unworthy of the empire.

III

Can we carry our inquiry farther? What is the basis of this patriotism? Marcian's administration strongly favoured the landed aristocracy. True, Marcian himself in the second of his Novels states his ideal of an Emperor's duty thus: 'Our care is to provide for the utility of the human race [*humani generis*]'. But he attached a somewhat restricted meaning to the term *humanum genus*, for Evagrius tells us bluntly that Marcian made it his policy 'to preserve the wealth of those possessing much untouched'.[22] In fact, his legislation was aimed almost exclusively at furthering the interests of the landed gentry. He restricted the number of senators liable for the expensive office of the praetorship, and he abolished the *follis*, the tax on the property of senators, to mention only two of his measures. It seems regrettable then that recent historians have not disagreed with Bréhier's conclusion that Marcian 'se révéla comme l'un des meilleurs empereurs qui ait régné à Constantinople' ('shows himself as one of the best emperors to have reigned at Constantinople').[23]

Now it is all but certain that the ill repute in which our extant authorities hold the government of Theodosius II is derived almost exclusively from the *Byzantine History* of Priscus. He too was responsible for the view, reported by later writers, that the reign of Marcian was another golden age,[24] as indeed for the landowning senate it probably was. On the other hand, we have seen above that the persons who are likely to have benefited from Theodosius' policy of subsidies to the Huns were the merchants, traders, and the like.[25] It would seem *a priori* likely that Priscus' condemnation of Theodosius II, the eunuch Chrysaphius and their foreign policy was largely due to his social attitude. Do the hints which have survived in his fragments support this view?

A passage of the utmost importance for the understanding, not only of Priscus' outlook, but also of the social basis for Chrysaphius' policy, has fortunately survived in the fifth of the historian's fragments. Priscus comments here on the taxes which Theodosius was compelled to levy after the great Hun raid of 441/3 in order to pay the sums pledged to Attila by Anatolius' Treaty of 443.[26] The historian contemptuously remarks that the government pretended to make this treaty voluntarily, but in fact did so on compulsion and owing to a crushing fear of its foes. The taxes had to be extracted more strictly than ever, he says, because of the foolish way in which the revenues were expended – much of the money, for instance, was squandered on shows in the hippodrome and the amphitheatre.[27] Everyone had to pay, says the historian; but he goes on to lament only the hardships of those who had been released from the land tax by imperial favour or by a decision of the law-courts. He bewails still more the fact that all senators were compelled to contribute a fixed sum of gold over and above their regular taxes. The effect of the severe taxation on the landed gentry is the only point against which Priscus really protests. There were striking changes of fortune, he says, for the tax-gatherers inflicted every indignity when collecting the money, so that those who had long been wealthy, οἱ πάλαι εὐδαίμονες, had to sell their furniture and the jewellery of their wives in the market-place. This calamity, he goes on, befell the Romans – he means οἱ πάλαι εὐδαίμονες among the Romans – in addition to the hardships caused directly by the war, so that many had recourse to suicide, by starving or hanging themselves.

Now it would appear certain that Priscus has greatly over-drawn the sufferings of the senatorial class in this highly coloured, rhetorical picture. The amount which Theodosius undertook to pay to Attila in 443 in a lump sum was 6,000 lb of gold,[28] and it was presumably this amount which the senatorial *ordo* was called upon to find. That the payment of such a sum should have brought the senatorial class to the verge of ruin, as Priscus would have us believe, is all but incredible. We may suggest that there were approximately 2,000 senators in the Eastern Empire at this time – the same number, in fact, as there were in the West at the same date[29] – and that the incomes of some of them, although admittedly very few, can scarcely have fallen very far short of the figures given by Olympiodorus for the incomes of Western senators a few years earlier, namely, 10, 15, and even 40 *centenaria* of gold per annum. Perhaps we should halve these figures. Perhaps Eastern senators numbered even less than a thousand, and perhaps their highest incomes amounted to not much more than 15 *centenaria* of gold. Even so, it would appear that an *ordo* containing such men would have been able to find 6,000 lb of gold, that is, 60 *centenaria*, without being reduced to selling their furniture and their wives' jewellery. It was rumoured[30] that Cyril of Alexandria could afford to disburse 2,000 lb of gold in bribes to state officials, and, although the rumour was doubtless false, it would have defeated its own purpose had it named an utterly impossible sum. Was the patriarch then in control of riches equal to one-third of the entire capital possessed by the whole senatorial *ordo*?

The sums paid by Theodosius to the Huns must be compared with those which other emperors of the same period judged it expedient to pay to other barbarians. We hear that Leo I (457–74) undertook to pay 2,000 lb of gold per annum to Theodoric Strabo in 473, and we are not told that there was any outcry in Constantinople when the agreement was made known.[31] Again, in 478 Zeno (474–91) consented to give Theodoric 2,000 lb of gold and 10,000 lb of silver in a lump sum, as well as 10,000 *solidi* per annum thereafter.[32] Although the treasury had then not yet recovered from Basiliscus' disastrous expedition against the Vandals in 468, we hear again of no outcry. From these examples it would seem that when Anatolius, in his first treaty with Attila, undertook to pay 2,100 lb of gold per annum (p. 94 above), he stipulated a sum which was quite usual in the treaties struck between the Eastern emperors and their northern neighbours. It should also be remembered that Marcian was not opposed to subsidies as such. We know him to have paid out considerable sums on his eastern frontier,[33] and we have seen that he was willing to present money to Attila, provided only that it was regarded as a gift and not as tribute (p. 147 above). It is very tempting to believe that what Priscus objected to was not the payment of money to the Huns, or even the size of the sums paid, but the manner in which the necessary amounts were raised inside the empire.

Another argument can be drawn from what we know of the expenses incurred by Leo's great expedition against the Vandals in 468, which cost the treasury more than 100,000 lb of gold, that is, 1,000 *centenaria* – 'whole seas . . . and rivers of money', in the words of a poet.[34] This expenditure reduced the state almost to bankruptcy for nearly a generation, but the money simply could not have been raised at all if the senatorial class was as poverty-stricken in 443 as Priscus wishes to suggest. Indeed, considering Marcian's abolition of the *follis* and his remission of arrears of taxes (a procedure, incidentally, which always favoured the wealthy), it seems scarcely credible that he should have left over 100,000 lb of gold in the treasury at his death, if the treasury had been empty and the upper classes drained dry at his accession.[35]

We have repeatedly had occasion to observe that Priscus' *Byzantine History* is primarily a literary effort, and not a scientific history. His indictment of Theodosius' taxation policy contains one of those *flosculi* against which we have had continually to be on our guard. He states that the senators, in order to raise the sums demanded of them by the emperor's tax-gatherers, had to sell, not only their furniture (ἔπιπλα), but also wives' jewellery (τὸν κόσμον τῶν γυναικῶν). I believe this statement to be nothing more than an illustration of Priscus' appreciation of Eunapius. The phrase, like the account of the Huns' manner of crossing into the Crimea at the outset of their career, is something which Priscus found in the work of Eunapius and took over with little change into his own book. For Zosimus, in a chapter where he is paraphrasing Eunapius and wishes to indict the financial policy of Theodosius I, writes as follows of that emperor's exactions: 'they gave not only money, but also women's jewellery and even all their clothes to pay the taxes demanded'.[36] The phrases in their contexts are too similar to allow us to suppose that the likeness between them is a mere coincidence. The fact is that Priscus knew and valued his Eunapius, the Eastern senators remained in possession of their valuables, and their wives continued to enjoy their trinkets.

The policy of Theodosius and Chrysaphius in raising money to meet Attila's demands in 443 struck at the pockets of the senatorial class; but, at their expense, it showed some regard for the well-being of the taxpayers as a whole. How else could the money have been raised without causing universal hardship in the Eastern provinces?

There is an excellent parallel to such a reaction on the part of the large landowning class towards a similar policy of buying off the barbarians by means of a capital levy rather than by engaging in a war: it too was a case in which the issue of the war would have been doubtful, and the expense involved would have been much greater than the capital sum whose payment made the war unnecessary. In 408 Alaric sent an embassy to Rome demanding payment for his recent services. The treasury was empty and the sum demanded by Alaric could not be raised at once out of the regular taxes. Hence, since peace at that time was altogether essential, Honorius' government considered it necessary to exact a contribution from those who possessed ready money, that is, the senators. The matter was put before the Senate and the question whether war should be declared upon the Goths was debated at Rome. During the debate the war party in the Senate asked Stilicho why he was refusing to fight, and why he was willing to purchase peace with a money payment to the disgrace of Roman honour. Stilicho defended his policy to such effect that, in the words of a Greek historian,

since everyone was convinced that he had made out a just case, the Senate resolved to pay Alaric 4,000 lb of gold so as to preserve the peace; the majority voted, however, not from choice, but because they were afraid of Stilicho. Indeed, Lampadius, a man of high birth and rank, shouted out in Latin, 'this is a bond of slavery not a peace.'[37]

Now the fact that the matter was debated in the Senate indicates that everyone knew beforehand that the senators would have to bear the expense if Alaric's terms were accepted. Hence their patriotic and warlike phrases merely concealed their anxiety for their purses.[38] We can scarcely be wrong in supposing that many Eastern senators saw the justice of Theodosius' case in 443, but only voted for it because they were afraid of Chrysaphius. The only difference was that the policy of 443 was supported by a handful of comparatively high-minded senators, Anatolius, Nomus, Senator, and the others, who themselves stood to lose by the policy which they advocated. Their opponents have found a mouthpiece in Priscus.

It is clear then that we must modify our statement that Priscus was a warm patriot. He disliked the seemingly timid foreign policy of Chrysaphius because the social class with which he sympathized stood to lose by that policy. He was loyal, not to the empire as a whole, but to a single class within it. It is difficult to avoid the impression that in this respect he marks a retrogression from the outlook of Olympiodorus, who was sharply critical of the grossly unequal distribution of wealth prevailing in the empire of his day, and even from that of Ammianus, who, despite his ties with some members of the Senate, was more than uneasy at their grotesquely large fortunes and the political use which they made of their economic power. Priscus' outlook approximates rather to that of his successor in the series of late Greek historians, Malchus of Philadelphia, who bitterly attacked the financial policy of Leo I,[39] largely because he paid subsidies to the barbarians so as to preserve peace;[40] yet Malchus seems to have admitted that Leo won great posthumous fame among 'the masses' (οἱ πολλοί).[41]

It seems fair to conclude then that a study of Priscus' character and outlook, in so far as they can be reconstructed from the remains of his work, reveals that his attack on the financial policy of Theodosius II and Chrysaphius results from prejudice and unfair partiality. This policy, as we have seen, was calculated to lay the exceptional financial burdens of the empire upon those who could best afford to sustain them. Priscus, a supporter of the senatorial *ordo*, misrepresents the endeavour of the emperor, exaggerates the burden shouldered by the senators, and implies that the entire population of the Eastern provinces was oppressed. It is sufficient to bear in mind that, if Theodosius and his ministers had in fact been oppressive tyrants, the emperor's name would not have been a symbol vividly remembered by the Greens in 583, over 130 years after his death.[42] Indeed, Priscus himself, in a curious passage of his work, seems to have been compelled to admit the wide support enjoyed by Chrysaphius. In the crisis of the eunuch's career in the autumn of 449, when his life was being demanded, not only by Attila, but also by the Isaurian Zeno, the master of soldiers in the East (pp. 133–4 above), Priscus tells us explicitly that 'everyone gave him good wishes and support'.[43] It is not our business to ask here why the historian felt it necessary to make this admission; it must have gone a long way towards destroying the case which he had been trying to build up in the earlier books of his history. It is only necessary to point out that, coming as it does from an enemy of Chrysaphius, its significance could scarcely be exaggerated.

IV

It may be objected, however, that Theodosius should not have remained content to buy off Attila. Why did he not face him boldly and put a stop to his exaction of tribute by firm military measures? Those who believe that Theodosius' government should have endeavoured to destroy the power of the Huns in a series of military campaigns have overlooked, I think, the essential nature of a conflict carried on by a settled, agricultural society, like that of the Romans, against a mobile, nomadic one, such as that of the Huns. Yet even as early as the fifth century BC the difficulties of such a struggle were fully realized by Herodotus, who writes (iv. 46. 3):

A people without fortified towns, living in wagons which they take with them wherever they go, accustomed, one and all, to fight as mounted archers, and dependent for their food not upon agriculture but upon their cattle, how can [the Scythians] fail to defeat the attempt of an invader not only to subdue them, but even to make contact with them?

In other words, the entire population and all the property of a nomadic community are so mobile that it causes them little trouble to disappear entirely out of the way of an approaching hostile army. Also, the cost of equipping a punitive expedition against a nomadic community is far greater than any return that could be expected from booty, captives, or the like. The Chinese court was racked for long ages by debates as to whether the Hsiung-nu should be fought or placated with 'gifts', and the wisest counsellors would ordinarily never countenance a policy of military expansion into the domains of the nomads. And so we find that throughout the entire history of the Huns no Roman government, either in the East or in the West, ever dispatched a punitive force against them – except once, and this one case is the exception that proves the rule: Marcian sent an army into Hun country in 452 when the bulk of the Hun forces was engaged in Italy, and it seemed possible to induce the subject Germans to rise against the small garrison which had been left to watch them (p. 163 above). When did such an opportunity present itself to Theodosius? If we blame the 'feeble and timid' Theodosius for sending out no such expedition, we leave ourselves open to the objection that we have overlooked the realities of the position in which he found himself. The cost of such an expedition would have been enormous, the results negligible, and the damage to the Huns minute. It is true that Attila, especially in his later years, had sacrificed some of his mobility. He derived tribute and food-supplies from fixed areas of central Europe, and therefore could not profitably have abandoned it.[44] Nevertheless, a temporary retreat, if he had been so minded, from part of it would have brought him comparatively little loss, while on the open plains of the steppe he would have had an excellent opportunity of destroying an entire Roman army. On the other hand, if we blame Theodosius for sending out no punitive force, we must remember that a nomad retaliatory expedition is apt to be conducted with such ferocity that the depopulation of large territories and even the destruction of agriculture itself might well be the only reward reaped in return for the expense of the original punitive campaign.[45]

It is scarcely a digression to indicate briefly here the difficulties in which the Romans found themselves when Hun prisoners fell into their hands. Their position is illuminated by a passage of Sozomen referring to the campaign of Uldin in Thrace in 409.[46] It will be recalled that the Huns on that occasion were supported by a large company of the Sciri, many of whom were captured by the Romans in the rout. Sozomen tells us the fate of the prisoners. It was impossible to leave them concentrated in Thrace, whence they could easily break out and recross the Danube. The government therefore sold some of them at a cheap rate – presumably no buyers could be found who were prepared to pay heavily for such *coloni*. The government accordingly was compelled to give others away gratis, merely binding the owners not to keep them in Constantinople or indeed in Europe: they were to be shipped across the sea. Even so, an enormous multitude of the Sciri could not be disposed of: landowners would not accept them even as a free gift, and the ecclesiastical historian saw numbers of them scattered over the foothills and spurs of Mount Olympus in Bithynia, presumably acting as tenant farmers on imperial estates. We have no such description of the fate of Hun prisoners, but it cannot be doubted that they presented their captors with even more difficult problems. They would have been of practically no use on the land; the only hope was that they would be willing to join the imperial army and serve as mercenaries against their fellow country-men. This hope apparently did not exist for the men of Asemus when they captured some of the Huns who assailed their city. It is significant to read that, as soon as they captured them, they put them to death.[47]

In all, it is idle to speak of the 'weakness' of Chrysaphius' policy on the Danube frontier. No other course was open to him than a policy of subsidies, and the 'strength' of Marcian in 452 was derived from an entirely new situation which arose in the Hun empire shortly after his accession. As for Marcian's policy in 451, we have already seen that it was characterized less by strength than by folly. It is true, of course, that the policy adopted by Theodosius' government was not always successful: it failed to avert the great invasions of 441–3 and 447. In 441 the policy which the emperor afterwards pursued had not yet been initiated. The government, accustomed only to comparatively minor raids, had not yet fully realized what war with the nomads meant: hence their hesitation about surrendering the Hun subjects who were alleged to be in the imperial service, and about handing over the bishop of Margus. The exaction of a capital levy from the senators illustrates the desperate anxiety of the government to maintain peace and prevent a repetition of the events of 441–3: the great invasion had shown them the correct policy to pursue. Within a few weeks of the restoration of peace Theodosius took steps to ensure that a similar invasion could never take place again, and we have a vivid memorial of his efforts in the Novel of 12 September 443 addressed to Nomus, a man who was henceforth to be so closely identified with his policy (p. 96 above). It is extremely unfortunate that, owing to the loss of the relevant part of Priscus' work, we do not know why the invasion of 447 was launched by Attila, but we have seen reason (pp. 98–9 above) to suspect that the blame did not lie on Theodosius and his ministers.

It is not difficult then to see why the financial and military policies of Theodosius and Chrysaphius have been misrepresented by our primary authority. Priscus' close association with Maximinus and especially with Euphemius, the powerful master of the offices, who reversed every aspect of the preceding administration's policy, would seem to indicate that, although he himself was not a member of the highest society in Constantinople, yet he certainly shared its outlook and resented its being called upon to endure alone the financial burden which Chrysaphius' policy imposed. Secondly, his inadequate understanding of military affairs rendered him both incapable of seeing the necessity for that policy and also unsympathetic to the group of comparatively enlightened senators whose understanding of the military position was greater than his. Chrysaphius' policy, which they supported, was calculated to save from increased financial hardship the great mass of the population of the East, which was suffering severely in these years from bad harvests, epidemics, and earthquakes.[48]

V

A final point calls for elucidation. If Theodosius' government, when directed by Chrysaphius, had in fact had the interests of the majority of the Eastern population at heart, why is it that the historical tradition is almost unanimous in condemning the eunuch? The answer is not difficult to find. Although other historians narrated the history of this administration, the *Byzantine History* of Priscus was universally recognized as the standard authority for the events of the years in question. This standard authority was biased and contained unfair judgements, as we have seen. Now the subsequent historians, whose works have survived, were in almost all cases orthodox Christian writers who, even before they read Priscus, were prejudiced against Theodosius and his minister on sectarian grounds; for Theodosius, in his later years, and especially Chrysaphius, the godson of Eutyches, were ardent and notorious heretics. Consequently, when these historians read Priscus' harsh strictures on the emperor and the eunuch, they accepted them gladly and uncritically, and incorporated them in their own works. At the same time, it is worth pointing out that the contemporary ecclesiastical historian Socrates is warm in his praise of the emperor. Admittedly it would have been unsafe for Socrates to publish a work which openly criticized Theodosius; but, if his attitude were critical, he could at least have removed the warmth from his eulogies.[49]

That Nestorius condemned Theodosius severely and for very personal reasons was to be expected. But he also draws our attention to a fact which helps us to understand the attitude of the orthodox Christian writers. In order to obtain money with which to pay Attila,[50] Theodosius, acting through Chrysaphius,[51] compelled the church to contribute, and Flavian, the patriarch of Constantinople (447–9), made his offering to the welfare of his flock with the utmost ill will. The emperor commanded, writes Nestorius (p. 342), that *whatever was due* should be exacted with insult[52] and that no respite should be granted unto him [Flavian], so that he was consequently constrained to send word unto the emperor that he had not possessions of his own, because he was poor, and that not even the possessions of the church, if they were sold, would suffice to pay the quantity of gold which was being exacted of him. But he had the holy vessels of the church, which he and the emperors his ancestors had placed therein, and he said, 'I must melt them down, because I am driven to do so by force'. But the Emperor then said, 'I want not to know this, but the gold I do want in any way whatsoever'.

Since he sought only *what was due*, the emperor's reply was not inapt. Flavian, however, proceeded to have the church vessels melted down in public so as to cause as much ill feeling as possible. Whatever the tactlessness of Theodosius' procedure, one would have thought that he had some moral claims upon the wealth of the church, for, as Nestorius (p. 363) himself admits, the people

had been worn out with pestilences and famines and failure of rains and hail and heat and marvellous earthquakes and captivity and fear and flight and all kinds of ills . . . A two-fold upheaval on the part of the barbarians and the Scythians, who were destroying and taking everyone captive, had shaken them and there was not even a single hope of rescue,

a passage in which the heresiarch refers to Attila's two invasions of 441–3 and 447.

These factors account for the unfavourable picture of Theodosius and Chrysaphius drawn by most of our orthodox Christian authorities. On the other hand, the Monophysite Zachariah of Mitylene mentions Theodosius often, always with respect and never with criticism; his abuse is reserved for Marcian. The humble John Malalas, also apparently a Monophysite, although he had Priscus' work to hand, thought so well of Theodosius that he writes: 'The Emperor Theodosius was held in high repute, being loved by all the people and by the senate.' His enthusiasm leads him into exaggeration in these last three words: the majority of the landowning class had little reason to love Theodosius.[53]

It is difficult to see how we can subscribe to Priscus' judgement on Chrysaphius, whom Theodosius loved, says John Malalas, 'as he was good-looking in every way'. In the end he lost his life not merely because he was charged with extortion – considering what his policies had been, this was inevitable as soon as a 'senatorial' emperor came to the throne. Charges against him could easily be found, for, in Bury's words, 'the system of raising revenue in the later Roman Empire was so oppressive that there is perhaps no Emperor' – and no minister, we may interpolate – 'whom a hostile critic could not have made out a case for charging with a deliberate design to ruin his subjects'.[54] But Chrysaphius was not merely executed for extortion; his financial policy aimed at the welfare of other elements in the population than the landowners. The failure of his religious policy marked an important stage of the process by which the empire lost the affections of the great masses of the Eastern provinces for ever and prepared the way for the Arabs. The humble tradesmen and artisans of the capital remembered his master with affection until at least the end of the sixth century. It is essentially because of the anti-senatorial character of their administration that our authorities paint so dark a picture of the attitude of Theodosius and Chrysaphius towards the Huns. Not the least portion of the blame must be borne by Priscus.

9

Conclusion

We have now tried to reconstruct the story of the political
and military activities of the Huns between the time of their
first assault upon the Ostrogoths and the disappearance of
Attila's sons in the confusion which followed their father's
death. We have also tried to describe the form of society in
which the Huns lived and the changes which transformed
that society and eventually brought about its downfall. In
both efforts, however, we have been gravely handicapped by
the deplorable state of the evidence. In the first case, for
instance, we are completely ignorant of the extent and
organization of the Hun empire in the years immediately
before Bleda and Attila became its leaders, and we have no
precise information as to the part played by Attila, still less
by Rua, in building up that empire and in expanding it.
When we turned to discuss Hun society, we found that only
an occasional and incidental phrase survived to throw a dim
light on a few of their institutions. Were it not for two or
three passing words of Priscus, for example, we could say
nothing whatever as to the type of family organization which
existed among the Huns. A sentence placed by the same
author in the mouth of one of his characters is the sole direct
evidence that the Huns extorted supplies of food from their
subjects – though admittedly in this case we could have

inferred the practice even in the total absence of any direct testimony.

It is very improbable, however, that any new literary evidence will make its appearance, and, since few startling revelations can be expected from the archaeological material, at any rate in the immediate future, it may be desirable to set down one or two conclusions of a general nature. We shall first discuss the current belief that, in some sense or other, Attila was possessed of genius, that he was, in fact, a 'great man', and that it was only his outstanding personality that kept the Hun empire together. Then we shall turn to the question of the general significance of the achievements of the Huns for the development of Europe. How would European history have been affected if the Huns had never come in contact with the Goths and Romans, and had instead directed their attention towards, say, the Persians or the Indians?

I

A view generally, if not universally, held by historians of the later Roman Empire is that the ascendancy of the Huns was entirely dependent on the genius of Attila. Without him, it is said or implied, there would have been no Hun empire comparable to that which he ruled; and when he died, the immediate collapse of the empire was inevitable.[1] Neither proposition, in my opinion, can be maintained.

The first is certainly false, because there was in fact an enormous Hun empire before Attila. We are explicitly assured that Attila ruled over more peoples than any of his predecessors, but the very source which mentions this implies simultaneously that the realm of Rua and Octar was by no means a small one, but was indeed comparable to his.[2] In fact we find that, a few years after Octar had been engaged somewhat to the east of the Rhine, Rua was interfering in Italian politics and threatening the East Romans on the

Danube. Their sphere of activity was obviously enormous. Attila therefore differs from Chinghis Khan in that he received his empire ready-made – or almost so – from the hands of his predecessors, whereas the Mongols of Chinghis' youth and even middle age were still the same petty, disunited pastoral tribes they had always been. It is regrettable that we know nothing of the process which united the Hun tribes into the confederacy which Attila subsequently led. Perhaps the founders of the confederacy were Rua himself and his brothers. If so, their services to Attila were as great as those of Chinghis to his successors, and entitle them to a measure of fame – or notoriety – greater than Attila's.

The second of these propositions, that the collapse of the empire was inevitable as soon as Attila died, is disproved by the very fact that Chinghis had successors as capable as himself. There is no inherent reason why a nomadic empire should not outlive its founder. To those who try to explain the Hun empire in psychological terms, a sufficient answer is that there was no psychological reason why Attila should not have been succeeded by an Ogdai or a Kublai Khan or a Tamburlaine. In a word, the circumstances of neither the beginning nor the end of the Hun ascendancy depended exclusively or even mainly on the personal character or abilities of any one individual.

What reason is there then to speak of the 'genius' of Attila? Was he a military genius? It may be doubted. True, he was able easily to defeat the East Romans in 441–3. But in 441 he penetrated their defences when there was nobody present to resist him,[3] and in 443 he merely defeated troops who had been hastily transhipped from Sicily, where they had been out-manoeuvred by the Vandals and had subsequently had their morale sapped by living in idle, passive conditions for several years on end. In 447, when Attila engaged the unimpaired forces of the East, he won a victory only at the cost of bloody losses. The one sentence of an ancient author which relates to the circumstances of the battle on the river Utus does not suggest that the victory was won by a military genius.[4] But let us waive these considerations. Let us suppose that, in fair and open fight, Attila twice trounced the armies of Eastern Rome. Was he therefore a military genius? Two victories over an army whose basis rested on the colonate and whose rear was no more hostile to the enemy than to its own forces do not entitle him to the term 'genius'. The true measure of his generalship is revealed by his fortunes in Gaul, when he fought the Western Germans whose society was not yet riven by such class struggles as paralysed the Romans. The saddles heaped into a funeral pyre on the plains of Champagne – even if the anecdote is mythical – are a symbol of his utter failure. On ground of his own choosing, with his forces at the peak of their success, facing disunited and suspicious allies, his generalship succumbed to the courage of a free peasantry.

Perhaps, then, when historians speak of the genius of Attila, they refer to his diplomatic abilities? Surely the judgement must be reversed. Success in the West in 451 was not impossible. Given a correct diplomatic preparation, Visigoths and West Romans alike could very probably have been overcome. Three conditions should have been fulfilled by a general in Attila's position in the summer of 449, and all three were brushed aside by him.

First, the Visigoths and West Romans should have been tackled separately. Attila seems at first to have been aware of this. It was his original plan to settle with the Visigoths while still claiming to be the friend of Ravenna. From his own point of view, it was of great importance to adhere strictly to this plan, for, whatever the limitations of Aetius in other respects, he was clearly a general of unusual ability. But, in fact, Attila allowed his plan to become obscured when he received the invitation of Honoria. His clumsy handling of her appeal united the West against him. Indeed, when we consider what the relations of Ravenna and Toulouse had been in the decades preceding 451, we may fairly conclude that only a bungler of the first order could have thrown Aetius and Theodoric into each other's arms. This indeed was a *coup de maître*.

Secondly, more use should have been made of Geiseric. For one reason or another the Vandal was very anxious that Attila should attack the Visigoths. Naval descents on Italy in 452, if not on Gaul in 451, should therefore have accompanied Attila's own thrusts on land. Yet we hear of no effort to stir Geiseric into activity, although he had spent his life in attacks on the Western Romans. History knows of few commanders who have thrown away so willing and so efficient an ally.

The third reason why it seems impossible to agree that Attila was a diplomat of exceptional ability is the most compelling of all, and can be stated very briefly. It is this: that after his flight to the Huns in 448 we hear no more of Eudoxius (p. 139 above). If Attila had put himself at the head of the Bagaudae, Visigoth and Roman alike could have been swept out of Gaul in a few months; but, in fact, the Armoricans are listed among Aetius' allies at the Catalaunian Plains.

Clearly the case has now been reduced *ad absurdum*. Attila could not possibly have appeared as the champion of a revolted peasantry. Parasitic marauders, such as the Huns, have other uses for peasants. In Attila's eyes the followers of Tibatto and Eudoxius were no different from the followers of his subjected German kings: they were simply potential suppliers of grain and livestock to feed his men. It is inconceivable that he should have used them as allies. Their purpose was to overthrow the landlords of Gaul. Attila had no desire to overthrow landlords as such: he was himself the largest landowner in Europe. The abilities of Attila, then, were limited by the limitations of the society which produced him. The Huns could never have produced a diplomat of genius, because the organization of their society was such that they could never really possess a true ally, and no one in Europe, not even Aetius himself, can have seriously believed that they could.

If we insist, then, that so striking a figure must have had some measure of greatness, we may turn to an observation of Mommsen's. Mommsen gave it as his opinion that Attila's greatest achievement was probably his strengthening of the central authority among the Huns.[5] Of this, to be sure, we cannot be entirely certain: we do not know to what extent the position of the military leader inside the confederacy had altered between the days of Rua and those of Attila. Nevertheless, it seems highly probable that in this matter Attila marked a distinct advance on his predecessor. Until the closing years of his life Rua had been content to rule only a portion of the Huns: his brother Octar, and doubtless Mundiuch too, had shared his power. But even when he became sole ruler on Octar's death in 430, he had been unable to compel *all* the Hun tribes to give him their allegiance.[6] The tribal leaders of the Amilzuri, Itimari, Tunsures, Boisci, and the others (p. 80 above) sought to preserve the independence they had enjoyed before the days of Rua's confederacy. They resisted the forces which were making for unity on the steppe, and Rua died before he could impose his authority over them. On the other hand, Attila's power was subject to no limitation after his murder of Bleda in 445, and we have seen that in 449, when Priscus visited him, his authority was absolute and autocratic (p. 178 above). It is difficult to believe that, as early as Rua's day, the Huns had surrendered their rude liberties so completely. We may agree then with Mommsen. Attila's greatness lay in his remarkable insight into the potentialities of Hun society. He saw the direction in which the changes taking place in that society in his day were tending. He realized more clearly than any of his predecessors that, if all the tribes could be united under an unquestioned and absolute leader, the Huns would form an unparalleled instrument for the exploitation of the peoples of central Europe. Without unity and a strong central power the Huns would have disappeared with as little stir as many a 'Scythian' people before them. Not only did Attila realize the potentialities of his people, but he also proved able to put his ideas into practice. It is unlikely that he instituted the λογάδες, for Uldin seems to have had similar subordinates (p. 63 above), and Berichus' father would appear to have been something like a λογάς in the generation before Attila (p. 179 above). But it seems very probable that Attila developed the institution and gave it its final form. Instead of relying on the unruly and divided tribal chiefs, he based his power on vassals like Onegesius and Berichus and Edeco, who were bound to him personally by an inviolable allegiance without the handicap of tribal obligations.

In the complete absence of a description of Hun society under Rua, no argument on these lines can be at all certain. Yet it is unlikely that Mommsen's judgement was far astray. But even if we subscribe to his view of Attila, we must admit that Rua had laid the foundations of his nephew's greatness.

II

Let us turn to the Huns as a whole. Before discussing the permanent effects of their ascendancy upon the future course of European history, it may be worthwhile emphasizing a fact which forced its attention on us more than once in earlier pages of this book: the continued existence of the Hun empire very quickly became a vested interest in many parts of Europe. In the West, Aetius, the champion of the landed aristocracy, maintained himself between 425 and 439 solely by means of Hunnic auxiliaries supplied by Rua and Attila, and continued to be on friendly terms with the Hun rulers until the eve of the campaign in Gaul in 451. Even after that, he seems to have thought it incredible that the Huns should undertake hostilities against him and his friends in Italy. He was probably looking forward to years of co-operation with Attila even after the Catalaunian Plains: otherwise he could scarcely have made the grotesque mistake of leaving the Alpine passes unguarded in the spring of 452. There can be no doubt that the great landowners, whose position was upheld by Aetius, entertained a similar attitude towards the Huns. True, Avitus disliked their unruly behaviour on his estate at Avitacum in 436 (p. 75 above) and the invasion of 451 was altogether terrifying, but who else, save the Huns, could have safeguarded his property from the encroachments of the Visigoths, Burgundians, and Bagaudae? It seems reasonable to suppose that in the thirties and forties of the century the landed aristocracy of the West were disposed to favour the continuance of a Hun empire which would lend them military support whenever they found themselves in difficulties. But, it may be pointed out incidentally, there were men in the West who felt differently. Aetius, naturally enough, made no attempt to create a diversion in the rear of his Hun friends when they attacked the Eastern Empire in 447. But we have already seen that he was criticized for his inaction (p. 102 above). Some men evidently felt that he had missed an excellent opportunity of ridding Europe of these barbarians for ever. It would be of profound interest to know who precisely these critics were. They were busy again, it seems, when Attila crossed the Julian Alps in the spring of 452 without meeting opposition,[7] and their general attitude may well have coincided with that of Salvian, who makes it perfectly plain that, in his opinion, it was better to live as an exile among the Huns than as a poor man in the Empire of Aetius.[8]

In the East it was not the landowning class that stood to gain from the existence of the empire of the Huns. On the contrary, the landowners did their utmost to induce Theodosius to fight Attila, and, when Marcian succeeded to the throne and made it his policy 'to preserve the wealth of those possessing much untouched', direct military action was taken almost immediately to overthrow the Hun domination of central Europe. In the East, as we have seen, it appears to have been the merchants, traders, and manufacturers who supported Theodosius. Such a conclusion should occasion no surprise, for, in his analysis of the forces which maintained

Chinghis Khan's empire, Fox writes thus (p. 132, cf. pp. 67, 106):

Nor must we leave out of account the influence of the merchants who flocked to Mongolia from Central Asia and the border regions of the Great Wall as soon as a stable state had been created by Chinghis. These merchants . . . were quick to see the great advantage which would come to them if a man of [Chinghis's] genius were to establish a firm rule over Northern China.

It is difficult to resist the impression that the same held good of the East Roman merchants in the days of the Huns. Even before the arrival of the latter, the frontier towns on the Danube had plied a considerable trade with the Visigoths who then lived directly north of the river. In fact, without this trade the Visigoths could scarcely live at all, for, after Valens' three campaigns in 367–9 Athanaric was ready to capitulate, we are told, 'because trade was cut off, so that the barbarians were distressed by the extreme scarcity of the necessities of life'.[9] But the Visigoths can have had very little to offer in return to the traders of these cities in comparison with the Huns of Attila's day, who were receiving 2,100 lb of golden Roman coins every year from Theodosius. Consider Eustace again, the merchant of Apamea (pp. 193–4 above). In the days of Perozes or Firuz, king of Persia (453–84), he was reduced to throwing in his lot with a small band of Huns on the Persian border, presumably in the hope of receiving some pickings from the plunder taken by his companions. In the peaceful days of Attila he would have been able to travel quietly and trade his Syrian wares anywhere he chose between the Caspian and the Rhine. As it was, we know that his life was one of risks and hazards; he must certainly have regretted the collapse of Attila's empire.

Finally, we have considered the possibility that some of the Germanic kings were comparatively well satisfied with their position under Attila. This, of course, can be no more than a suggestion, but if in fact they were dissatisfied, we can only say that they were peculiarly blind to the advantages of their bondage.[10]

In all this it will be observed that the arrival of the Huns released no new social or productive forces that might have transformed the condition of the Roman Empire. It was not possible for them, as it was for some of the Germanic kings[11] – and indeed for the Eastern Emperors themselves in the long run – so to alter the position of the peasantry as to make possible their eventual liberation. None the less, further research into the social history of the Eastern Empire may well show that, at a critical time, they played an important, if unwitting, part in the preservation of the East. One of the greatest dangers in all ancient societies was the fact that, owing to the low productive methods available, land had an inevitable tendency to concentrate rapidly into a very few hands, and we know that the paralysis of the West in the fifth century was largely due to this extreme concentration of land. The estate-owners were so strong that the government stood powerless before them. In the East, however, the landlords were opposed, as they were not in the West, by a comparatively powerful and wealthy class of merchants, traders, craftsmen, and the like. We have seen reason to suppose that the existence of the Hun empire, and the policy adopted by Theodosius and Chrysaphius towards that empire, tended to strengthen this class of merchants and craftsmen at the expense of the landed aristocracy. When the social relationships existing within the Eastern Roman Empire have been more fully analysed, it may well appear that the ascendancy of the Huns was thereby an important factor in postponing the struggle between the government and the landowners which racked Constantinople at a later date and finally, after many vicissitudes, resulted in the victory of the landlords. Of course, the issue was not without its complications. The merchant of Viminacium had little reason for gratitude towards Theodosius, and the wars of 441–3 and 447 caused untold damage and loss to the traders of the frontier towns. Yet that same merchant had prospered during the thirties in Viminacium, which he certainly would not have done had Marcian succeeded to the throne twenty years earlier and had begun his provocative measures when Attila was still a young man. And despite the devastation of the frontier towns, their trade must have continued, for, as we have seen, the Huns would have perished without it. In the present state of our knowledge, no certainty can be attained on considerations like these. But the sceptical may be asked: In the long run who was it that benefited from the 2,100 lb of gold that reached the Huns every year? After all, the Huns extorted the money because they wanted to spend it.

III

The question of the results and significance of the Hun ascendancy has been discussed by Bury, whose conclusions are accepted by Alföldi and others.[12] Bury argues that the existence of the Hun empire 'helped to retard the whole process of the German dismemberment of the Empire', and that it did this in two ways. In the first place, the Huns, by conquering the Germanic peoples of central Europe and holding them in check, eased the pressure on the Roman frontiers for many years. True, the Huns themselves devastated the Roman provinces both in the East and in the West on several occasions, but, in Bury's opinion, these devastations were no worse than those which would have been carried out by the Germans if the Huns had not been there. In fact, soon after the beginning of the fifth century Italy was almost completely free from barbarian attacks launched from the Danube basin. It was only in 452 that such attacks were renewed. Again, we know that after the death of the usurper John in 425 the plundering raids of the Germans into Gaul were considerably restricted, and this was certainly due to the Huns' conquest of the Germans who had hitherto been pressing on the Roman frontier. In the second place, both the Eastern and particularly the Western Empire were provided with considerable numbers of Hunnic auxiliaries, who, whatever the social implications of their activities, were, as Bury says, 'an invaluable resource in the struggle with the German enemies', such as the Visigoths and Burgundians.

It will be noticed that, in one important respect, this view coincides with the conclusions reached in the previous section: it was Bury's opinion that the Huns, so far from hastening the collapse of the Roman Empire, actually delayed it. We came tentatively to this conclusion by examining the Huns in relation to the *internal* condition of the Eastern, but not the Western, Empire; Bury reached it after a consideration of the *external* relations of the Empire as a whole. Yet it may be suggested that Bury's view should be modified. Granting that the Germans were held in check when Attila was leader of the Huns, the same cannot be said of the periods before and after his career. It is difficult to imagine that, if the Huns had never appeared, any such cataclysms would have shaken Europe as were caused by the two great westward drives of the nomads c.376 and c.405. These two dates are landmarks in the process by which the Empire fell. When the Goths crossed the lower Danube and fought at Adrianople, and when the Vandals, Alans, and Sueves crossed the Rhine, the Roman Empire very quickly became something basically different from what it had been, say, in the time of Julian (361–3). These two westward thrusts of the Huns drove the Germans far deeper *and far earlier* into Gaul, Spain, and even Africa than would have been possible for them if the Huns had not been at their heels. Take the case of Alaric. Can we suppose that he would have been content with a miserable career as half-friend and half-foe of the Romans, half in their pay and half cheated out of it, if the rich lands of the Danubian plain had been available to his men? He has caught our imagination by his capture of Rome in 410; but we must not forget that throughout his career he was a man for whom retreat was impossible. In his search for land, upon which his followers could settle and grow their crops in peace, he never dared to turn towards the north, and he died with his problem still unsolved. Again, in the years which followed Attila's death the Ostrogoths were reduced to outright starvation as a result of their experiences at the hands of the Huns. They were compelled by their sheer want of food to obtain land and money from the Romans. How different their history would have been if they had been allowed to live on peacefully north of the Danube and in southern Russia, where they might have continued for many years to exploit the numerous races included in the empire of Ermanarich.

Hence, even if the Germanic invasions were retarded between 430 and 455, they were accelerated both before and after those dates. Without the appearance of the Huns there would have been no Visigothic kingdom of Toulouse, no Ostrogothic kingdom in Italy, no Vandal kingdom in Africa *as early as in fact there were*. That Germans would eventually have set up their kingdoms in Gaul, Italy, and Africa is of course undeniable; but without the Huns they would have done so at a more leisurely pace.[13]

The Huns played an important role in European history for less than a hundred years. But we have seen that, despite its brevity, their appearance had profound consequences for the subsequent development of western Europe and may have had considerable influence on the East. But the effects, which we have tried to trace, were all indirect. They were caused by the displacement of other peoples and by the trade of the Romans. Did the Huns make no *direct* contribution to the progress of Europe? Had they nothing to offer besides the terror which uprooted the Germanic nations and sent them fleeing into the Roman Empire? The answer is, No, they offered nothing. Their society was such that they could make no contribution like those of the Germans, the Persians, and the Arabs. They were mere plunderers and marauders. A character in Priscus briefly and admirably describes what they did: 'Being themselves contemptuous of agriculture,' he says, 'they descended upon the Gothic food-supply and snatched it away like wolves, so that the Goths occupied the position of slaves and toiled for the sustenance of the Huns.'[14]

Afterword

In the winter of 1991, some digging in the back garden was interrupted by a phone call inquiring whether I might be interested in helping Edward Thompson produce a revised edition of *A History of Attila and the Huns* for Blackwell's 'Peoples of Europe' series. Professor Thompson was very keen to do the job thoroughly, and take full account of all the relevant historical and archaeological literature which had appeared in the meantime. At this point, he had already been ill, however, and felt that he was not capable of undertaking the task unaided. It was with great pleasure that I accepted. Unfortunately, Professor Thompson died before we had been able to take our collaboration beyond a few meetings and exchanges of thoughts, and this has decisively shaped the nature of the revisions which the reader will find separating this second edition of *Attila and the Huns* (renamed *The Huns* in line with the rest of the series) from the original.

The author wanted to recast much of the text, and professed himself ready to follow any suggestions I cared to make. Such an attitude was entirely characteristic of him, in its total lack of defensive sensitivity with regard to his own work. If our collaboration had been fated to continue for longer, I would anyway have been deeply hesitant about proposing changes to another scholar's work, particularly to a work such as this, stamped indelibly with its author's vigorous coherence. After his death, it would have been presumptuous of me in the extreme even to consider making wholesale changes. As a result, my working principle has been to leave the text intact and unchanged, except where I have the author's specific instructions to do otherwise.

Some of these instructions were communicated verbally. That quotations from the original sources were, in the first edition, made in Latin and Greek he dismissed with a laugh, and the comment that they reflected 'a young man's vanity'. Given that the book was published in 1948, I rather think that this reflects the standard conventions of a different era, where a much more widespread knowledge of the classical languages could simply be assumed. Many more instructions have been transmitted via a xeroxed copy of the first edition, carrying the author's annotations in the margins. It particularly distressed him, for instance, that in his account of Attila's feast, he had misunderstood Priscus to imply that the Hun's leading lieutenant, Onegesius, was not seated on the right – the seat of honour – of his king, and he had spent a few lines commenting on this supposed fact. Among the annotations, I found a disgusted 'Oh God. Onegesius *was* seated on the right of Attila.' I doubt very much that anyone else will have taken as much account of this small slip as the author did himself.

With the author's comments and marginalia as my guide, I have been able to put into effect at least some of his wishes. All quotations from the original sources have been translated into English, except for the occasional footnote whose meaning is directly transmitted in the text. Published translations of the major relevant sources are listed under 'Primary Literary Sources' in the further reading list below; I have on occasion adapted them, and other translations are my own. Quite a few small deletions of one kind or another have also been made from the 1948 edition of the text, again only in accord with the author's expressed wishes. What I have specifically not done, however, is alter the text to take account of more recent work, even where Professor Thompson's marginalia indicate that he would have done so. Instead, it seemed to me much more appropriate to produce an afterword, which would draw the reader's attention to some of the most important items in subsequent literature on the subject.

What follows makes no claim to be comprehensive, but neither have I felt the need, working this way, to confine comment only to works specifically mentioned to me by the author. For convenience, I have divided the material thematically, considering in turn literary sources, secondary historical works, and archaeological and anthropological writings. Some of the items, of course, cross these over-neat boundaries, in which cases I have made an arbitrary decision about where to include them. To my certain knowledge, Professor Thompson was well acquainted with most of the historical and archaeological literature and indicated a wish to take account of it, so that my comments will on occasion draw specifically upon his notes, both verbal and marginal. A bibliography of all items mentioned in this afterword is given under 'Secondary Works' in the further reading list.

Literary Sources

There have been no dramatic finds of major new literary sources for the history of the Huns since 1948. A great deal of very important work, however, has been completed, and would ideally have been reflected in a fully revised version of *Attila and the Huns*. Welcome and necessary new editions have appeared of many of the major historical narratives which form the core of the source material on which the book is based. In particular, a new Budé edition (with French translation) of the historian Zosimus has been produced by F. Paschoud, and, by R. C. Blockley, a new edition of the fragments of Eunapius, Olympiodorus, and Priscus, the latter in particular a central text underlying many pages of

Thompson's book. Blockley's work poses, however, one technical question, since it renumbered the fragments, abandoning the system used by older editions (Dindorf and Muller). After some reflection, I have retained here the old numbers, since many readers will probably still be using older editions, and Blockley has provided convenient tables cross-referencing the older editions with his renumberings. Very valuable too have been revised editions of minor sources, too numerous to mention individually, although I would draw attention to the new edition of the poet Merobaudes (with English translation) by F. M. Clover, and the new *Sources Chrétiennes* edition of Callinicus' *Life of St Hypatius*. I have broken with my normal practice elsewhere in revising two footnote references to the *Life*, to follow the *SC* numbering system (ch. 2, nn. 95 and 96).

Beyond actual editions, the appearance of an English translation is worth signalling, at least in one major instance. In 1948, the only available translation of Priscus was in Latin. Since then, two English translations of this fundamental source for Hunnic history have become available, the first by C. D. Gordon in 1966, the second by Blockley as part of his new edition of the text. Blockley also produced the first English translation of the fragments of Eunapius, and, in addition to Paschoud's French version in the Budé edition, there is now an excellent English translation of the historian Zosimus by R. T. Ridley. Many of the minor sources have also been made more accessible by the appearance of translations into modern European languages.

All this effort put into study of the texts has been equally fruitful in terms of secondary studies of individual authors, their literary styles and techniques, and their purposes as historians. The new literature in this field since 1948 is immense, and it is neither possible nor appropriate to discuss it at any length here, or even list it all, since the new editions of the texts are extremely good sources of bibliography. The various volumes of Paschoud's Zosimus, for instance, provide a comprehensive and updated listing of studies relevant to this important author, as do Blockley's new edition and its companion volume of essays for Priscus, Eunapius, and Olympiodorus. Before moving on, however, let me add a couple of more specific comments. First, Professor Thompson signalled in his marginal annotations that he wished readers now to consult for further information on the historian Olympiodorus, not his own study in *Classical Quarterly* for 1944, but that of John Matthews in the *Journal of Roman Studies* for 1970, 'Olympiodorus of Thebes and the history of the West (AD 407–425)'. Rather than change the text, I have thought it best to signal this point here. More generally, the marginalia indicate that he was well aware of the further contributions to the study of the major sources incorporated in O. J. Maenchen-Helfen's book, *The World of the Huns*. Much more must be said about this remarkable work below, but for the moment I would note in particular its contributions to understandings of Ammianus Marcellinus' famous digression upon the Huns, and of the sources underlying Eunapius' account of their background and origins. Over Ammianus, the authors differed considerably in their interpretations (cf. Maenchen-Helfen, pp. 9–15), and I am sure that Maenchen-Helfen would have received a typically good-spirited if none the less combative rejoinder. In the case of Eunapius, Thompson wanted to acknowledge Maenchen-Helfen's work in uncovering further the classical sources used by Eunapius. In particular, in the case of the 'royal Scythians' (p. 14 above), and 'Snub-nosed men' (p. 21 above), readers were to have signalled to them the importance of Maenchen-Helfen, pp. 5–9.

Historical Studies

Since 1948, a number of general books on the Migration Period, with more or less concentration on the history of the Huns, have been produced, particularly in France, where there seems to be at least one per scholarly generation. In even broader vein, the history of the Huns is also sometimes discussed alongside that of other great nomadic empires, particularly in the well-known study of Grousset. Amongst such general syntheses, I would single out just two. The first is that of Lucien Musset, since 1975 conveniently available in the English translation of Edward and Columba James. This not only provides useful bibliographical information (arranged by subject), but also attempts to summarize the state of scholarship on particular topics, highlighting the issues which remain contentious. A more detailed narrative account has been provided more recently by the study of E. Demougeot, an extensive introduction in itself, and also transmitting substantial amounts of bibliographical information in its footnotes. Neither of these handbooks, however, amounts to a detailed re-evaluation of Hunnic history *per se*; Demougeot was able to devote only about thirty-five pages, for instance, to the high point of Hunnic history in the fifth century. For the really detailed response to Thompson's work, the reader must turn to more specific studies.

Three major scholarly historical studies of the Huns, based primarily on written sources, have been published since Thompson's *Attila and the Huns* first appeared.[1] A shorter book on the subject by the German scholar Franz Altheim was followed about a decade later by a much bigger collaborative project, in five volumes, again under the same author's direction. About a decade later still, Otto J. Maenchen-Helfen published another large book on the subject. My purpose in this section is to highlight the significant ways in which these books differ from Thompson's, both in general shape and scope, and in important points of interpretation. In doing this, I will not pass any judgements on the likely correctness of this or that view, but underline the importance of Thompson's work in the light of subsequent literature. This, I hope, will be a useful service to the reader, and go part of the way towards fulfilling Professor Thompson's desire to revise his work, by making clear what choices he would have had to make.

Of these three major historical studies, the first, Altheim's personal monograph, is distinguishable from Thompson's study primarily by the breadth of its coverage. On the origins and early movements of the Huns before the last quarter of the fourth century, *The Huns* has little to say. This was deliberate. The author felt that an article by Maenchen-Helfen (see p. 1, n. 1 above) had undermined by then traditional equations between the Huns and the nomadic Hsiung-nu confederation who had earlier been a powerful presence on the fringes of China. He also saw little of value in the earliest Roman reports on the subject. As he concludes (p. 26 above), 'Not only the origin of the true Huns, but also their movements and activities before the last quarter of the fourth century, remain as profound a mystery to us as they were to Ammianus.' By contrast, in Altheim's study, two out of a total of eight chapters (only seven are listed in the book's table of contents) deal with the history of the Huns prior to their attacks on the Goths in *c*.370. Indeed, these two chapters amount to over a third of the book, and there is even a final chapter which deals with developments on the Steppes subsequent to the defeat and disappearance of Attila's empire.

As this suggests, Altheim's book has a very different vision of the subject from that of Thompson. Thompson's is essentially a study of the Huns in contact with the Roman world and its fringes between *c*.370 and *c*.470. Altheim was concerned to, and believed (where Thompson did not) that the sources were available to set this particular phase of Hunnic history in a much broader context. His coverage of the period where the two books overlap is slighter; Altheim's book makes no attempt to provide, as does Thompson, a thoroughgoing critique of the Roman literary sources, and devotes much less attention to matters of historical detail in this period. On the other hand, he offers an invigoratingly broad perspective, and the chance to contemplate Hunnic origins in the light of both a greater wealth of information and what we know of subsequent patterns of movement across the Steppe.

Exactly the same vision informs Altheim's later and much larger-scale collaborative contribution to the subject. Again, what is really remarkable about this work, for present purposes at least, is how minimal an overlap with Thompson's study there actually is. In five volumes, each of three hundred pages plus, no more than about half of one volume concerns itself with the subject matter at the heart of *The Huns*. The bulk of the first volume covers much the same ground, but in much more detail and via a variety of contributors, as the first two chapters of Altheim's own study: origins and history of the Huns prior to their impact upon the fringes of the Roman world. Only chapters 13–15 of this book, dealing with the Huns' attacks on the Goths, and the organization of Hunnic society, tackle subjects which were of concern to Thompson.

The next two volumes in the series part company with Thompson entirely. The second volume is devoted to the history of the collision of the Hephthalites (or Ephthalites) with Sassanian Iran in the fourth and fifth centuries AD (very much the same time period as that in which the Huns were plaguing the Roman Empire and its European neighbours). The Hephthalites are sometimes known as the Hephthalite Huns, and this volume proceeds from the conviction that their attacks upon the Persians and those of the Huns upon the Roman Empire were closely related phenomena. His two brief references to them (pp. 41 and 87 above) suggest that Thompson would not necessarily have been averse to such a view, but his is a book devoted to those Hunnic tribes who came into contact with the Romans. Volume 3 deals with religious contacts between the settled worlds of the Mediterranean and the Near East and peoples of the Steppe, and is very wide-ranging indeed. The first chapter deals with missions to the Huns, but further chapters deal, amongst other things, with Avars (who infringed upon the borders of Europe about a century after the collapse of

Attila's empire), internal Sassanian religious developments, and the spread of Nestorian Christianity.

With volume 4 in the series (*The European Huns*), we return again to territory covered by Thompson, but not without continuing detours. The first one hundred and eighty pages (out of a total of about three hundred and fifty) are devoted to miscellaneous contributions on Iranian historical background, and paganism and Christianity (the latter including, for instance, a chapter on pagan *Germanic* gods). The remaining eight chapters consider the westward movement of the European Huns, the defeat of the Burgundians, Attila's campaigns, and the collapse of his empire. There is much of interest here, and the chapters do provide another view of the subject matter covered by Thompson. The surprising thing, however, is that, even in this five-volume project, so little space is devoted to Attila and his forebears that Thompson's consideration of the subject is certainly more detailed. Even in this volume, for instance, another sixty pages are spent considering the *Nibelungenlied* (reflecting in some way – precisely how is highly controversial – the Huns' attacks upon the Burgundians) and the poetic genres to which it belongs. The fifth and final volume, likewise, ranges far beyond Thompson's brief, with contributions about a whole range of later nomadic groupings whose movements affected Europe and the Near East.

In sum, Altheim's larger collaborative project is very similar in profile to his own earlier book. It offers a different, broader vision of Hunnic history to that of Thompson, driven by a different set of priorities. As a result, despite all the pages of its five volumes, it certainly does not make redundant Thompson's detailed and coherent study of one part of this material. Whether it really supplements Thompson, by setting his study of what might be termed 'the European Huns' in a well-established, broader context, is a matter for individual readers to decide.

The third and most recent of the major works devoted to

the Huns since the publication of the first edition of Thompson's book, the study of Otto Maenchen-Helfen, is, in some senses, much more directly a 'competitor' of Thompson's book than either of Altheim's projects. Its author was a very remarkable man. As the fragments of the preface he intended for his book explain, he spent some months in 1929 living with Turkish-speaking nomads in north-western Mongolia. He also spent time in Nepal, was an expert in the history of Asian art, and possessed really wide-ranging philological abilities, being equally at home in Greek, Russian, Persian, or Chinese. It is hardly surprising, then, that his work should share the same desire as that of Altheim to set the history of the 'European Huns' in the broadest context possible of Asiatic Steppe nomads in general, and their relations with empires and civilizations at either end of the Eurasian Steppe. While, as we have seen, it was an early article of his which convinced Thompson that the standard equations of Huns and Hsiung-nu were misconceived, Maenchen-Helfen was not content, as was Thompson, to leave the question of Hunnic origins and early history with this negative conclusion. Thus many pages of *The World of the Huns* are devoted to archaeological and anthropological evidence, much of it from the territories of the former Soviet Union, which might shed some further light on the matter. Indeed, it is one of the major contributions of his book to draw at great length on the writings of Russian-speaking commentators, whose conclusions would not otherwise be available to those unable to read them in the original. At the same time, however, unlike Altheim, Maenchen-Helfen, also subjected the history of the 'European Huns' to the same degree of scrutiny as Thompson had done. *The World of the Huns* thus supplies another narrative reconstruction and analysis of the impact of the Huns upon the world of the Roman Empire and its neighbours.

Before comparing and contrasting the two studies, however, it is extremely important to take full account of another significant feature of Maenchen-Helfen's book. As the editor's note explains, the author brought a 'beautifully typed' manuscript to the offices of California University Press in early January 1969, and, very unfortunately, died just a few days later. Upon investigation, the delivered manuscript turned out to represent not a completed book, but only a first batch of chapters. The manuscript also came without a contents page (although a draft of one 'of unknown age' was unearthed), and some further chapters were brought to publishable form by the editor from materials he found in the author's study. The more closely one scrutinizes *The World of the Huns*, in fact, the more clear it becomes that it represents a far from finished work. Some footnotes are missing or incomplete, but, much more important, the book is highly episodic. The different chapters, or indeed sections of chapters, contain very detailed and closely argued treatments of particular problems, but do not tend to run smoothly into one another, while other sections do not come to any kind of formal conclusion. I suspect, therefore, that many linking paragraphs and summarizing conclusions remained to be written at the time of the author's death. Likewise, the order of material is far from straightforward. The book opens with a detailed discussion of the historical value of some of the major Roman literary sources which describe the first impact of the Huns on the fringes of Europe. It then goes on to reconstruct in detail the history of the 'European Huns' between *c*.370 and *c*.470. In this, its structure closely resembles that of Thompson's book (sources, then reconstruction): so closely that I wonder if the resemblance was deliberate. After this, there follow a number of thematically arranged sections on economy, society, warfare, religion, art, race, language, and evidence for Huns in eastern Europe before 370. Some of the thematic sections follow on well enough from the history, but the final three sections on race, language, and pre-370 European Huns are really addressing the overall question of Hunnic origins and history prior to their impact upon the fringes of the Roman Empire. It has thus been placed after (some two hundred pages after) the material it should logically precede, and this, combined with the fact that no overall conclusions are drawn from these last three sections, again suggests to me that *The World of the Huns* as published is still some way from the final destination to which its author, had he lived, would have brought it. As I know from experience, these features of the book make it extremely difficult, amongst other things, for students to use.

Be that as it may, there remain some two hundred pages (the first four sections on literary evidence, history, economy, and society) where there is very considerable overlap between Maenchen-Helfen's work and that of Thompson. Indeed, Maenchen-Helfen was explicitly responding to some of Thompson's arguments. An afterword such as this would be an entirely inappropriate occasion for me to venture my own opinions on who is more likely to be correct, and I will not do so. I will, however, highlight where, in my reading of the two works, the main differences lie. This, I hope, will make it easier for subsequent readers to make the necessary comparisons and draw their own conclusions.

The first major area of contention between them concerns the ethnographic digression on Hunnic society and customs written by the Roman historian Ammianus Marcellinus in *c*.390 AD. Both agree that it is the only early source of information worth taking seriously: the question is how seriously. For Thompson, while not complete or first-hand, the digression is 'highly vivid and consistent', and he consequently takes it at face value, except where there is explicit reason not to (pp. 10–11 above). While insisting on its merits, Maenchen-Helfen is more suspicious, considering it highly coloured by classical traditions of ethnographic writing, and hence considerably misleading. This fundamental difference in approach leads to rival historical interpretations in two areas. First, Thompson concluded from Ammianus' account of the Huns' total reliance upon their flocks that, in *c*.370, they were at the so-called 'lower

stage of pastoralism', with few craftworking skills and a
total reliance on the productive abilities of others for luxury
goods, and even weapons. Maenchen-Helfen rejects Ammianus' account as at this point a *topos* of classical ethnographic
descriptions of nomadic life in general, and attempts to prove
that the economy of the Huns was marked by considerably
greater differentiation and productive capacity. Second, these
competing visions of the Huns' economic capacities stimulate
correspondingly different visions of Hunnic social structure.
Much of the argument here also turns on the interpretation
of a critical sentence in Ammianus' description, which
reports (xxxi. 2. 7): 'Aguntur autem nulla severitate regali,
sed tumultuario primatum ductu contenti, perrumpunt
quicquid inciderit' ([The Huns] are not subject to the
authority of any king, but break through any obstacle in their
path under the improvised command of their chief men). In
Thompson's view, as his account of their economy would
imply, this suggests that Hunnic society was deeply
egalitarian in *c*.370. They did not have kings, nor even a
proper aristocracy, but elected only temporary leaders in
time of warfare. Maenchen-Helfen's interpretation is quite
otherwise. As we have seen, he does not believe that
Ammianus' account should be read literally, and points to
evidence for substantial social differentiation among the
Huns (as *his* account of their economy would imply), and to
the fact that one late source, Jordanes, reports, against
Ammianus, that Hunnic attacks upon the Goths in *c*.370 were
master-minded by a king called Balamber (on Balamber, see
further below). Both Thompson and Maenchen-Helfen
would agree that Hunnic society developed fast in the face
of its contacts with the Roman world after *c*.370, but they
thus have very different views of its starting point.

The other main area of disagreement between them
concerns the most famous Hun of them all, Attila: both
specific aspects of his career, and its overall interpretation. In
the chapters on Attila, Thompson was concerned, amongst
other things, to debunk the view that the Hun king was a

leader of genius, whose personal qualities alone explain the
sudden rise and equally dramatic collapse of the Hunnic
empire. Rather, he sought to explain this phenomenon by the
unleashing, through proximity to the Roman Empire, of
broader forces of social and economic development, which
had already produced a powerful empire before Attila's
lifetime. At the same time, Thompson also made a series of
more specific criticisms of Attila's record as leader. He was a
diplomatic bungler who, when invading the West in 451,
managed to cause a whole series of initially disunited
enemies to combine against him. More than that, most of his
military victories came when there was no opposition worth
talking about (esp. pp. 226-31 above). Maenchen-Helfen, it
seems to me, is basically in agreement with Thompson on the
historical importance of forces standing outside the control
of any specific individual. Very much against Thompson,
however, he argued that those processes culminated in the
career of Attila, and that via his unprecedented military
successes, Attila created a much more powerful Hunnic
empire than had existed in previous generations. He quite
specifically did not want to portray Attila as 'another
Alexander', but clearly felt that Thompson had overplayed
his arguments for Attilan incompetence in both the military
and diplomatic spheres. In the latter case, for instance,
Maenchen-Helfen argued that Attila's relations with the
Western Empire had always been strained, and that no great
blunder was involved in the decision to attack the West, or
indeed the comprehensively hostile response it provoked
from Western powers (pp. 94ff).

Aside from this, two important questions of historical
reconstruction also separate the two accounts. First, when
did Attila (and, in the first instance, his brother Bleda) come
to power over the Huns? Much of the answer to this turns on
the date of what seems to be an exploratory Byzantine
embassy to Attila and Bleda, conducted, amongst others, by
one Epigenes. In his record of this embassy, Priscus refers to
Epigenes as *Quaestor*, a post we know he did not hold until

after November 438 (when he was still a more junior *Magister memoriae: Nov. Theod.* i. 7). Thompson thought Priscus' reference a mere slip and that the embassy should be placed in 434/5, when he considers the new Hunnic leaders to have taken power (pp. 79–83 above; cf. Appendix B). For Maenchen-Helfen, however, Priscus' embassy must be taken at face value, and the accession to power of the new leaders thus placed more c.440 than c.435 (pp. 91–4).

Second, there is considerable disagreement over the narrative reconstruction of Attila's Balkan campaigns against the Byzantines in the 440s. Thompson and Maenchen-Helfen are by no means the first to attempt to solve problems created by mutually contradictory sources, and neither adopts a solution not previously championed. Here, the argument turns on the degree of credibility accorded the Byzantine chronicler Theophanes. Largely following his account, and arranging the various fragments of the historian Priscus around Theophanes' outline, Thompson argues that, aside from an initial incursion in 441/2, Attila mounted two further hugely successful attacks into the Byzantine Balkans in 443, when a Roman army was defeated in the Chersonesus, and 447, when he threatened the walls of the imperial capital (pp. 86–103 above). In Maenchen-Helfen's view, stimulated by a vigorous rebuttal of Theophanes' accuracy, there was only one further assault after 441/2, the campaign of 447, which saw Attila both approach the walls of Constantinople and defeat a Roman army in the Chersonesus (pp. 108–25). As a consequence, where Thompson would place an important peace agreement after the 443 campaign (Priscus frag. 5; Blockley frag. 9.3), Maenchen-Helfen is convinced that it was a consequence of the battles of 447.

There are, of course, a host of other comparisons worth making between the two most recent accounts in English of the Huns in Europe. I will only briefly draw attention to two others, however, which seem to me of particular importance. First, thanks to his knowledge of oriental sources, Maenchen-

Helfen provides a much more detailed account of the Hunnic raids through the Caucasus into the Persian and Byzantine Empires in 395 (pp. 51–9). Thompson's marginalia make it clear that he was aware of this, and would have wished to strengthen his own account by drawing appropriately upon Maenchen-Helfen's reconstruction. Second, while their narrative reconstructions of the career of the Hunnic king Uldin (*fl. c.*400–10) are similar, they come to different conclusions as to his significance. Maenchen-Helfen sees him as much less powerful than Attila, but none the less an important precurser, whose empire is an important indicator of the steady build up of Hunnic power on the fringes of Roman territory (pp. 59–72). Thompson sees him, however, as only 'a relatively minor figure', whose activities bear no direct relation to the dramatic subsequent victories of Attila (*passim, esp.* pp. 63–7).[2] There is much more that could be said, but rather than allow this afterword to become to too great an extent merely a comparison of Thompson and Maenchen-Helfen, it is important to move on to consider other, shorter contributions to the reconstruction and analysis of Hunnic history which have appeared since the first publication of Thompson's *Huns*.

Again, I make no claim to be comprehensive. On matters of straightforward narrative reconstruction, there have been a number of contributions in a variety of contexts. Although not specifically about the Huns, a book by the Hungarian scholar Lazlo Várady attempted to recast standard arguments concerning the Huns' involvement in the Middle Danubian area. It seems only fair to bring to the reader's attention the fact that the book received a whole series of critical reviews.[3] More recently, Brian Croke has taken further Maenchen-Helfen's arguments about the chronology of the reign of Rua (or Ruga), predecessor of Attila and Bleda, and attempted to add further twists to the story of relations between the Huns and largely the eastern half of the Roman Empire in the 420s. It is perhaps not out of place also to signal here my own interest in the chronology of the Hunnic impact on the fringes of the Roman Empire. Contrary to received views, I have attempted to argue that the Huns did not reach the Danube en masse in the 370s, but only some thirty years later, viewing the Hunnic invasions as more of a process than a single event, even if two main phases of movement are detectable (Heather, 'The Huns and the end of the Roman Empire in western Europe').

The reign of Attila and the significance of its various phases have continued, naturally enough, to receive attention. Gerhard Wirth has written about relations between the Huns and Byzantium in the earlier part of Attila's reign, a reinterpretation of some important information in Priscus. F. M. Clover has likewise reinterpreted a critical moment later in the reign, Attila's decision to attack the West, and the diplomatic manoeuvring which accompanied it. There have also been more specific studies of Attila's reign. Among these, I would just pick out the controversy over the location of Attila's camp as visited by the historian Priscus as part of a Byzantine embassy. The field is currently held by Robert Browning's study, arguing that the Byzantines found Attila not on the Great Hungarian Plain in the Middle Danubian basin, but in Wallachia, north of the Lower Danube. Thompson himself wrote on this subject, advocating a Middle Danubian location, and when the two sets of arguments are placed side by side, it seems to me, it is not clear which of them is correct. I would urge the reader, therefore, not simply to discount Thompson as has been the modern trend.

Finally, there have been a whole series of studies focusing on Hunnic society and its development. Much of this work stems from Ammianus' famous digression upon the Huns, and this itself has been much discussed. As we have already seen, Maenchen-Helfen took a rather more critical view of this important passage than did Thompson, but both agreed that it has substantial historical value. More recently, the digression has received rather rougher treatment. A whole series of studies, reflecting a broader strain of new work upon the classical ethnographical tradition in general, have argued that it is little more than an agglomeration of inherited description and judgement, with very little historical value (Richter, Shaw, and Wiedemann). Their arguments have not gone unchallenged (cf. Matthews, *The Roman Empire of Ammianus*, pp. 332–42).

More specifically, how one interprets certain sections within Ammianus' digression largely dictates one's overall vision of the development of Hunnic society in the period *c*.370–470. The broad 'shape' of Hunnic society in the age of Attila (*c*.450) is clear enough from the surviving fragments of Priscus. These demonstrate beyond doubt the existence of both an absolute monarchy among the Huns at this time, and an attendant nobility or aristocracy. Much more problematic is Ammianus' description of Hunnic society. As we have already seen, Maenchen-Helfen considered that Thompson had misinterpreted Ammianus' enigmatic phrasing about the Huns' leadership in arguing that Hunnic society was fundamentally egalitarian in *c*.370. Others have been of the same opinion. In particular, the first appearance of Thompson's book stimulated a surge of interest from Hungarian scholars, arguing for a less egalitarian vision of the starting point of Hunnic society in the Migration Period. In doing so, they were not only putting forward the case for a different interpretation of Ammianus' words, but drawing upon archaeological evidence, in particular the occasional finds of symbolic golden bows (on these, see below). Together, these writings form another major body of argument, an important supplement to the debate between Thompson and Maenchen-Helfen (Harmatta, 'The golden bow of the Huns' and 'The dissolution of the Hun Empire'; Laszlo). Again, I should perhaps declare a personal interest. Study of the text of Jordanes' *Gothic History* has led me to reinforce, on the basis of different arguments, a conclusion reached by others, namely that the supposed Hunnic king Balamber, who, according to Jordanes, led the Hunnic attacks upon the Goths in *c*.370, is actually a confused reminiscence of the Gothic king Valamer (Heather, 'Cassiodorus and the rise of the Amals'). There have, of course, been many other historical studies of relevance. There is a distinct danger, however, of this afterword turning into a book, and I hope that readers will be able to find their way to the other studies via the footnotes of the works discussed or at least mentioned here.

Archaeological and Anthropological Studies

In Hunnic archaeology, the 1956 monograph of the German scholar Joachim Werner still provides a key starting point. Thompson, of course, was well aware of Werner's work, and his marginalia (and personal comments) indicate that he would have wanted to take proper account of it, particularly in chapter 1 on sources and the possible contribution of archaeological evidence to understandings of the Huns, which, in 1948, Thompson felt to be minimal (pp. 7–9 above). In his study, Werner systematically collected and commented upon the available archaeological evidence for the Huns, adopting a thematic approach, so that its constituent sections deal with particular artefacts or customs which have some claim to be associated with the Huns. Indeed, in some cases, Werner was concerned firmly to establish these associations by demonstrating that the custom or artefact had moved west into eastern Europe from the lands of the Steppe at precisely the same time as the Huns were making their impact. In particular, sections on cranial deformation (pp. 5–18) and the spread of the use of large bronze cooking cauldrons and female diadems (pp. 57–81) drew heavily on the findings of scholars from the then Soviet Union to make the case for such an association. Otherwise, Werner drew together the evidence for items such as the reflex bow characteristic of the Huns, and the other equipment and armaments of nomadic cavalrymen from the Hunnic period. A final section was devoted to the extremely rich, so-called 'princely' graves (German *fürsten-gräber*) of the era of Attila (*c*.450).

Werner's study remains an indispensable place from which to begin, even after forty years, but much work has been done since. This subsequent work has not only expanded (at least in some areas) the archaeological database, as it were, but also challenged some of the assumptions underlying Werner's work. A convenient summary (in German) of subsequent finds down to *c*.1980 was made by the Hungarian scholar Istvan Bona ('Die archäologischen Denkmaler der Hunnen and der Hunnenzeit'). Since then, occasional finds of Hunnic materials have continued to be made. In particular, I would draw the reader's attention to the publication of a staggeringly rich Hunnic grave found south-west of the Danube at Pannonhalma, which produced a rich array of personal belongings, weapons, and horse equipment, most of which had been plated in gold (Tomka).

A second and more recent work (again in German) by Istvan Bona, however, has now become an indispensable source of information on Hunnic archaeology. The book is entitled *The Hunnic Empire (Das Hunnenreich)* and could in some senses have been discussed above with the historical studies, since it is cast as a broad history of the Huns in Europe and gives much space to matters such as Hunnic attacks of the 370s and Attila's campaigns of the 440s. In these sections, however, precise reference is not made to the primary sources, and the historical reconstruction is essentially dependent on the work of Thompson and Altheim. The fundamental contribution of the work thus lies in the access it gives the reader to the current state of the archaeological evidence, on two levels. First, there are substantial sections dealing specifically with Hunnic finds, customs, weapons, etc. In particular, the book gathers together important evidence from the former Soviet Union for what might be Hunnic or Hunnic-related burials from the period before their impact upon Europe. Second, not only in these sections but throughout, the book is copiously illustrated with maps, photographs (a few in colour), and analytical drawings. More than that, the illustrations are carefully explained and analysed in a full sixty pages of notes at the end of the book (pp. 234–94). Between them, photographs and notes add up to a very full dossier of archaeological materials on the Huns. Also worth noting is the book's substantial annotated bibliography (pp. 216–33). All in all, Bona's book is an invaluable, up-to-date guide to Hunnic archaeology.

The relative lack of directly Hunnic finds remains, even after modern efforts, quite striking. The archaeological contribution to the subject is not now as 'minimal' as it was in 1948, but only about one hundred burials have been identified, for instance, which have any reason to be thought of as Hunnic, in that they have produced reflex bows, cauldrons, diadems, or other characteristic items (about seventy from modern Hungary and another twenty-five or so from the former Soviet Union: Bona, *Das Hunnenreich*, pp. 134–9). There are two obvious possible explanations for this. First, beyond Europe, the operation of the nomadic economy will have meant that the Huns operated in small groups dispersed over very wide areas. Likewise, their tenure of lands in the Middle Danube (modern Hungary) was of little more than fifty years, or two generations in duration (*c*.410/ 420–65). The Huns also buried their richer population members (always the easiest to identify archaeologically) in highly visible burial mounds which were already, it seems, being pillaged in the fifth century (Priscus frag. 2; Blockley frag. 6.1). Since Hunnic numbers are unlikely to have been enormous anyway, one answer to the relative paucity of evidence is thus that the probabilities of retrieval are relatively low.

The second possible line of explanation would turn the discussion more towards developments in archaeological method and interpretation, which have transformed the discipline as a whole since the time that Werner wrote. Werner was working within a well-established interpretative framework which considered objects placed with the physical remains to be basically an accurate guide to that individual's identity. The basic assumptions here, obviously enough, are that the different political groups known from the literary record all had their own distinguishably different physical cultures, and these were directly reflected in burial rites. Since the 1950s, and particularly the 1960s, this assumption has been fiercely challenged, and a great deal of evidence assembled to show that, in some cases at least, the tri-partite relationship between physical culture, identity, and burial rite is much more complicated than simple equations might imply. For instance, status – whether claimed or established – affects burial rites, different ethnic or political groups can have essentially the same material culture, and, within broad physical cultural assemblages, only a very few articles may have possessed significance when it came to expressing identity. A particular case in point is the significance of the spread of the custom of cranial deformation west into Europe in the fourth and fifth centuries AD. This was taken by Werner as a basic guide to the spread of Hunnic migration, although he did also argue that its distribution within Europe shows that the habit was adopted at least by some Burgundians, but a recent study has provided an alternative explanation less dependent upon supposing a direct equation between custom and people (Buchet). In a more general sense, this line of explanation would suggest that relatively few 'Huns' have been identified because investigators have been looking for the wrong thing. The few burials full of reflex bows and the equipment of nomadic cavalry might represent, for instance, only a political elite defining themselves by a distinctive material culture, while the bulk of the Huns were buried in a totally different manner. .

The relevance of all this is well illustrated by the other area of archaeological study relevant to our concerns here. If Huns are, or seem to be, in short supply in the archaeological record, their Germanic subject peoples are not. The Hunnic empire of Attila comprised not only Huns, but also a very large number of largely, but not totally, Germanic subject groups, such as Goths, Gepids, Sciri, Rugi, and Suevi. Study of the remains of these groups had already made important beginnings by the time Werner wrote. It was clear to him, for instance, that the so-called *fürstengräber*, with which he closed his monograph, belonged to some of the leaders of these groups. Since the 1950s, however, the quantity of available evidence has mushroomed, and this has generated in its wake important advances in historical analysis. Again, I will not attempt to be comprehensive, but will merely provide a brief overview and some introductory bibliography.

A whole series of cultural horizons have now been identified (in chronological order, the so-called Villafontana, Untersiebenbrunn, and Domolospuszta/Bacsordas horizons), which succeeded one another in the Middle Danubian region in the first half of the fifth century. Two features of this material have particular historical importance. First, they demonstrate the emergence, west of the Carpathians, of what has come to be known as the 'Danubian style', which consists of a number of characteristic objects (large brooches with semi-circular heads, plate buckles, earrings with polyhedric pendants, and gold necklaces), characteristic weapons (saddles decorated with metal appliqués, long straight swords suitable for cavalry use, and particular kinds of arrow), and some new burial habits (cranial deformation and the deposition in burials of broken metallic mirrors). From the literary sources, we know that many different Germanic and other groups occupied the Middle Danube in the Hunnic period. The Danubian style, however, is common to the entire region, and it is quite impossible to place the different subject groups of the Huns on the basis of the archaeological evidence. The Hunnic empire thus managed to generate some unity in physical culture within its domain.

Second, the majority of burials contain few grave goods, or none at all. A minority, however, are richly endowed in the extreme, producing a vast array of gold fittings and ornamentation, particularly garnet-encrusted jewellery. The cultural horizons, indeed, are all named after such burials. As has often been argued, the gold wealth of these burials demonstrates that not only Huns, but also the elites of the various subject peoples, shared in the wealth generated by the predatory activities of the Hunnic empire. Puzzles still remain. In particular, debate still rages over the relationship of this material found west of the Carpathians to other remains from lands further east, north of the Black Sea, which were at least partly under Hunnic control. Despite such caveats, a new and convincing picture has emerged since Thompson wrote of the archaeological importance of the Hunnic Empire in generating new norms in central Europe (Bierbrauer, Tejral, Kazanski, and Kazanski and Legoux).

Matching these archaeological advances, there has been, since 1948, similarly profound extensions of anthropological and ethnographical understandings of nomadism. Thompson had read all the literature available to him at the time, but much work has been done since. In the early 1980s, for instance, Rudi Lindner attempted to apply anthropologically derived perspectives particularly to the Huns. This study first draws attention to the relatively restricted grazing room available on the Hungarian Plain (where the Huns were concentrated from *c*.420 at the latest) compared to the wider reaches of the Steppe. It then goes on to argue, the crux of the paper, that there was simply insufficient pasture west of the Carpathians for the Huns to maintain enough horses (each rider needing a string of ten remounts or more to be effective) to continue to operate as nomadic cavalry. Subjecting contemporary literary sources and the archaeological remains to intense scrutiny, Lindner finds no conclusive evidence that the Huns were still nomadic cavalry in the time of Attila (*c*.450), and concludes that, in adapting to their new environment, the Huns gave up their horses. This is a profoundly important argument, and I am unaware of any scholarly reply.

More generally, I would above all draw the reader's

attention to the fundamental study of the Russian scholar A. M. Khazanov, available conveniently in English translation since 1984. This is the first general, comparative account of pastoral nomadism in all its forms and geographical contexts, drawing equally on both ancient and modern Chinese and western literary sources, Russian observations of Eurasian nomadic societies, together with archaeological information, and an extensive knowledge of modern anthropological literature. The end result is a thematic comparative account of the subject, with chapters on such subjects as food production, historical origins, types of relation with the outside world, and possibilities, forms, and limits of state formation. There is, however, at the same time a particular emphasis on the Eurasian Steppe nomad, the larger classification in which we must place the Huns. Khazanov's earlier work concentrated on the Scythians, and, in the longer chapters subdivided by geographical region, Eurasian Steppe nomads receive more extensive treatment than any other particular group (their food production, origins, and state structures are discussed at respectively pp. 44–53, 90–7, and 233–63).

Overall, the book is concerned to advance two main arguments. First, nomads can remain nomads only by establishing a very particular set of relations with the outside world. Second, nomadism is not susceptible to any linear pattern of evolutionary development, tending rather to demonstrate circular or repetitive social patternings. The second of these goes well beyond Thompson's interests, which were focused very firmly on one particular nomad group, but the first greatly extends a line of argument to which Thompson himself subscribed (esp. p. 48 above). Khazanov devotes very little space to the Huns *per se* (a total of three brief comments), but the importance of his work can hardly be overstated; it introduces the broader context in which the history of the Huns must now be seen. The book also comes with a valuable introduction by Ernest Gellner, sketching in the Marxist ideological context of Khazanov's work.

Rather than attempting any further listing or categorization of my own, I would simply urge the reader to follow up Khazanov's footnotes for further guidance to the anthropological literature. Alternatively, I have personally found a recent volume by R. J. Cribb, on the problems and opportunities facing the archaeologist interested in nomadism, very helpful. Again, the book is thematic in approach. Chapters on methodological questions combine with particular studies, and extensive bibliographical reference in the footnotes, to provide both alternative, wider perspectives on the Hunnic problem, and plenty of information on further reading.

In writing this afterword, I am conscious that there is much that I have failed to cover. My aims, however, have been two-fold, and, in these at least, I do hope to have succeeded. First, I wanted to provide sufficient coverage of more recent scholarly literature in the main areas of relevance to Thompson's *Huns* to enable interested readers to follow up their own particular concerns. Second, it seemed to me desirable to make clear the relationship of Thompson's work, and the series of arguments of which it is composed, to the main historical studies which have been published subsequently. For the history of the Huns in eastern and central Europe in the period *c.* AD 370–470, as I hope to have made clear, Thompson's work remains fundamental. Subsequent scholars such as Maenchen-Helfen and Bona have taken their agenda from *The Huns*, and, in their writings, have engaged in extensive dialogue with it. Despite the approach of its fiftieth birthday, therefore, the book retains its importance as a, or, arguably, *the* central text shaping argument in the field (in Bona's characterization, a 'classic' and 'the first modern study of Hunnic history': *Das Hunnenreich*, p. 217), even if, on occasion, one might want to modify some of its conclusions. On a whole series of counts, therefore, it has been a great pleasure to help see this second edition of *The Huns* through to publication. I am only sorry that the author himself did not live long enough to see this project come to fruition, but am extremely happy to have had some chance to pay back just a little of the huge scholarly debt which I owe him.

Peter Heather
University College London

Acknowledgement

Much of the work involved in my contribution to this second, revised edition of *The Huns* was completed during my tenure of a Senior Fellowship at Dumbarton Oaks in autumn/winter 1994/5. I would like to express my profound thanks to the trustees for this award.

Appendix A

The Songs of the Huns

On the songs mentioned by Priscus[1] the reader should consult H. M. Chadwick, *The Heroic Age*, esp. pp. 84ff, idem, *The Growth of Literature*, i, p. 576, and, for the relations of such primitive singers with their audience, G. Thomson, *Marxism and Poetry* (London, 1946), pp. 22ff. Chadwick quotes an interesting parallel to the duet from *Widsith*, 103ff: 'Then Scilling and I began to sing with clear voices before our victorious lord; loudly rang out our music as we played the harp. Then it was openly confessed by many brave-hearted and experienced men that they had never heard a better song.' In our passage, however, nothing is said of an accompaniment. Chadwick[2] is inclined to believe that the two men were professional minstrels, and this seems probable enough. But one may be permitted to doubt Chadwick's view (accepted by Klaeber, p. 261) that the songs were rendered in the Gothic language. It is highly unlikely that there were any Goths present at the banquet, and it is impossible to believe that the Scourge of God had taken the trouble to learn Gothic. Even if he had, why should his minstrels sing his praises in a foreign language? I would also dissent from Chadwick's view[3] that, in listening to these songs, Attila 'was following Gothic custom', if by this we are to understand that the custom was not native to Hunnic society; rather, I would repeat the view expressed in another connection by Chadwick himself[4] that 'similar poetry is the outcome, or rather the expression, of similar social conditions'. Schröder's view that the songs sung by the barbarian girls as Attila rode into his village[5] were Gothic is in my opinion untenable.

By these criticisms I do not wish to conceal my debt to Chadwick's masterly volumes.

Appendix B

The Causes of the War of 441

A new view of the chronology of the events recounted in Priscus, frag. 1, has been proposed by Ensslin.[1] He points out that on 20 December 435, when serving on the commission which drew up the Theodosian Code, Epigenes was *Magister scriniorum*,[2] but on 15 November 438 he was *Magister memoriae*.[3] He therefore concludes that Epigenes' quaestorship, and consequently his embassy to Attila and the signature of the Treaty of Margus, must date from the end of 438 or later, for Priscus explicitly describes him in this fragment as quaestor.[4] This argument has been accepted by E. Stein[5] who, however, for an unstated reason dates the embassy to a year not earlier than 436.

I have rejected this argument. It seems incredible that Priscus, in this extract, should have given us a review of some five years of Romano-Hun relations without any chronological indication. The manoeuvres of Plintha to be allowed to conduct the negotiations with Attila are represented as following directly on his intrigues with regard to the negotiations with Rua. If Ensslin is correct, then Priscus is guilty of inconceivably bad writing. Furthermore, if this theory be accepted, it follows that Attila and the Romans waited for four years at least (434–8) before establishing diplomatic contacts with each other. This was not the way of the Huns. It seems much simpler to suppose that Priscus has prematurely described Epigenes as quaestor than to believe that frag. 1 covers four or five years of frontier history. Considering that Priscus wrote his book more than thirty years later, such a slip would be pardonable. In addition, with the traditional chronology of these years we can explain why the war of 441–3 was fought at all.

In 443 Attila demanded that the East Roman government should pay him 6,000 lb of gold in a lump sum. Why did he choose precisely this figure? Why not 5,000 lb or 7,000 lb? And why on this occasion alone did he demand the payment of a lump sum at all? The answer to these questions in my opinion is simple. The Peace of Margus was signed in 435, Theodosius paid none of the annual tribute, which had been fixed at 700 lb of gold, and Attila in 443 therefore demanded the arrears, fixing 6,000 lb as a round sum. Explicit evidence in favour of this reading of the events will be found in Priscus[6] where Attila expressly says that the war was caused by the non-payment of the tribute. If the Treaty of Margus dated only from 438 or 439, how did he arrive at the 6,000 lb?

Appendix C

Valips

Our only source of information about Valips is Priscus, frag. 1 *a*, where we are told how he seized Noviodunum. Who was he? Mommsen *ap.* Wescher[1] suggests that Valips' expedition, undertaken by the Rugi alone, was intended to be preparatory in some way to Attila's great invasion of 441. E. Polaschek[2] suggests that Valips was a Hun, but for three reasons this seems unlikely: (1) there is little room for a Hun commander capable of acting independently of Attila and Bleda on the Roman frontier at this date; (2) it is not likely that a foreigner other than Attila and Bleda could have incited the Rugi to go to war with the Romans at this time; (3) it is incredible that a Hun at this date would have shut himself up in a city and courted a siege, as Valips does here. I believe that Valips was a chieftain of some Rugi settled *inside* the Roman Empire; a study of Priscus' usage will show that the word νεωτερίζειν, which he uses at p. 278. 9, always implies a rebellion, not a foreign invasion. Consequently I have not subscribed to Mommsen's suggestion. Rappaport[3] errs in saying that the Rugi undertook this raid in company with the Huns: Priscus does not say that.

It is impossible to date the incident precisely. It must fall after 434, the date with which Priscus' narrative began. Again, since frags. 1 *a* and 1 *b* appear in the manuscript in the order in which they occurred in the original work, the siege of Noviodunum by Valips must be dated before the siege of Naissus by Attila in 441.

We can only say then that Valips took Noviodunum sometime in the period 434–41. L. Schmidt[4] dates Valips *c*.435, but gives no evidence. For some interesting remarks on the Rugi see Reynolds and Lopez[5] and add that Germanic philologists have also failed to offer a convincing etymology of Valips' name.

Appendix D

The Campaign of 441–3

Fragments 1 *b*, 2, and 3 are all that remain of Priscus' account of the great Hun invasion of the Eastern Empire in 441–3. Güldenpenning[1] puts frag. 3 before frag. 2 because (1) at the end of the former we hear of the capture of some forts of which Priscus speaks again at the beginning of frag. 2; (2) the beginning of frag. 3 tells of Attila's demand that the Romans should restore some Huns who had deserted to them, and this was his usual plea at the commencement of a war; (3) the Huns only cross the Danube in frag. 2: there is no mention of their crossing it in frag. 3, and therefore frag. 2 refers to a later stage in the campaign than frag. 3.[2]

This transposition is accepted by Bury[3] and by E. Stein[4] but not by Seeck.[5] I believe Seeck to be right in rejecting it.

The first of Güldenpenning's arguments can scarcely stand. There is no reason to suppose that the φρούριον (fort) of frag. 2 is one of the φρούριά τινα (some forts) of frag. 3. Why should the Roman ambassadors of frag. 2 complain to Attila of the capture of only one φρούριον if in fact several φρούρια and the large city of Ratiaria had also fallen? The Huns say, in reply to the ambassadors, ὡς οὐκ ἀρξάμενοι, ἀλλ' ἀμυνούμενοι ταῦτα δράσειαν ('that they had done these things not to initiate trouble, but as a response') (frag. 2). Surely this statement could only have been made at the beginning of a campaign? As for the third argument, the Huns *must* be across the river in frag. 3, for Ratiaria lay on the southern bank. The decisive phrase has been overlooked by Güldenpenning. In frag. 3 Attila sends a letter to Theodosius 'concerning the fugitives and the payments of tribute, all which had not been handed over to him on the pretext of the current state of war'. The last six words show that the war was already in progress and that frag. 3 did not tell of how it broke out.

But if the war begins in frag. 2, how does it come about that negotiations are in progress in frag. 3 and hostilities are at a standstill? The words τοῦδε τοῦ πολέμου ('the current state of war')[6] show that fighting has already taken place. When Attila says to the Romans εἰ . . . πρὸς πόλεμον ὁρμήσειαν ('if . . . they prepared for war'), we see that further fighting may well break out, as in fact it did. Evidently a temporary truce has been arranged. This is confirmed by Count Marcellinus, s.a. 441, who tells us that Aspar, the *Magister militum*, made a truce for one year with the Huns after the invasion had begun. I conclude then that frag. 2 tells of the beginning of the invasion of 441, and that frag. 3 tells of the breakdown of Aspar's one-year truce. Güldenpenning is right, however, in saying that frag. 1 *b* refers to events later than those of frags. 2 and 3.

Appendix E

Chronological Note on
the Years 449–50

The standard histories show some confusion as to the date of
Anatolius' final treaty with Attila. No date at all is given by Seeck.[1]
Bury[2] dates it loosely to '449–450'. The *CMH*[3] has '449?' I believe
that we can reach some certainty, if we remember that John of
Antioch, frag. 199, is a direct continuation of Priscus, frag. 14, as
was pointed out by E. W. Brooks.[4]

Since it is John's custom merely to transcribe his authorities
verbatim, it follows that we have in his frag. 199 Priscus' own
account of what happened when Anatolius returned from his
negotiations. Theodosius suspected the Isaurian Zeno of plotting a
rebellion and took measures to forestall him: he sent a certain
Maximinus to Isauropolis and dispatched a naval expedition to the
East. But in the midst of these activities, which cannot have
occupied more than a couple of months, the emperor received
news of Honoria's message to Attila, inviting him to attack the
Western Empire. Now Bury[5] has shown beyond doubt that this
news reached Theodosius about June of 450: therefore Anatolius'
final embassy to Attila must be dated to March or April of that
same year. But it is clear from Priscus, frags. 12–13, that Anatolius
set out not very long after Maximinus and Priscus had returned. I
have little doubt that Maximinus' embassy must be dated to the
autumn of 449, and Edeco's mission to Constantinople to the
spring or early summer of that year.

It is clear from this, I hope, that the traditional date of

Maximinus' embassy, 448, is improbable: an entire year cannot have elapsed between it and that of Anatolius. The chronology of the relations of the East Romans with the Huns in the last years of Theodosius, in my opinion, is correctly set out in the following table:

447   The invasion of the Eastern Empire by Attila.

448   Peace negotiations conducted by Anatolius (Marcellinus, s.a. 448).

449   Outstanding questions discussed by Edeco in Constantinople and by Maximinus in Attila's headquarters (Priscus, frags. 7–8).

450   Complete peace settlement arranged by Anatolius and Nomus.

This dating of Maximinus' embassy was first proposed by Tillemont,[6] but has been neglected since. Observe further that we have evidence in J. Fleming[7] that Martialis was *Magister officiorum* and that Zeno was *Magister militum per Orientem* in 449. Both of them are in these offices in Priscus, frags. 7–8, but we have no evidence that they held them in 448.

A final point calls for comment: who was the Maximinus whom Theodosius sent to Isauropolis in the early summer – doubtless at the beginning of the campaigning season – of 450? I think there can be little doubt that this was Priscus' friend, though the matter is not discussed in Ensslin's biography of Maximinus.[8] If Priscus had introduced a new Maximinus in the lost portion of his work which lay between frag. 12 (where the ambassador is last mentioned) and frag. 14+John, frag. 199, the Maximinus in the latter extract would require an adjective or a qualificatory phrase of some kind so as to distinguish him from the Maximinus who had dominated the narrative hitherto. In fact, he is given no qualification and hence must surely have been identical with the ambassador.

Priscus says in frag. 16 that he was in Rome on the eve of Attila's campaign in Gaul, that is, he was there in 450. But he refers in the first person plural to what he saw there – 'we saw, when we were in Rome . . . ' What is the meaning of the plural? Who was in Priscus' company on this occasion? We need have little hesitation in subscribing to the general view that it was Maximinus. Priscus was his *assessor* in 449 and again in 452–3, and he is unlikely to have been *assessor* to anyone else in the meantime. But if Maximinus was at Isauropolis in May (or thereabouts), the visit to Rome must be dated to the end of the year – say, November or December. The purpose of the embassy to Rome then was probably connected with the discussions between the two emperors occasioned by Honoria's intrigue with Attila. Beyond that we cannot go.

It has been pointed out by Ensslin[9] that on 8 November 450 a certain Maximinus *comes* was given a letter by Pope Leo at Rome to deliver to some churchmen at Constantinople, and that this Maximinus was Priscus' friend, in Ensslin's opinion, is very probable.[10] Now, Leo says that he is sending the letter *per illum nostrum Maximinum comitem* ('through our Count Maximinus), a very unlikely phrase if Maximinus was a pagan. Ensslin in fact believes that both Maximinus and Priscus were Christians; but I must admit that I do not find his arguments convincing and hesitate to accept this identification.

Appendix F

The Site of Attila's Headquarters

The only clue to the approximate site of Attila's chief village is provided by Priscus' statement that the journey to it involved the crossing of the rivers Δρήκων (Dreccon), Τίγας (Tigas), and Τιφήσας (Tiphesas), p. 300. 2.[1] That the ambassadors did not cross the Theiss is maintained by Güldenpenning,[2] Diculescu,[3] M. Fluss,[4] and by many others. They all place Attila's camp in the steppe north of Körös – see, for example, Güldenpenning[5] and Diculescu[6] – but no reasons are given. Now the Theiss had a vast variety of names in ancient writers and a further crop appears in medieval times: see the list given by J. Melich.[7] It will at once occur to the reader that none of the forms listed by Melich has the -γ- which appears in Priscus' Τίγας, and therefore Müllenhoff, cited by Melich, follows Tomaschek in supposing that Τίγας is a copyist's error for Τίσας. Fluss, P.-W. vi, 1469, agrees that Τίγας is corrupt and suggests Τίζας. This is having it both ways. Either (1) Τίγας is not the Theiss and Attila's camp *was* near Körös, or (2) Τίγας is an error for Τίσας or the like, in which case the ambassador *did* cross the Theiss and Attila's camp was *not* near Körös. In view of Priscus' statement that these were the largest rivers in the neighbourhood, I find it hard to believe that the Theiss is entirely omitted. If the second of these alternatives is rejected, we must suppose, it seems, that Priscus had never heard of the Theiss, which appears unlikely.

There is not enough evidence to identify the other two rivers with certainty, and an enormous number of guesses has been offered.[8] We can only say that, if we are right in supposing Priscus' Τίγας to conceal the name of the Theiss, the Τιφήσας should probably be equated with some river lying west of the Theiss.

Appendix G

The Alleged Gothic Names
of the Huns

Bury is following the vast majority of scholars when he writes as follows:[1] 'The most notable fact in the history of the Huns at this period is the ascendancy which their German subjects appear to have gained over them. The most telling sign of this influence is the curious circumstance that some of their kings were called by German names.' The German names of the Huns have become a matter of dogma among historians, but I must confess myself sceptical after examining the lists given by Moravcsik in his *Byzantinoturcica*. He has collected all the known Hun names without exception and has added a bibliography of studies of them. Now it is clear from his work that, for every scholar who claims such and such a Hun's name as Germanic, there is at least one other scholar who claims it as Turkish or the like. The names are so numerous, and this variation of opinion is so regular, that one is forced to the conclusion that the evidence is simply inadequate to allow us to reach any certainty. And it is easy to see why this must be so, for the bases on which the philologists are working are in many cases too insecure to permit scientific deductions to be drawn. Take the name of Ὀνηγήσιος (Onegesius) Hodgkin,[2] observing that it is unlikely that a Hun of such authority would have had this Greek name, suggests that this is a Greek form of some such name as Onégesh. On the other hand, Marquart[3] believes that the name is Gothic and is equivalent to Hunigis. It is clear that both proposals involve the assumption that Priscus thought the name sounded somewhat like a Greek name which was familiar to him and consequently *altered* it and made it into that Greek name. This assumption is unavoidable; but we can go farther. In a late document[4] Onegesius apparently is mentioned again, but this time the author who mentions him is not a Greek speaker, but a German speaker, and Onegesius becomes Hunagasius. This writer too has failed to give us the exact sounds which made up the man's name, but has altered them and given them a Germanic flavour.[5] Take as a second example the one Hun name which resembles a Latin word. Donatus was a Hun 'king' who lived north of the Black Sea and was visited by Olympiodorus *c*.412.[6] It is out of the question that he bore a Latin name. Olympiodorus, our sole authority for him, when he heard the name, thought that it resembled a Latin word which he knew – he was familiar with the Latin language – and so *altered* the name to a more congenial sound than the original. The point of all this is that the names given in our Greek texts, which we try to derive, have not been preserved in a phonetical transcription, but have been subjected to various alterations by our authorities. In fact, most Hun names must have reached our Greco-Roman authorities from oral Gothic sources, and so will have undergone a double alteration: they will have been approximated first to Germanic sounds and then to Greek or Roman ones. I do not wish to suggest that *all* Hun names have been changed out of recognition, but how can a philologist expect to derive such a name as *Rua*, which also appears as *Ruga, Rugila, Roilas*, etc?

In the text, then, I have not suggested that any Hun ever bore a Germanic name, and there is no ancient evidence that any Hun ever did. But there is excellent evidence for the reverse: the Goths often took on Hunnic names.[7] Those who are as sceptical of the philologists in this matter as the present writer is will welcome the article by Reynolds and Lopez listed in bibliography 8 below.

Notes

Introduction

1 Maenchen-Helfen, pp. 222–43.
2 Ed. of Gibbon, vol. iii, Appendix 6; but Bury later inclined to accept the identification: cf. his *Later Roman Empire*², i, p. 101.
3 J. Darkó, pp. 479ff; Moravcsik, *Byzantinoturcica*, i, pp. 28–9, ii, pp. 199–204.

1 Sources

1˙ Procopius, *BG.* viii. 19.8: 'the Huns are absolutely unacquainted with writing and unskilled in it up to the present time, and they neither have any writing-master nor do the children among them toil over their letters at all as they grow up'.
2 Jordanes, *Get.* iv. 28, v. 43: so too among the earlier Germans celebration in song was 'the people's one memorial and record of the past', Tacitus, *Germ.* ii. 3, cf. *Ann.* ii. 88. 4. On the Hunnic songs see Appendix A.
3 Cf. Lattimore, pp. 70, 329.
4 See Werner, pp. 236–8; Maenchen-Helfen, pp. 239ff; cf. Minns, p. 72.
5 For this see Nestor and Plopsor, pp. 178ff.
6 xxxi. 2. 1.
7 See Franz von Schwarz, *Turkestan, die Wiege der indogermanischen Völker*, Freiburg-im-Breisgau, 1900, p. 89, n. 1. The story is also told of the early Hungarians, a fact which still occasions pain to some Hungarians: see A. Solymossy, 'La Légende de "la viande amortie sous la selle"', *Nouvelle Revue de Hongrie*, xxx, 1937, pp. 134–40.

8 Maenchen-Helfen, p. 234; cf. Alföldi, *Gnomon*, ix, 1933, p. 565.
9 Maenchen-Helfen, p. 234, n. 76.
10 Amm. xxxi. 2. 11 'ad omnem auram incidentis spei novae perquam mobiles' ('strongly inclined to sway to the breeze of every new hope'); Livy, xxix. 3. 13 'gente ad omnem auram spei mobili atque infida'.
11 *Skythien und der Bosporus* (Berlin, 1931), p. 103.
12 For further information about this interesting author see *Classical Quarterly*, xxxviii, 1944, pp. 43–52, and Haedicke, P.-W.s.v.
13 Zosimus begins to use Olympiodorus as his source at v. 26.
14 Moravcsik, *Ung. Jbb.* x, 1930, pp. 53ff; Thompson, *CQ.* xxxix, 1945, pp. 92–4.
15 *Menschen die Geschichte machten*, i, p. 229, cf. p. 230.
16 *Later Roman Empire*, edn 1 (1889), i, p. 223; the remark does not recur in edn 2.
17 I am glad to note that this conclusion has already been reached by Reynolds and Lopez, p. 48.
18 Priscus, pp. 341. 16; 291. 4. If Edeco was a German, why had Chrysaphius to speak to him through Bigilas, the interpreter of the Hunnic language?
19 Priscus, pp. 287. 19; 297. 26: see p. 111, ch. 5, n. 26 below.
20 Cf. N. H. Baynes, *Journal of Roman Studies*, xii, 1922, p. 225.
21 Ed. of Gibbon, vol. iii, Appendix I, p. 483; *Later Roman Empire²*, vol. ii, p. 418.
22 Ed. of Jordanes, p. xxxiv f.; but I see no reason for believing that *Get.* iii. 21 on the Screrefennae is from Priscus. Mommsen denies, for unconvincing reasons, that the account of Bleda's death in *Get.* xxxv. 181 is derived from Priscus.
23 p. 358. 8, Bonn; cf. *Chron. Pasch.* p. 587. 9, Bonn: but see p. 24 below.
24 ii. 16, 'most accurate', cf. i. 17.
25 ii. 1; v. 24.
26 See Appendix E.
27 The contrary is argued unconvincingly by J. Haury, ed. of Procopius, vol. i, pp. vii–viii.
28 Procopius, *BG.* viii. 5. 10; *BV.* iii. 4. 30; cf. Gibbon, *Decline and Fall*, vol. iii, p. 468, n. 50.
29 Alföldi, *Gnomon*, ix, 1933, p. 563 n., has promised us a new volume of *Hunnenstudien*.

2 The History of the Huns before Attila

1 Amm. xxxi. 2. 1.
2 See Vasiliev, pp. 24ff.

3 Zosimus, iv. 20 (a slightly different version); Sozomen, vi. 37; Jordanes, *Get.* xxiv. 123–5 (Priscus is expressly mentioned as his source); Procopius, *BG.* viii. 5. 7ff; Agathias, v. 11, etc.

4 Frag. 41; Vasiliev, l.c.

5 Sozomen, vi. 37. 3; Aeschylus, *PV.* 681, cf. 729ff.

6 e.g. Vasiliev, p. 30; L. Schmidt, *Geschichte*, pp. 251ff. There is a considerable literature in Hungarian on this story which is inaccessible to me: see *Byzantion*, vi, 1931, p. 679.

7 Zosimus, iv. 20. 3; the βασίλειοι Σκύθαι, Herodotus, iv. 20. 1ff, etc.; the σιμοί, id. iv. 23. 2.

8 Philostorgius, ix. 17 (p. 123. 12ff); Herodotus, iv. 17 and 105. For Eunapius and Philostorgius see Bidez's edn of the latter, p. cxxxviii.

9 *Hist.* i. 2. 45; vii. 33. 9ff.

10 Jerome, *Ep.* lxxvii. 8; Herodotus, i. 103ff. Contrast the restraint of Ambrose in Migne, *PL.* xv. 1898.

11 *BG.* viii. 5, I.

12 *De adm. Imp.*, p. 123, Bonn.

13 Ed. Bonn, p. 27. 566, 574ff.

14 *Alleg. Iliad.* proleg. 427.

15 Libanius, *Ep.* 369. 9; Sidonius, *Ep.* viii. 2. 2.

16 *Ep.* i. 6. 2.

17 *Get.* xxiv. 121ff.

18 On this word see J. de Vries, *Altgermanische Religionsgeschichte*, vol. i (Berlin and Leipzig, 1935), p. 264, cited by Maenchen-Helfen, p. 245.

19 *Contra*, Maenchen-Helfen, pp. 244–51, who believes the tale to be based on the Christian, or late Jewish, legend of the fallen angels. Herbert, p. 281 n., refers to an English parallel in the *Faerie Queene*, bk. 2, c. 10, st. 8.

20 So Diculescu, p. 19.

21 Malalas, pp. 282. 18, 303. 3, Bonn; cf. Zonaras, xii. 30.

22 *Vita Constantini*, ed. H. G. Opitz, *Byzantion*, ix, 1934, p. 586.

23 *v.* 752: besides Φροῦνοι, the MSS also give Φρουροί, Φρούριοι, etc.: see Müller, *ad loc.*; Maenchen-Helfen, p. 248.

24 See W. W. Tarn, *The Greeks in Bactria and India* (Cambridge, 1938), pp. 84ff.

25 Dionysius, *v.* 730: see Kiessling, P.-W. viii. 2953ff; Maenchen-Helfen, pp. 250ff.

26 See the lists in Moravcsik, *Byzantinoturcica*, vol. ii, pp. 199–204.

27 John Lydus, *De Mag.* iii. 52; Seeck, *Untergang*, v, p. 466.

28 Amm. xxxi. 4. 1–4.

29 Ib., 2. 13 and 16.

30 Ib., §§ 17–25, 'they did not know the meaning of slavery'.

31 On its extent see L. Schmidt, *Geschichte*, pp. 240ff.

32 Sozomen, vi. 37. 5, 'The Huns first made an attempt to attack the Goths with a few soldiers. But afterwards they raised a powerful army, and conquered the Goths in battle, etc.', Vasiliev, pp. 23ff.

33 Amm. xxxi. 3. 2.

34 Ib., § 3; Sozomen, l.c. Jordanes' narrative in *Get*. xlviii. 249 is merely saga, and cannot be accepted as historical: see L. Schmidt, *Geschichte*, pp. 253–7.

35 Jordanes, l.c., § 248.

36 Amm., l.c.

37 Amm. xxxl 3. 4–8.

38 Ib., §§ 7–8.

39 Ib., § 8.

40 Amm. xxxi. 4. 3, *aspernanter*.

41 On the date of the crossing see Seeck, *Untergang*, v, p. 466. The figure of 200,000, given by Eunapius, frag. 42, is much exaggerated; Amm. xxxi. 4. 6 says expressly that all efforts to count the Goths failed.

42 On the site see W. Judeich, 'Die Schlacht bei Adrianopel', *Deutsche Zeitschrift für Geschichtswissenschaft*, vi, 1891, p. 5, n. I.

43 Amm. xxxi. 8. 4f.

44 Ib., 16. 3.

45 Id., 12.17 mentions a band of Alan cavalry.

46 Paneg. Lat. xii (ii), 11. 4; cf. Victor, *Epit*. 47. 3; Philostorgius, xi. 8.

47 *Chron. Min*. i, p. 243; Victor, *Epit*. 48. 5; Zosimus, iv. 34. 6.

48 Victor, *Epit*. 47. 3; cf. Ausonius, *Prec. cos*. 31.

49 Marcellinus, s.a.

50 Cf. Alföldi, *Untergang*, ii, pp. 66ff, 71ff.

51 Ambrose, *Ep*. 24; Migne, *PL*. xvi. 1081; cf. Ensslin, *Phil. Wochenschr*. xlvii, 1927, col. 847.

52 Claudian, *De cons. Stil*. i. 110; Ausonius, *Epigr*. xxvi. 8.

53 Claudian, *In Rufin*. ii. 26ff, 36; Philostorgius, xi. 8; Sozomen, viii. 25. 1; Caesarius, *Dial*. i. 68 (Migne, *PG*. xxxviii. 936), who says that the enemy was 'often seen in tens of thousands'.

54 See p. 42. Claudian's rumour is repeated by Socrates, vi. 1. 6; Joshua Stylites, ix (p. 8, trans. Wright); and cautiously ($\dot{\epsilon}\lambda\dot{\epsilon}\gamma\epsilon\tau o$) by Sozomen, viii. 1. 2.

55 Claudian, *In Rufin*. ii. 28–35; *In Eutrop*. i. 16ff, ii. 569–75.

56 Ib., i. 243–51; Joshua Stylites, ix, xii (pp. 7ff, 12, Wright).

57 Philostorgius, xi. 8; Socrates, vi. 1. 7; Sozomen, viii. 1. 2.

58 *Epp*. lx. 16, lxxvii. 8.

59 Joshua Stylites, ix (p. 8, Wright), 'all Syria was delivered into their hands by . . . the supineness of the general [$\sigma\tau\rho\alpha\tau\eta\lambda\dot{\alpha}\tau\eta\varsigma$] Addai' (i.e. Addaeus).

60 Claudian, *In Eutrop.* ii. 572, *nullo obstante.*
61 Ib. i. 242 *Getas.*
62 Ib. ii. 223–5.
63 Ib. 572.
64 Ib. 122.
65 See, for example, Gibbon, *Decline and Fall,* iii, p. 262, ed. Bury.
66 vii. 37. 3.
67 Procopius, *De Aed.* iv. 6. 33, who says that it was restored by Justinian, having fallen down from neglect; cf. Amm. xxxi. 11. 6: modern Kula in Bulgaria.
68 Sozomen, ix. 5: see pp. 63, 219–20.
69 *CTh.* xi. 17. 4 = xv. I. 49.
70 *CTh.* vii. 16. 2, of 24 April 410.
71 Ib. 17. I, to Constans, the Magister militum per Thracias.
72 Themistius, *Or*, xviii 223B; cf. Van Millingen, *Byzantine Constantinople*, p. 42.
73 *CTh*, xv. I. 51, cf. Socrates, vii. I. 3; Dessau, *ILS.* 5339.
74 *Selected Essays*, pp. 234 ff.
75 Marquart, *Ērānšāhr*, p. 97, believes that they returned from Atropatene past Baku, crossed the lower Daghestan, and so reached the pass of Derbend.
76 Socrates, vii. 18. 4.
77 *Chron. Min.* ii, p. 75, s.a. 422 *Hunni Thraciam vastaverunt*: cf. Seeck, *Untergang*, vi, p. 86.
78 Paneg. Lat. xii (ii). 32. 4.
79 Paneg. Lat. xii (ii). 32. 4.
80 Ib. 35ff; Seeck, *Untergang*, v, p. 215.
81 Ambrose, *Ep.* 24 (Migne, *PL.* xvi. 1081).
82 Zosimus, v. 22. 1–3; *Chron. Min.* ii, p. 66; cf. Alföldi, *Untergang*, ii, p. 69. That payments were made to the Huns even before this may result from Synesius, *De Regno* xi (Migne, *PG.* lxvi. 1081). For the aftermath of this incident see p. 60–1.
83 Zosimus, v. 19. 6f. (from Eunapius); see p. 93.
84 *Chron. Min.* i, p. 652 'exercitum . . . hostium circumactis Chunorum auxiliaribus Stilicho usque ad internicionem delevit'; ib. ii, p. 69 'captivos . . . singulis aureis distrahentes'; Zosimus, v. 26. 4.
85 Greg. Tur. ii. 8; cf. Ensslin, l.c., col. 850.
86 Merobaudes, *Paneg.* ii, 3ff, 127ff.
87 Zosimus, v. 45. 6, cf. 37. 1 (both from Olympiodorus).
88 Ib., 50. 1ff, from Olympiodorus: see p. 53.
89 Philostorgius, xii. 4 (p. 150, Bidez): *Chron. Min* i, p. 471. 658; Greg. Tur. ii. 8: On this figure see p. 55.

90 Claudian, *In Rufin.* ii. 76 f.; *Chron. Min.* i, p. 650 *Chunorum, quo fulciebatur, praesidio.*
91 Zosimus, v. 34. I.
92 Claudian, *In Rufin.* i. 328; Theodoret in Migne, *PG.* lxxxiii. 1405; cf. Herodotus, i. 216.
93 Claudian, *In Rufin.* i. 324; Priscus, p. 348. 9; Sozomen, vii. 26.8; Amm. xxxi. 2.2, cf. 11; Jerome, *Ep.* lx. 16, lxxvii. 8; Jordanes, *Get.* xxiv. 121; Procopius, *BP.* i. 3. 5; Zachariah, p. 152, transl. Hamilton and Brooks.
94 xxxi. 3. 8: see Eunapius, frag. 42 init. on the Goths.
95 Callinicus, *Vita S. Hypatii*, 3.8–11: see p. 30.
96 Ib., p. 64. 21ff.
97 Sozomen, vii. 26. 6.
98 Ib., § 7 'it is said'(λέγεται), § 9 'they say' (φασί).
99 Sozomen, vii. 26. 6, §§ 6–10.
100 Ib., § 8.
101 Theodoret, *HE.* v. 31; see *Hermathena*, lxvii, 1946, p. 75.
102 Jerome, *Ep.* cvii. 2; Orosius, vii. 41. 8; Theodoret in Migne, *PG.* lxxxiii. 1405, cf. 1009.
103 *Apoth.* 430ff: he calls the Huns 'Geloni'.
104 See, for example, Procopius, *BG.* v. 10. 29; Agathias, v. 13, p. 368, Dindorf.
105 pp. 224, 152, Hamilton and Brooks.
106 Saffet, p. 9.

3 Hun Society before Attila

1 xxxi. 2. 3 *cuiusvis pecoris* ('any kind of animal') – but not pigs: see G. F. Hudson *ap.* Toynbee, *A Study of History*[2], iii, p. 11 n.; cf. Parker, p. 83.
2 Lattimore, pp. 74–5 and esp. 413; Peisker, p. 331.
3 Amm., l.c., § 5; Jordanes, *Get.* v. 37 'Now the Hunuguri are known to us from the fact that they trade in marten skins'; cf. Justin, ii. 2. 9 (of the Scythians), and other passages cited by Wagner-Erfurdt on Amm. xxxi. 2. 5.
4 Amm., l.c.; Fox, p. 114.
5 Amm., l.c., § 6: a description of such *galeri* or *tiarae* will be found in Jerome, *Ep.* lxiv. 13.
6 Amm. xxxi. 2. 21; Priscus *ap.* Jordanes, *Get.* xxiv. 123, who may, of course, have misrepresented him; cf. Claudian, *In Rufin.* i. 327 *praeda cibus*, 'the chase supplies their food' (Platnauer).
7 Amm. xxxi. 2. 3.
8 Ib. 2. 10; Sozomen, vi. 37. 4, is absurd to endow them with an interest in γεωργία (farming).

9 xxxi. 2. 8; Tac. *Germ.* vi. 5, vii. 3.

10 Peisker, p. 334.

11 *Later Roman Empire*[2], i, p. 102; Peisker, p. 333; cf. Fox, p. 43.

12 Priscus, p. 298. 29.

13 Amm. xxxi. 2. 4.

14 l.c., § 7.

15 Fox, pp. 77, 106; cf. Seeck, *Untergang*, vi, p. 280. 9.

16 Amm. xxxi. 2. 25; cf. the *duces* of the Germans in Tac. *Germ.* vii. 1–2.

17 Amm. xxxi. 2. 7.

18 Lattimore, pp. 66–8.

19 Fox, p. 43.

20 See the very illuminating graph in Hobhouse, etc., p. 237.

21 Fox, p. 47, and see Priscus, pp. 309. 3, 321. 2, cf. 326. 13.

22 Parker, pp. 12, 15, 159, *et passim.*

23 Quoted without disapproval by H. Leclercq, *Dict. d'arch. chrét.* VII. ii. 2793, s.v. 'Huns'.

24 Those who, despite Ammianus' description of the methods of producing food at the disposal of the Huns, believe their numbers to have been anywhere near this figure should ponder over some observations uttered by a Chinese general in AD 11 and recorded in Parker, pp. 57ff: see also Lattimore, p. 438.

25 p. 38; Zosimus, v. 50. I, from Olympiodorus.

26 *Ap.* Zosimus, v. 45. 6: see p. 38.

27 Agathias, p. 367. 22, Dindorf.

28 Amm. xxxi. 2. 11.

29 Philostorgius, xii. 14: see p. 39.

30 p. 281. I.

31 p. 284. 14; cf. p. 344. 22.

32 pp. 292. 7, 296. 5.

33 p. 313. 1.

34 Jordanes, *Get.* xxxv. 182 'His army *is said* to have numbered five hundred thousand men.'

35 Procopius, *BV.* i. 5. 18–19; note Fox, p. 147.

36 I take the phrase from Peisker, p. 350.

37 Bury, *Later Roman Empire*, i. pp. 103 ff.

38 *Untergang*, v, p. 214.

39 Note Zosimus, v. 22. 3, discussed pp. 60–1; Procopius, *BP.* i. 21. 16, *BV.* iii. 18. 17, and the passages cited at ch. 2, n. 104.

40 Amm. xxxi. 2. 2; Claudian, *In Rufin.* i. 325; Sidonius, *Carm.* ii. 245 (transl. Anderson); Jordanes, *Get.* xxiv. 127–8; Jerome, *Ep.* lx. 17; cf. Procopius, *BP.* i. 3. 4.

41 Amm. xxxi. 2. 6; Zosimus, iv. 20. 4; Jerome, *Ep.* lx. 17; Suidas, s.v.

ἐν τῷ βαδίζειν σφαλλόμενοι τούτεστιν οἱ Οὖννοι; Priscus, pp. 277. 5, 304. 16, etc.

42 See a good example in W. P. Webb, *The Great Plains* (Oxford, 1931), pp. 167ff.

43 Amm. xxxi. 2. 6 'certainly hardy but ugly'; Jerome, *Ep.* lx. 17; Lattimore, p. 58.

44 Orosius, vii. 34. 5 '[the tribes] were equipped with Roman horses and arms'.

45 Amm. xxxi. 2. 6; Claudian, ib. 330ff. 'of incredible swiftness, they often return to battle quite unexpectedly'; Zosimus, iv. 20. 4 'they wrought immense slaughter by wheeling, charging, retreating in good time, and firing arrows from their horses'; Jerome, *Ep.* lxxvii. 8 'Hunorum examina . . . pernicibus equis huc illucque volitantia'; Agathias, i. 22.

46 Sidonius, *Carm.* ii. 266ff: 'Shapely bows and arrows are their delight, sure and terrible are their hands; firm is their confidence that their missiles will bring death, and their frenzy is trained to do wrongful deeds with blows that never go wrong.'

47 Cf. Jerome, quoted p. 31, and Nestorius quoted p. 68. On their tactics see E. Darkó, pp. 449ff. It is significant that the Persians had less to fear from them: see p. 35.

48 Amm. xxxi. 2. 9: see p. 7.

49 Amm., l.c. *lacinia* (lasso). Some good examples will be found in the references cited by Wagner-Erfurdt, ad loc. I regret that I cannot consult Gy. Moravcsik, 'A hunok taktikájához', *Körösi Csoma-Archivum*, i, 1921–5, pp. 276–80: one gathers from *Byzantion*, vi, 1931, pp. 685ff, that the author shows from Byzantine writers that other peoples systematically used the lasso in warfare.

50 Cf. p. 43 above; Sozomen, vii. 26. 8.

51 Lattimore, pp. 64ff; Alföldi, *Funde*, p. 19.

52 Olympiodorus, frag. 18; Amm. xxxi. 2. 9; Sidonius, *Carm.* ii. 266–9; Jordanes, *Get.* xlviii. 249; Procopius, *BG.* i. 27. 27.

53 Aetius: Greg. Tur. ii. 8, cf. p. 38 above. Scythian bows: Claudian, *iii cos. Hon.* 27; Vegetius, i. 20, with Alföldi, *Funde*, p. 24.

54 This seems to be implied by Orosius, vii. 34.5, quoted above; cf. the shield in Sozomen, vii. 26.8.

55 See p. 43: Zosimus, v. 22.3 (from Eunapius) φυγάδες γὰρ οἰκέται καὶ ἄλλως τὰς τάξεις ἀπολιπόντες.

56 Vegetius, i. 20; see p. 60.

57 Leo, *Problemata*, vii. 9, p. 48, ed. Dain. Leo is drawing verbally on Urbicius, vii. I, in Jo. Scheffer, *Arriani Tactica* (Uppsala, 1664), p. 137.

58 Procopius, *BG.* viii. 19. 14.

59   xxxi. 2. 11 and 12.
60   Jordanes, *Get.* xxiv. 130; xlviii. 248, 249, cf. L. Schmidt, *Geschichte*, pp. 253–7. The attempt of Marquart, *Streifzüge*, pp. 368f, to combine the saga of Jordanes with the history of Ammianus seems to the present writer to be unconvincing. Observe that a Germanic name like Balamber is impossible among the Huns at this – or perhaps any – period: see Appendix G.
61   vi. 37. 5, quoted at ch. 2, n. 32.
62   Frag. 18: see pp. 11–12.
63   Zosimus, v. 22. 1.
64   P.-W. viii. 2601.
65   Cf. Alföldi, *Untergang*, ii, p. 67.
66   I take the date, but not the interpretation, of Jordanes, *Get.* xxxiii. 173–5 from Diculescu, pp. 53–5.
67   *Untergang*, ii, p. 69.
68   *Untergang*, vi, p. 282.
69   *Later Roman Empire*, i, p. 104 n. He is also inaccurate in his remark (op. cit., p. 271) that Rua 'seems to have brought together all the tribes into a sort of political unity': cf. Jordanes, *Get.* xxxv. 180. Similarly, Grousset, p. 117, misleadingly says that it was Balamber who led 'the Huns' across the Volga and the Dnieper: even Attila on his accession was not ruler of *all* the Huns (Priscus, frag. 1).
70   Amm. xxxi. 3. I *uberes pagos*.
71   *The Bazaar of Heracleides*, p. 366, transl. Driver and Hodgson.

4 The Victories of Attila

1   Jordanes, *Get.* xxxv. 180. For the various forms of his name in our authorities see Seeck, P.-W. (*Zw. R.*) i. 1157, and note that the form *Roilas* is found in John of Nikiu, § 85, transl. Charles: cf. Appendix G.
2   See pp. 38, 40. For these events see *Chron. Min.* i, pp. 473ff, 658; ii, p. 22, with J. de Lepper, *De rebus gestis Bonifatii Comitis Africae* (Tilburg, 1941), pp. 107–9.
3   *Chron. Min.* ii, p. 76, cf. Jordanes, *Get.* xxxii. 166, and see Ensslin, *Phil. Wochenschr.* xlvii, 1927, pp. 846ff.
4   Priscus, p. 286. 25; *Chron. Min.* i, p. 660 'Rugila king of the Huns, with whom peace had been made, dies'.
5   Priscus, p. 296. 31; Cassiodorus, *Var.* i. 4. 11.
6   For these see *Chron. Min.* i, p. 658, s.a. 433.
7   p. 33. See H. de Claparède, *Les Burgondes jusqu'en 443* (Geneva, 1909), pp. 26–9, but cf. Coville, pp. 101–4.
8   Jerome, *Chron.* s.a. 2389 (misunderstood by Orosius, vii. 32. 11, who gives them 80,000 *warriors*, and so Bury, op. cit. i. p. 106); Amm. xxviii. 5. 9.

9 Claparède, pp. 29–34, but his conclusions cannot be pressed, cf. Coville, p. 104.

10 Sid. Ap. *Carm.* vii. 234ff.

11 *Chron. Min.* i, p. 475, s.a. 435; ii, p. 22, s.a. 436; Sidonius, l.c., with Anderson's note.

12 *Chron. Min.* ii, p. 23, s.a. 437; i, p. 660, s.a. 436, cf. p. 475. I follow Waitz, pp. 3ff. Bury, op. cit. i, p. 249, n. 3, rightly says that 'the number of 20,000 is of course an exaggeration'.

13 Socrates, vii. 30. 1–6: Reading, ad loc., denies the historicity of the story, which is not mentioned, for example, by Bury, op. cit., or by Seeck, *Untergang*; but see Coville, pp. 99ff.

14 Sid. Ap. *Carm.* vii. 322; Procopius, *BG.* v. 12. 11; cf. Claparède, pp. 33ff.

15 Id. p. 33, n. 4.

16 Sid. Ap. *Carm.* vii. 234ff, 241ff.

17 Ib., 248ff.

18 Ib., 251ff.

19 Prosper, s.a. 436.

20 *Chron. Min.* i, p. 475 s.a.

21 Ib., p. 476 s.a.

22 *Chron. Min.* ii, p. 23, s.a. 438; cf. Mommsen, *Ges. Schr.* iv, p. 535.

23 Salvian, *De Gub. Dei*, vii. 9. 39 'praesumeremus nos in Chunis spem ponere, illi in deo'.

24 Prosper, s.a. 439.

25 Salvian, vii. 9. 39ff.

26 Prosper, s.a. 439. For the two battles outside Toulouse see A. Loyen, pp. 47–50.

27 Cf. A. Loyen, *Bulletin de la société archéologique et historique de l'Orléanais*, xxii, 1935, p. 502.

28 For their social organization see the well-known passage of the *Querolus*, p. 58, ed. Hermann. Hermann, *Revue belge de philologie et d'histoire*, vii, 1928, pp. 1217ff., doubts that the reference is to the Bagaudae, but adduces no convincing reason. No doubts are expressed by F. Lot, *La Gaule* (Paris, 1947), pp. 472ff.

29 Seeck, *Untergang*, vi, p. 115; for Amandus, etc., see id. P.-W. ii. 2766ff.

30 *Chron. Min.* i, p. 660 'omnia paene Galliarum servitia in Bacaudam conspiravere'.

31 Ib., cf. Sidonius, *Carm*, vii. 246 f. 'Litorius . . . elated by the conquest of the Aremoricans'.

32 *Later Roman Empire*, i, p. 250.

33 *Paneg.* ii. 8ff, cf. John of Antioch, frag. 201. 3 (from Priscus).

34 See the excellent summary of Aetius' ruinous career in E. Stein,

Geschichte, i, pp. 501–17.

35 Theodoret, *Ep.* 22, Sakellion.

36 The names are given in Priscus, p. 276. 7, cf. Jordanes, *Get.* xxiv. 126, who seems to distinguish them from the Huns: but who else could they have been? They are regarded as Huns by Tomaschek, P.-W.i. 1835; Kiessling, ib. viii. 2603; Seeck, *Untergang*, vi, p. 461, etc. The Itimari are identified by Marquart, *Streifzüge*, p. 356 n., with the *Dirmar* of Zachariah of Mitylene, p. 328.

37 *Chron. Min.* ii, p. 73, s.a. 418, corrected by Seeck, *Untergang*, vi, p. 484.

38 Socrates, v. 23. 12; Sozomen, vji. 17. 14.

39 Priscus, p. 276. 14–24.

40 April or May 434: see *Chron. Min.* i, p. 660, with Seeck, *Untergang*, vi, p. 460.

41 Socrates, vii. 43; Theodoret, *HE.* v. 37. 4; John of Nikiu, lxxxiv, § 85. It was a Dean of Manchester who first explained how the miracle arose: see Herbert, pp. 325ff. This text of Ezekiel did good service again during the first Russian attack on Constantinople in 860–1, cf. A. A. Vasiliev, *The Russian Attack on Constantinople in 860* (Mediaeval Academy of America), 1946, pp. 166–8.

42 Theophanes, p. 102. 16, explicitly describes Bleda as the elder, a piece of information which undoubtedly goes back to Priscus, Theophanes' source for the Huns. Priscus, curiously enough, always mentions Bleda second in the extant fragments; but in *Chron. Min.* i, p. 660, s.a. 434, we read 'Rugila, king of the Huns, dies; Bleda succeeds him', and Marcellinus, s.a. 442, has *Bleda et Attila.*

43 Priscus, frag. 11 = Suidas, s.v. Ζέρκων. Zerco reappears on p. 129.

44 *Decline and Fall*, iii, pp. 418ff.

45 For the date see Appendix B. Observe the power of the East Roman Senate, cf. Helm, pp. 397ff.

46 *CIL.* iii. 8140.

47 Priscus, pp. 276. 24–277. 10.

48 Priscus, p. 277. 11–27: on the date see Appendix B.

49 Ib., p. 278. 1.

50 Romulus *ap.* Priscus, p. 312. 19.

51 *Decline and Fall*, iii, p. 421. Hodgkin, p. 42, n. 2, asks whether this northward drive of the Huns had any effect on the migrations of the English to Britain between the years 430 and 450.

52 Priscus, p. 312. 20.

53 See the passages of Prosper and Jordanes cited at ch. 4, n. 107.

54 Priscus, p. 277. 29 Καρσῷ, cf. Procopius, *De Aed.* iv. II. 20; *Itin. Ant.* 224. 4, etc.; despite G. Tocilescu, *Arch.-epigraph. Mitth. aus*

Oesterreich–Ungarn, xiv, 1891, p. 16, it seems doubtful whether the correct form was *Carsium*. Patsch, P.-W. iii. 1616, overlooks Priscus here.

55 See Appendix B.
56 Cf. Bury, *Later Roman Empire*, i, p. 72, n. 2.
57 Priscus, p. 278. 4–20: see Appendix C.
58 p. 34, cf. Vegetius, iv. 45.
59 *Nov. Val.* ix, of 24 June 440.
60 E. Stein, pp. 436, 440.
61 *Vita S. Danielis Styl.* 56.
62 Theophanes, A.M. 5942 (wrong date), cf. Bury, op. cit. i, p. 255, n. 3.
63 Prosper, s.a. 441.
64 For this Persian invasion see Bury, op. cit. ii, pp. 5ff.
65 See p. 83: on the chronology of Priscus, frags. 1 *b*, 2, and 3, see Appendix D.
66 Priscus, p. 280. 5–7.
67 Priscus, by his use of the terms ὀλιγωρίας (contempt) and κατωλιγώρουν (rejection of arbitration) at p. 280. 9. 19, tries to shift the blame on to the Huns.
68 Procopius, *De Aed.* iv. 5. 17: observe that Priscus said nothing of the circumstances of the capture of this important city, a striking illustration of his lack of interest in military affairs.
69 See E. Gren, p. 61.
70 Priscus, frag. 2.
71 Theophanes, AM 5942, p. 102. 22, cf. Not. Dign. xli. 33 'praefectus militum . . . contra Margum in castris Augustoflavianensibus', but the exact site cannot be determined: see Patsch, P.-W. iv. 951.
72 Procopius, *De Aed.* iv. 5. 13; Marcellinus, s.a. 441.
73 Priscus, p. 302. 20. That Sirmium fell in this invasion, and not that of 447, was shown by Alföldi, *Untergang*, ii, p. 96. On Justinian, *Nov.* xi, see E. Stein, *Rhein. Mus.* lxxiv, 1925, pp. 355ff.
74 Marcellinus, s.a. 441.
75 Prosper, s.a. 441 'Siciliae magis oneri quam Africae praesidio fuere'.
76 Procopius, *De Aed.* iv. 5. 6.
77 Marcellinus, s.a. 441; John of Antioch, frag. 206.
78 Priscus, p. 281. 11.
79 See A. Blanchet, pp. 97ff.
80 Ib., p. 101, n. 2.
81 Ib., p. 102.
82 Priscus, frag. 3.
83 Ib., pp. 281. 23; 318. 32. It is the modern Artscher in Bulgaria.
84 Ib., p. 318. 32, cf. Not. Dign. Or. xlii. 43; xi. 38.
85 On its site see R. Roesler, pp. 843ff.

86   Amm. xxi. 10. 5 *copiosum oppidum.*
87   Procopius, *De Aed.* iv. 1. 34; 4. 122.
88   For Priscus' literary account of a siege see *CQ.* xxxix, 1945, pp. 92–
4. He says that he saw a bridge connecting Naissus with the left
bank of the river, and he asserts that this was constructed by the
Huns so that their forces could approach the city easily. I find this
hard to believe. Is it likely that Attila would have wasted time in
bridge-building in the middle of a campaign, even if he had with
him men competent to carry out such an operation? And was this
great city entirely unconnected with the left bank of the river
throughout antiquity until the nomads linked it up? Finally, the
nomads were already on the same side of the river as Naissus. The
sentence referring to the construction of the bridge is probably
nothing more than an unhappy guess on the historian's part.
89   Priscus, p. 290. 3 Σερδικῆς δῃωθείσης: see p. 114.
90   Theophanes, p. 102. 21ff.
91   Ib., p. 102. 24.
92   Ib., p. 102. 25ff. On its site and importance see Agathias, p. 371,
Dindorf. It was not far from the village of Melanthias, which lay
only seventeen miles from the capital.
93   Priscus, p. 282. 25.
94   Ib., p. 284. 9–15. Note the valour of Asemus in AD 593: the citizen
militia mentioned in Theophylactus, vii. 3, may have been first
organized in the days of Attila.
95   Priscus, pp. 282. 26–283. 3. Theophanes, p. 103. 4, gives the amount
of the annual tribute as 1,000 lb of gold: but Priscus was his source!
He agrees with his source as to the sum of 6,000 lb.
96   *Chron. Pasch.* i, p. 583. 18, Bonn; Marcellinus, s.a. 443.
97   On the λογάδες of Attila see pp. 179ff.
98   Priscus, p. 284. 1–9.
99   Ib., pp. 284. 26–285. 28.
100 Cf., for example, Malchus of Philadelphia, frag. 3, p. 389. 9ff,
Dindorf.
101 *Nov. Theod.* v. 3, of 26 June 441.
102 Marcellinus, s.a. 441, cf. Procopius, *BP.* i. 15. 21.
103 E. Stein, i, p. 436, takes τά Αἰθιοπικά ἔθνη (the Ethiopian peoples)
of Priscus, p. 286. 16, to be the Blemmyes and Nobadae who lived
south of Egypt; but in frag. 21 Priscus refers to these peoples by
their correct names, and there seems to be no reason why he should
call them Ethiopians here.
104 Priscus, frag. 6.
105 *Nov. Theod.* xxiv.

106 So Marcellinus, s.a. Prosper, *Chron. Min.* i, p. 480, dates the
murder two years after the invasion of the Eastern Empire, which
he records s.a. 442; but, since that invasion, in fact, ended in 443, he
also points to 445. The *Chron. Gall. a. cccclii* (ib. i, p. 660) dates
the event s.a. 446, but its record of these years is very inaccurate.

107 Prosper, l.c. 'he compelled his [i.e. Bleda's] followers to obey him
[Attila]'; Jordanes, *Get.* xxxv. 181 'Bleda, who ruled over a great
part of the Huns, having been killed, Attila united the whole of the
Hunnic people to himself'.

108 So E. Troplong, p. 546.

109 Priscus, p. 314. 12 (from which it is clear that in 449 the sword had
only recently been discovered); Jordanes, *Get.* xxxv. 183 (= Priscus,
frag. 10). Although Priscus has in mind Herodotus, iv. 62, the truth
of his story cannot be doubted.

110 Priscus, p. 306. 16ff.

111 Frag. 4, which appears misplaced in Müller and Dindorf. It occurs
between frags. 1 and 8 in the *De Legat, Romanorum*, and can
therefore refer to any time between 435 and 449.

112 For his career see Seeck, P.–W. s.v.

113 Priscus, p. 284. 32, with which cf. p. 346. 30. Ensslin, P.–W. (Ζω. R.),
v. 1966, thinks he was only a Dux.

114 Marcellinus, s. aa. 443, 444, 445, 446.

115 Ib., s.a. 447.

116 Jordanes, *Rom.* 331.

117 Priscus, frag. 43 = Evagrius, *HE.* ii. 14; Theophanes, AM 5930;
Malalas, p. 363; Marcellinus, s.a. 447.

118 A. van Millingen, *Byzantine Constantinople* (London, 1899), p. 46;
cf. Marcellinus, s.a. 447; Preger, *Scriptores Originum Constanti-
nopolitanarum*, pp. 150, 182.

119 Dessau, *ILS.* 823; *Anth. Pal.* ix. 690.

120 Priscus, p. 320. 5. This problem and the career of Zeno are
discussed in *Hermathena*, lxviii, 1946, pp. 18–31.

121 Callinicus, op. cit., p. 139. 21ff; Nestorius, op. cit., pp. 366ff.

122 Theophanes, p. 102. 20.

123 Marcellinus, s.a. 447 'many of the enemy were killed'; cf. Jordanes,
Rom. 331.

124 *Chron. Pasch.*, p. 586. 4, Bonn; Jordanes, *Get.* xvi. 92; Zosimus, iv.
10. 3; Procopius, *De Aed.* iv. II. 20, p. 148.

125 *Rom.* 331.

126 Marcellinus, s.a. 447.

127 *Vita S. Hypatii*, p. 139. 21ff.

128 *Chron. Min.* i, p. 662: see p. 232.

5 Peace on the Danube Frontier

1 I date this war to 448, because it is clear from Priscus, p. 298. 25, that it had only recently ended in 449; cf. the order in which the invasion of 447 and this war are mentioned at p. 306. 10. Priscus called them the Ἀκάτιροι, (Akatiroi) cf. Marquart, *Streifzüge*, p. 41, n. 1, who shows that the form Ἀκάτζιροι, (Akatziroi) is due to the copyists.

2 See Marquart, op. cit., pp. xxiff, 40ff; Toynbee, p. 132; Moravcsik, *Byzantino-turcica*, ii, s.v. 'Akatziri'.

3 Jordanes, *Get.* v. 36; Marquart, l.c., p. xxii.

4 Priscus, p. 310. 31.

5 Ib., pp. 341. 15, 346. 7.

6 Tomaschek, P.-W. s.v. 'Acatziri'; Marquart, op. cit., pp. xxiv. 41; Kiessling, P.-W. viii. 2604, and cf. now K. H. Menges, *Byzantion*, xvii, 1945, p. 261.

7 Jordanes, l.c.; Priscus, p. 298. 29.

8 Priscus, p. 298. 30ff.

9 Ib., p. 299. 6 συμβασιλεύοντες.

10 Ib., p. 306. 10 μάχαις.

11 Ib., p. 299. 1–18, cf. p. 310. 29. For the name of Attila's eldest son cf. Jordanes, *Get.* l. 262.

12 Marcellinus, s.a.

13 The reference in Priscus, pp. 296. 15, 327.3, can scarcely be to the peace of 443.

14 Priscus, pp. 286. 32–287. 7; E. Stein, *Geschichte*, p. 439.

15 Stein, p. 439, says that the amount of the tribute was not raised. This may be, but I do not know that there is any evidence for the statement.

16 Priscus, pp. 301. 32; 302. 5. For a full account of his career see Ensslin, P.-W. xviii. 1012 f. Romulus Augustulus was, of course, a usurper.

17 Historians sometimes call him Vigilius, Vigilans, or Vigilas: see Gibbon, ch. 34; Dindorf, *Hist. Gr. Min.* i, Index, s.v.; Alföldi, *Nouvelle Revue de Hongrie*, xlvii, 1932, p. 237, etc. It is safer to retain Bigilas with Bury, op. cit. i, p. 279; Güldenpenning, p. 351, n. 102 *b*, says that the name is Gothic, and it should be noted that Jordanes, *Rom.* 336, speaks of a Gothic chief called Bigelis.

18 Priscus, p. 289. 5; Not. Dign. Or. vi. 52, p. 33 Seeck.

19 Priscus, pp. 293. 32; 296. 15.

20 Ib., pp. 294. 32; 312. 1; 318. 26.

21 Procopius, *BG.* viii. 11. 9; *BP.* ii. 28. 42.

22 Priscus, pp. 286. 22–287. 12.

23 Theophanes, p. 100. 16; Malalas, p. 363. 4. Helm, p. 415, takes the ἕτεροι οἶκοι of Priscus, p. 287. 16, to be the quarters, μητᾶτα, assigned to Edeco as an ambassador by the Magister Officiorum; but they are doubtless merely the residence of Chrysaphius: so Hodgkin, p. 57. Chrysaphius did not hold the highest office open to a eunuch, that of *praepositus*; he was content to remain *primicerius sacri cubiculi* (Nicephorus Call. *HE.* xiv. 47). But through his influence the responsible functions of *spatharius* were now attached to this office, and Chrysaphius is usually referred to as *spatharius* by our authorities: Stein, i, p. 445 f.; cf. *Coll. Avell.* 99. 5 (p. 441, 12, ed. Günther), *Chron. Pasch.* i, p. 590. 6, Bonn; *Vita S. Daniel. Styl.* 31, and that is the meaning of ὑπασπιστής in Priscus, p. 287. 17, and Evagrius, ii. 2 (p. 39. 3), who characteristically avoid the technical term.

24 *Vita S. Danielis*, 31.

25 John of Antioch, frag. 191; Suidas, s.v. Θεοδόσιος (both from Priscus).

26 Priscus, pp. 287. 12–288. 6. Priscus' source was doubtless Bigilas, cf. p. 15.

27 Ib., p. 288. 6–31.

28 Priscus, pp. 288. 32–289. 32. The ἀγγελιαφόροι are the *agentes in rebus*, also called μαγιστριανοί because they were under the direction of the Magister Officiorum.

29 For other cases of Roman ambassadors travelling on horseback cf. Plintha and Epigenes, pp. 82–3; Priscus, p. 277. 7; Menander, frag. 20, etc.

30 *CTh*, I. i. 6. 2, where he is described as 'spectabilis comes et magister sacrorum scriniorum'. On the identification see Ensslin, *Byz.-neugr. Jahrbb.* v, 1926–7, pp. 2–3.

31 *Nov. Theod.* i. 7 (15 Feb. 438).

32 Priscus, p. 290. 4. Similarly, Plintha had nominated Epigenes in 435, p. 82. It would be interesting to know who had nominated Olympiodorus in 412.

33 On the semi-official relationships of the *assessores* (legal advisers) to their superiors see Seeck, P.-W. i. 424.

34 Ensslin, ib., p. 8.

35 Amm. xvii. 5. 15 *ut opifex suadendi*; Priscus, p. 276. 29; Procopius, *BP*. ii. 24. 4, *BG*. v. 3. 30, etc.

36 Priscus, pp. 295. 1ff, 312. 1, 318. 26.

37 Ib., p. 288. 5 τῶν ἀλλῶν συμπρεσβευτῶν.

38 Priscus, p. 305. 9 ὑπηρέταις, p. 295. 31 οἳ μετὰ τῶν ὑποζυγίων. On such servants see Helm, p. 403, who overlooks the present case.

39 *CTh*. vii. i. 9; xii. 12. 2, etc. Helm, p. 413.

40 Priscus, p. 290. 18 'But we turned the conversation to other things and by our friendly manner calmed their anger.'
41 Cf. *CQ*. xli, 1947, p. 62.
42 Priscus, pp. 290. 5–291. 9.
43 Ib., p. 294. 9–16.
44 Anon. Vales. 2.
45 Cf. *CQ*. ib., p. 63.
46 Priscus, p. 291. 9–15.
47 Ib., p. 292. 32, 'We were shocked by this unreasonable question and looked at each other.'
48 Ib., pp. 291. 15–293. 13.
49 Ib., p. 293. 13–26.
50 Ib., pp. 293. 26–294. 1.
51 Priscus, p. 294. 17–31.
52 Ib., pp. 294. 31–296. 3.
53 Jordanes, *Get.* xxxv. 182.
54 Priscus, p. 297. 2 τοὺς σφετέρους θεράποντας.
55 Ib., pp. 296. 4–297. 13.
56 Priscus, pp. 297. 13–298. 25.
57 Ib., p. 295. 15.
58 Ib., p. 303. 24. See Appendix G.
59 Ib., p. 298. 23–7; p. 299. 18–22.
60 The old view (e.g. Herbert, p. 381 n.) that Ἐσκάμ in Priscus, p. 299. 30, is accusative and that Attila married *his own* daughter is impossible: this would not have been 'according to the law of the Scythians' (κατὰ νόμον τὸν Σκυθικόν), as Priscus puts it, a phrase in which he refers simply to the polygamy practised by the Huns, or at any rate by their rulers.
61 See Appendix F.
62 The northern barbarians prized pepper very highly, and in his treaty with the Romans in 408 Alaric demanded 3,000 lb of it, Zosimus, v. 41. 4.
63 Priscus, p. 301. 29 τῆς Νωρικῶν ἄρχων χώρας, Eugippius, *Vita S. Severini*, 20, etc.
64 Ib., pp. 299. 23–302. 6. On Constantius see p. 139. There is little likelihood in the view of Gibbon, iii, p. 436, and Hodgkin, p. 73, that Attila arranged this meeting for scenic effect, so that he 'might enjoy the proud satisfaction of receiving, in the same camp, the ambassadors of the Eastern and Western Empires'.
65 Priscus, pp. 303. 12–304. 2. The view of Attila's 'camp' adopted here is that suggested in *Journal of Hellenic Studies*, lxv, 1945, pp. 112–15; see also bibliography 4 below. Those scholars who suppose that the whole village was surrounded by a palisade (for which

there is no evidence in Priscus) have mistaken the nature of Hunnic warfare.

66 Priscus, pp. 304. 2–305. 3.
67 Ib., p. 305. 19, does not warrant us to follow Alföldi, *Menschen die Geschichte machten*, p. 231, and others, in believing that Latin was, with Hunnic and Gothic, a third '*Umgangssprache*' in the camp.
68 On this see Procopius, *HA*. vii, pp. 44ff., Haury.
69 Priscus, p. 305. 32 τότε δὴ γελάσας ἔλεγε Γραικὸς μὲν εἶναι τὸ γένος. The word Γραικὸς here means a native of Greece proper.
70 Priscus, p. 305. 12–32: see pp. 203ff.
71 Ib., pp. 309. 12–310. 26.
72 On the form of her name, which is printed as Κρέκα in the editions, see J. Markwart, p. 89, n. 1.
73 Priscus, p. 312. 5ff.
74 Ib., pp. 310. 26–311. 29; with p. 311. 24 cf. Jordanes, *Get.* xxxv. 182 'he [*sc*. Attila] was haughty in his walk, moving his eyes here and there, so that the power of his proud spirit was visible in the movement of his body'.
75 Priscus, pp. 311. 30–314. 16. On this sword see p. 97. Constantiolus must have been a pagan.
76 Priscus, pp. 314. 17–315. 10.
77 Ib., p. 315. 11–25: see *JHS*. 1.c.
78 Priscus, p. 303. 24.
79 On the 'polychrome' style of decoration described by Priscus, p. 316. 32, see Alföldi, *Germania*, xvi, 1932, p. 136, and *Funde*, pp. 12ff, who states that it was very widespread in Europe at this time; but we need not believe that it was the work of the Huns themselves.
80 Priscus, pp. 315. 25–317. 20: see Appendix A.
81 Ib., p. 317. 20–3.
82 Priscus, pp. 317. 23–318. 17.
83 Ib., p. 318. 18 ἐπὶ πολὺ μὴ βουληθέντες τῷ πότῳ προσκαρτερεῖν.
84 Ib., pp. 318. 20–320. 20.
85 Priscus, pp. 320. 21–322. 5: this remark of Maximinus is discussed in *Hermathena*, lxviii, 1946, pp. 22ff.
86 Priscus, p. 321. 21
87 Ib., pp. 320. 21–323. 14.
88 Ib., pp. 325. 29–326. 17.
89 Priscus, pp. 319. 27–320. 13.
90 Ib., p. 326. 19–26.
91 Ib., p. 326. 17ff.
92 Ib., frag. 13.

93 Ib., pp. 327. 22–328. 22.
94 Malalas, xiv, p. 366.

6 The Defeats of Attila

1 On the date 440 see J. de Lepper, *De rebus gestis Bonifatii*, pp. 110ff.
2 *Chron. Min.* ii, p. 24, s.a. 446; p. 25, s.a. 449; see Seeck, *Untergang*, vi, p. 303.
3 Sidonius, *Carm.* v. 210.
4 See Constantius, *Vita Germani*, 28. 40, passages which are carefully discussed by W. Levison, 'Bischof Germanus von Auxerre und die Quellen zu seiner Geschichte', *Neues Archiv der Gesellschaft für ältere deutsche Geschichtskunde*, xxix, 1903, pp. 97–175, at pp. 133ff. Levison concludes that Constantius made a slip when he mentioned Tibatto, but to the present writer this seems unlikely.
5 Constantius, op. cit. 40.
6 *Chron. Min.* i, p. 662, s.a. 448.
7 *CTh.* xiii. 3, etc.
8 *De Gub. Dei*, v. 21.
9 Priscus, pp. 295. 4; 301.31; 319.25. Seeck, P.-W. iv. 1102, believed the Italian tombstone of *Constantius dux* (Bücheler, *Carm. Epigr.* ii. 1335) to have belonged to this Constantius; but the words 'he was the horror of the Pannonian peoples', though doubtless a reference to the Huns, can scarcely be applied to a man of whom we only know that he served Attila in the capacity of a secretary. The stone is agreed to date from the early fifth century, but the name was then a very common one.
10 So Herbert, p. 376 n.
11 Priscus, p. 302. 10. 27.
12 Ib., p. 325. 19.
13 Ib., p. 313. 30ff, cf. *CTh.* vi. 22. 4; viii. 5. 44, etc.
14 Ib., p. 302. 7.
15 Ib., pp. 302. 7–303. 9.
16 Ib., p. 312. 10.
17 I take the embassy to Valentinian mentioned in Jordanes, *Get.* xxxvi. 185, to be earlier than the Honoria affair, cf. Prosper, s.a. 451 (*Chron. Min.* i, p. 481).
18 Jordanes, *Get.* xxxvi. 185 *dudum bella concepta.*
19 John Lydus, *De Mag.* iii. 43, p. 132 Wuensch. *Contra*, Bury, *Later Roman Empire*, i, p. 290; E. Stein, *Geschichte*, i, p. 494.
20 Seeck, *Untergang*, vi, p. 301, believes that by invading Gaul Attila hoped to cut off the Visigothic kingdom as a source from which the armies of West Rome could be recruited. But, while Aetius lived, is

it likely that a single Visigoth from the kingdom of Toulouse fought in the imperial armies?

21 Prosper, l.c. After the events of 451 and 452 it was inevitable that this should be disbelieved.

22 John of Antioch, frag. 199 *ad fin.*

23 Jordanes, l.c.: see p. 76.

24 See Bury, *JRS.* ix, 1919, pp. 1–13.

25 Marcellinus, s.a. 434; but John of Antioch, frag. 199 (i.e. Priscus) says nothing of this.

26 On Herculanus see Seeck, *Untergang*, vi, p. 466 (n. on p. 298. 8).

27 John of Antioch, frag. 199 τῶν βασιλικῶν καὶ αὐτὴ ἐχομένη σκήπτρων.

28 Ib., cf. Bury, art. cit., p. 12. The other sources for Honoria's action are Marcellinus, s.a. 434, and Jordanes, *Rom.* 328, *Get.* 224.

29 Priscus, pp. 328. 28–329. 3, cf. p. 330. 6–10.

30 Priscus, p. 329. οὐ γὰρ θηλειῶν, ἀλλὰ ἀρρένων ἡ τῆς Ῥωμαϊκῆς βασιλείας ἀρχή.

31 Ib., p. 329. 3–14.

32 For the long hair of the Merovingian princes see Agathias, p. 144. 19ff; Greg. Tur. iii. 18, vi. 24, viii. 10.

33 Priscus, pp. 329–330. 1.

34 Ib., p. 329. 14–17.

35 For a different judgement of Marcian's policy see, for example, Bury, *Later Roman Empire*, i, p. 290.

36 Priscus, p. 329. 19.

37 Prosper, s.a. 451.

38 Jordanes, *Get.* xxxvi. 184.

39 Greg. Tur. ii. 6 *Chuni a Pannoniis egressi.*

40 Jordanes, *Get.* xxxv. 182, but he adds *ferebatur* (it is said), an indication of Priscus' caution.

41 Sidonius, *Carm.* vii. 319ff; see A. Loyen, p. 52.

42 Damascius *ap.* Cobet's Diogenes Laertius (Didot), p. 126.

43 Priscus, p. 329. 19.

44 Note Priscus' phrase τοῦ πρὸς φράγγους πολέμου πρόφασις ([Attila's] excuse for war against the Franks), p. 329. 23, and see Mommsen, p. 542.

45 Schmidt, *Geschichte*, i, p. 245; Sidonius, *Carm.* vii. 325f.

46 Priscus, p. 330. 1 τὴν ἐκστρατείαν ποιούμενος.

47 Ib., frag. 16.

48 Malalas, xiv, p. 358; *Chron. Pasch.* i, p. 587: they also transfer the battle from the Loire to the Danube.

49 Priscus, l.c.

50 Jordanes, *Get.* xxxvi. 189 (from Priscus, cf. Mommsen, praef., p.

xxxvi), cf. Sidonius, *Carm.* vii. 333 *prope contemptum hostem* (a foe [i.e. the Huns] the Goths almost despised).

51   Ib., 332ff; Jordanes, *Get.* xxxvi. 187–8. Sidonius' enthusiasm for his father-in-law grows as his poem progresses, and in *vv.* 352, 547ff, he seems to imply that the Goths intended to stay neutral until Avitus induced them to fight. This is contradicted by Jordanes–Priscus and by Sidonius himself, *v.* 333.

52   Sidonius, *Carm.* vii. 327–30.

53   *Nov. Valent.* 33.

54   *Get.* xxxvi. 191.

55   So Bury, *Later Roman Empire,* i. p. 292, n. I.

56   Sidonius, *Carm.* vii. 547. He tells us that some three or four years later Armorica was suffering from Saxon sea-raiders, *Carm.* v. 369. F. Lot, *Les Invasions germaniques* (Paris, 1945), p. 108, doubts whether in fact the Armoricans took part in the battle at all.

57   *Vita Lupi* 5 (p. 297) 'cum diversa urbium loca simulatae pacis arte temptaret', which seems likely enough, although the source is all but valueless.

58   Jordanes, *Get.* xxxvii. 194.

59   Sidonius, *Ep.* viii. 15. 1 'the attack on Orleans, when the city was invaded but never plundered', *Vita S. Aniani,* 9ff.

60   So Bury, op. cit. i, p. 293, n. I.

61   The ancient evidence for the site of the battle is conveniently set out in Bury's Gibbon, iii, Appendix 28: but in his *Later Roman Empire,* i, p. 293, n. I, Bury rightly says that there is no evidence for connecting the skeleton found at Pouan in 1842 with the battle against Attila. See the relevant works listed in bibliography 5.

62   *Vita S. Aniani,* 7, p. 113; Bury, l.c. i, p. 292, n. 5.

63   Jordanes, *Get.* xxxvii. 196ff.

64   Ib., 198, 200ff.

65   *Get.* xli. 217. I doubt if Attila could have fed an army of even 30,000 men.

66   Damascius, l.c. (see p. 136, n. 2), § 63.

67   Jordanes, *Get.* xli. 215ff.

68   *Chron. Min.* i, p. 302.

69   Priscus, frag. 18.

70   Seeck, *Untergang,* vi, p. 273.

71   Ib., p. 301, citing Mansi, vi, pp. 557 *d,* 560 *c.*

72   *Chron. Min.* i, p. 662 'despairing of bringing ruin to Gaul, Attila sought out Italy in great rage'.

73   Jordanes, *Get,* xlii. 219.

74   *Chron. Min.* i, p. 482 'having restored the forces which he had lost in Gaul, Attila aimed to invade Italy via Pannonia'. The season is

conjectural; Seeck, op. cit., p. 311, supposes that he crossed the Alps in winter, which seems very unlikely.

75 *Chron. Min.* l.c. 'nihil duce nostro Aetio secundum prioris belli opera prospiciente, ita ut ne clusuris quidem Alpium, quibus hostes prohiberi poterant, uterentur, hoc solum spebus suis superesse existimans, si ab omni Italia cum imperatore discederet' (Prosper).
76 Amm. xxi. 12. 1.
77 Jordanes, *Get.* xlii. 219–21. The siege is also mentioned by the writers of the *Chron. Gall. a. dxi* and the *Addit. ad Prosp. Haun., Chron. Min.* i, pp. 663, 302; by Count Marcellinus, ib. ii, p. 84, Cassiodorus, ib. ii, p. 157, Procopius, *BV.* i. 4. 30–5, and later writers. For the legend of the chaste Digna who killed herself somewhat dramatically rather than allow the barbarians to lay hands on her, see Paul, *Hist. Rom.* xiv. 9.
78 *Chron. Min.* i, p. 662 'whose [i.e. Italy's] inhabitants from fear abandoned the soil, and from terror their fortifications'.
79 Paul, xiv. ii; Jordanes, *Get.* xlii. 222; *Chron. Min.* i, p. 302.
80 Suidas, s. v. Μεδιόλανον, cf. id., s. v. κόρυκος.
81 Jordanes, *Get.* xlii. 222 'as Priscus the historian reports'.
82 Prosper, s.a. 452 'cum hoc plenum dedecoris et periculi videretur', etc.
83 *Chron. Min.* i, p. 482.
84 *Later Roman Empire*, i, p. 295. For other examples of clerical embassies see Helm, p. 398, n. 3, and above, p. 76.
85 *Chron. Min.* i, p. 474.
86 Sidonius, *Ep.* i. 9. The embassy is reported by Prosper, *Chron. Min.* i, p. 482; Jordanes, *Get.* xlii. 223; Paul, xiv. 11.
87 On him see Seeck, *Untergang*, vi, p. 469 (n. on p. 312. 10).
88 Hydatius, *Chron. Min.* ii, pp. 26ff. 'The Huns, who had been plundering Italy and who had also stormed a number of cities, were victims of divine punishment, being visited with heaven-sent disasters: famine and some kind of disease. In addition, they were slaughtered by auxiliaries sent by the Emperor Marcian and led by Aetius, and at the same time they were crushed in their settlements by both heaven-sent disasters and the army of Marcian. Thus crushed, they made peace with the Romans and all returned to their homes.'
89 Priscus, frag. 9; Jordanes, *Get.* xliii. 225.
90 Ib., xlix. 254 'post innumerabiles uxores, ut mos erat gentis illius'.
91 Ib., *sine ullo vulnere.* Jordanes expressly names Priscus as his source in this passage.
92 Ib., 225.
93 Cf. Schröder, p. 242, with Jordanes, *Get.* xlix. 256.

94 v.l. *orbis.*

95 Jordanes, *Get.* xlix. 257. Attempts to reconstruct the Gothic (which of course was not the original) are ridiculed by Schröder, pp. 243ff. For an example see F. Kluge, pp. 157–9. F. Klaeber, p. 259, thinks that the song is a composition of Priscus or even Jordanes, which is surely impossible.

96 Jordanes, l.c., 258.

97 Ib. The symbolic significance assigned to the metals may be due to Priscus or his informants.

98 H. M. Chadwick, *The Heroic Age*, p. 53. For similar rites among the Bulgars see Marquart, *Streifzüge*, pp. 205ff, and for the unhappy picture of the Huns as Homeric scholars see the *Transactions of the Connecticut Academy of Arts and Sciences*, xxv, April 1922, pp. 340ff. The suggestion is not rejected by Klaeber, p. 263. It is to be observed that Jordanes does not profess to give a complete account of the funeral, *Get.* xlix. 256 'pauca de multis dicere non omittamus'.

99 References in Maenchen-Helfen, p. 255. Jordanes, *Get.* lii. 269, also tells us that the Huns called the Dnieper (or more probably the Danube – see Macartney, p. 108) *var*, and in Mommsen's Index to his Jordanes we read (s.v. 'Danaper'): 'vocabulo *var* pro fluvio Hungari adhuc utuntur', but the point is much debated.

100 *Chron. Min.* ii, p. 86: the tale reappears in the *Chron. Pasch.*, p. 588. 3, Bonn. See Chadwick, op. cit., pp. 37ff, and *The Growth of Literature*, i, pp. 185ff.

101 *The Pardoner's Tale*: the story doubtless arrived at Chaucer from Priscus via Cassiodorus, Jordanes, Paulus Diaconus, and Landolfus Sagax, *Hist. Misc.* xv. 8. The circumstances of Attila's death excuse those who believed the rumour. It is not easy to see what excuse can be devised for those recent writers who suggest that, since Attila and Ildico so closely resemble Holophernes and Judith, the entire tradition must be suspected: see Klaeber, pp. 257–8, Maenchen-Helfen, p. 244. That Priscus should have turned to Herodotus and Thucydides when he had no information as to the movements of distant tribes or the course of obscure battles was natural enough by the standards of his time. But that he should have failed to find out the circumstances of Attila's death and should instead have introduced into his work the story of Judith and Holophernes is incredible.

102 Jordanes, *Get.* xlviii. 253.

103 Jordanes, l.c., § 255 'hoc Priscus istoricus vera se dicit adtestatione probare'.

104 Cf. the story in Evagrius, *HE*. ii. 1, designed to explain his policy of non-interference in Africa.

105 Jordanes, *Get.* 1. 259.

106 *Chron. Min.* i, p. 482 'certamina de optinendo regno exorta sunt'.

107 Ib., pp. 185, 482; Jordanes, *Get.* 1. 259; *Vita. S. Severini*, 1.

108 Cf. Paulus Diaconus, *Hist. Rom.* xv. 11, and see Ensslin, *Byz.-neugr. Jbb.* vi, 1927–8, pp. 151ff; Macartney, p. 112.

109 Jordanes, *Get.* 1. 263.

110 Ib., 262 *multos gravesque conflictos*: for a discussion of the name Nedao see Diculescu, pp. 64ff.

111 Jordanes, l.c. 'aliarum gentium quae Hunnis ferebant auxilium': it would seem from § 265ff that these included some of the Sciri, Alans, Rugi, and perhaps Ostrogoths, cf. Ensslin, art. cit., p. 150.

112 Jordanes, l.c. *inopinata victoria*.

113 Ib., 264 'when the Goths perceived the people of the Huns occupying its [*suis*] ancient abodes'; see Macartney, pp. 107ff, who rightly, I think, takes *suis* here to refer to the Huns.

114 Jordanes, *Get.* lii. 268, cf. 264, and see Ensslin, art. cit., p. 152.

115 Jordanes, l.c. 269, reading *Danubii* or the like (with Macartney, p. 108) for Mommsen's *Danabri* – the bulk of the manuscripts are against Mommsen here. For the natural strength of this region Macartney compares Amm. xvii. 13. 4.

116 Jordanes, l.c. 265: see p. 33.

117 See Mommsen's note on Jordanes, op. cit. 266.

118 Sidonius, *Carm.* ii. 239ff. Seeck, *Untergang*, vi, p. 358, dates the incident to the winter of 466/7.

119 Sidonius, op. cit. 269ff.

120 John, frag. 209 (source not Priscus); Anon. Vales. 45.

121 To the names of those who have accepted the identification cited in Reynolds and Lopez, p. 48, n. 40, add those of Seeck, P.-W. v. 1939 (cautiously); Güldenpenning, p. 350; L. Schmidt, *Geschichte*, p. 298; E. Stein, *Geschichte*, p. 440; and W. Ensslin, P.-W. xvii, 1888, s.v. 'Odoacer', who says that the identification 'can now scarcely be doubted'. But Reynolds and Lopez alone draw the necessary conclusion that Odoacer was a Hun: see their suggestive article *passim*.

122 *Get.* liv. 277.

123 See pp. 129–30. On the name Dengizech – Jordanes, *Get*, liii. 272, has *Dintzic* – see Markwart, p. 83, who believes it to be a Turkish diminutive, but is unable to identify it.

124 Jordanes, *Get*, liii. 272 f. The names of the Ultzinzures (on which see p. 202) and Bittugures are known to Agathias, pp. 201. 6, 365. 9, Dindorf.

125 Priscus, frag. 36.

126 Ib., frag. 38.

127 Chron. Pasch., p. 598. 3, Bonn; Marcellinus, s.a. 469.
128 Macartney, p. 113; see p. 170.
129 Evagrius, HE. iii. 2, but the chroniclers do not think it worthy of mention.
130 Diculescu's opinion (p. 63), that these Goths, here found collaborating with the Huns, had also fought for them at the Nedao, is not impossible.
131 Priscus, frag. 39.
132 Sidonius, Carm. v. 475.
133 Ib., 485ff, 499.
134 Priscus, frag. 29. Seeck, Untergang, vi, p. 350, and Ensslin, P.-W. xiv. 1447, seem to be certainly right in taking these 'Scythians' to be Huns.
135 Howorth (1889), p. 722.
136 This nation is only known from Priscus, frags. 30, 41 (cf. Suidas, s.v.) and Zachariah of Mitylene, p. 328. Bury, ed. of Gibbon, iv, Appendix 15, p. 538, n. 5, is tempted to suppose that Priscus has erred and that the Kotriguri are meant. This is hazardous.
137 The doubts of de Boor as to the authenticity of the extract from Suidas printed in Priscus' frag. 30 at p. 341. 6–14, Dindorf, carry little weight, as was shown by Moravcsik, Ung. Jbb. x, 1930, pp. 53ff.
138 Moravcsik, art. cit., p. 58.

7 Hun Society under Attila

1 Priscus, pp. 276. 13, 277. 23: see pp. 83–4.
2 Ib., p. 277. 21.
3 Ib., p. 282. 25–30: see p. 94.
4 Ib., p. 319. 5.
5 Ib., p. 277. 15 and 22.
6 Ib., p. 306. 7.
7 Priscus, p. 326. 9. Theophanes, p. 102. 15, calls him Μούνδιος, but Jordanes, Get. xxxv. 180, xlix. 257, has Mundzucus. Müllenhoff ap. Mommsen's Jordanes, Index s.v. (p. 152), derives the name from the Germanic Mundevechum, but this is very doubtful.
8 Priscus, p. 289. 30.
9 Ib., p. 311. 22.
10 Ib., p. 298. 28.
11 Ib., p. 311. 26.
12 Ib., p. 298. 1.
13 See p. 85, cf. p. 94.
14 Priscus, p. 286. 22 ἀνὴρ Σκύθης, μέγιστα κατὰ πόλεμον ἔργα διαπραξάμενος, p. 291. 4 Ἐδέκωνα δὲ τὰ κατὰ πόλεμον

ἄριστον. He, like Onegesius, is called ἐπιτήδειος or λογάς without distinction: cf. p. 287. 30 with p. 292. 30, and p. 304. 15 with p. 306. 6, 9.

15 Ib., p. 320. 25. The only other λογάδες whom we know by name are Onegesius, Scotta his brother, and Orestes, but there were more, cf. p. 292. 30.

16 Ib., p. 315. 28.

17 In the Anon. Vales. 38 we read: 'Orestes was a Pannonian, who joined with Attila at the time when he came to Italy, and was made his secretary.' This cannot refer to the invasion of 452: when had Attila been in Italy before? Perhaps with Aetius in 433: see p. 71.

18 For the former see Priscus, pp. 286. 6, 328. 2, etc., and for the latter pp. 292. 30, 318. 24.

19 Ib., p. 286. 6.

20 Priscus, p. 287. 32, cf. p. 311. 20.

21 Ib., p. 310. 18.

22 Ib., 14–18.

23 Ib., p. 288. 18.

24 Ib., p. 320. 25.

25 Ib., pp. 299. 17, 320. 25; see p. 107.

26 Ib., pp. 315. 25, 319. 22.

27 Ib., p. 291. 3.

28 Ib., p. 348. 8.

29 Jordanes, *Get*. lii. 268, cf. l. 260, 263; Priscus, pp. 326. 25, 348. 10. Attila even compares Theodosius to a slave, ib., p. 326. 13.

30 Priscus, p. 296. 26.

31 *Get*. xxxviii. 199.

32 Ib., 200; xlviii. 253.

33 Ib., 249.

34 See, for example, Peisker, pp. 341ff.

35 Priscus, p. 304. 2 ff.: see p. 124.

36 Ib., p. 304. 15.

37 Ib., p. 311. 5ff: see p. 126.

38 Ib., p. 301. 1: see p. 121.

39 Menander Protector, frag. 43 (p. 85. 15, Dindorf).

40 Malalas, p. 430. 20ff; Theophanes, p. 175. 12ff, de Boor.

41 Priscus, p. 304. 12, 24.

42 Jordanes, *Get*. xlix. 254 'post innumerabiles uxores, ut mos erat gentis illius': Priscus, p. 299. 31 (quoted on p. 269, ch. 5, n. 60), where Σκυθικόν does not denote the rulers alone, one would think; cf. Salvian's *Chunorum impudicitia, de Gub. Dei*, iv. 68. We have direct testimony to the polygamy of Attila (Priscus, p. 299. 30), Bleda (ib., p. 301. 2), and Onegesius (ib., p. 310. 16).

43 Lewis H. Morgan, *Ancient Society* (New York, 1877), pp. 465ff.
44 Priscus, p. 306. 8.
45 Ib., p. 286. 6 *et al.*
46 Ib., p. 290. 22.
47 Ib., pp. 316. 24, 27, 304. 17.
48 Ib., pp. 301. 17, 311. 32, 304. 17.
49 Ib., p. 317. 1.
50 Ib., p. 315. 23, cf. 311. 8: they have an abundance of linen, p. 304. 4, 8.
51 Ib., p. 301. 17.
52 Ib., pp. 316. 20, 317. 2, cf. p. 304. 12: they also had fish, p. 294. 23.
53 Ib., p. 317. 9.
54 Peisker, p. 340.
55 Priscus, p. 300. 9, 11; on *camum* see CQ. xli, 1947, p. 63.
56 Priscus, p. 316. 23.
57 Ib., pp. 315. 10, 318. 18.
58 Ib., p. 316. 15, 22.
59 Ib., p. 315. 20, 21, 30, etc.
60 Ib., p. 316. 16.
61 Amm. xxxi. 2. 10 *carpenta*, cf. § 4.
62 Priscus, p. 300. 9.
63 Cf. Fox, p. 9.
64 Amm. xxxi. 2. 6; Jordanes, *Get.* v. 37; see p. 258, ch. 3, n. 3.
65 See Lattimore, pp. 68–70.
66 Priscus, p. 316. 29, 328. 7.
67 Lattimore, p. 64; cf. Amm. xxxi. 2. 9.
68 Fox, pp. 41ff.
69 p. 50. 1ff., Dindorf.
70 Menander, frag. 9.
71 Chadwick, *Heroic Age*, p. 444.
72 Libanius, *Or.* lix. 66.
73 Claudian, *In Rufin.* i. 327 *vitanda Ceres.*
74 Lattimore (1938), p. 12.
75 Priscus, pp. 298. 16, 328. 7.
76 Lattimore, p. 69.
77 *Nouvelle Revue de Hongrie*, xlvii, 1932, p. 237.
78 Moisil, p. 208, who gives a different interpretation of the evidence.
79 Zachariah of Mitylene, p. 152.
80 See Macartney, p. 113, n. 4; Hirth in bibliography 8.
81 *Get.* v. 37.
82 Priscus, p. 277. 18: see p. 83.
83 Ib., p. 287. 3: see p. 108.
84 Priscus, p. 291. 19.

85 Ib., p. 297. 3ff.
86 Ticeloiu, pp. 84ff.
87 Cf. Lattimore, pp. 71, 210, 519 *et al.*; Stein, *Geschichte*, i, p. 435.
88 See p. 31 and cf. especially Joshua Stylites, cap. 9 (p. 7, Wright); cap. 18 (p. 12).
89 Priscus, p. 345. 25ff. See pp. 171–2.
90 *CJust.* iv. 41. 2, with Kruger ad loc., and Seeck, *Regesten*, p. 124. 27. The law was still in force under Justinian, cf. Procopius, *HA.* xxv. 2ff; *BP.* i. 19. 25ff.
91 Priscus, frag. 38.
92 Fox, p. 106.
93 For this word see Eugippius, *Vita S. Severini*, x. 2 *latrones quos vulgus scamaras appellabat*, with the references collected by Knoell in his index s.v.
94 Jordanes, *Get.* lvii. 301. See Ensslin, P.-W. xvi. 559ff, on Mundo, but I see no reason to believe him to have been of mixed Hunnic and Gepid blood.
95 Cf. Reynolds and Lopez, p. 44.

8 Roman Foreign Policy and the Huns

1 *CJust.* i. 14. 4 (AD 429).
2 *Ep*, 32, Sakellion.
3 *De Prov.* I *init.*, ap. Migne, *PG.* lxxxiii. 556ff. There is a translation of this passage of Priscus (p. 307. 7ff) in A.J. Toynbee, *Greek Civilization and Life* (London 1924), pp. 130–6.
4 Macrobius, *Sat.* ii. 4. 18, whose banqueters, as one might expect, have no fault to find with the sentiment.
5 Theodoret, *Ep.* 44; Procopius, *De Aed.* i. 3. 14.
6 Priscus, p. 282. 17ff; see p. 98.
7 Ib., p. 285. 4 κατεπτηχότες: see pp. 94–5.
8 Evagrius, *HE.* i. 18.
9 Priscus, p. 327. 9ff, 19ff.
10 See Mansi, vi, p. 1024 *b* τότε τὰ τῆς οἰκουμένης ἐν χέρσὶν ἔχοντι πράγματα.
11 See J. Fleming, 'Akten der ephesinischen Synode vom J. 449', *Abh. d. Ges. d. Wissenschaften zu Göttingen*, xv. i, 1927, p. 15.
12 Priscus, p. 315. 1: see p. 127.
13 p. 286. 8, cf. 283. 7ff.
14 Ib., p. 286. 17.
15 Frag. 5: see p. 93.
16 Priscus, p. 336. 1ff.
17 Ib., p. 340. 6.
18 Ib., p. 337. 19.

19 Ib., p. 348. 26: see pp. 173–4.
20 Priscus, p. 285. 27.
21 Ammianus: see J. Mackail, *Classical Studies* (London, 1925), p. 182.
22 *HE.* ii. 1.
23 *Šišićev Zbornik* (Zagreb, 1929), p. 88.
24 Theophanes, AM 5946 καὶ ἦν ἐκεῖνα τὰ ἔτη κυρίως χρυσᾶ τῇ τοῦ βασιλέως χρηστότητι John Lydus, *De Mag.* iii. 43 (p. 132) Μαρκιανὸν τὸν μέτριον.
25 See p. 194. It seems to have been in their interests that Theodosius made his repeated attempts to win back North Africa from the Vandals: see Bury, *Later Roman Empire*, ed 1 (1889), vol. i, p. 162.
26 Priscus, p. 283, 5–32.
27 With this assertion cf. Socrates, *HE.* vii. 22. 12 and 15.
28 Priscus, p. 282. 27.
29 J. Sundwall, *Weströmische Studien* (Berlin, 1915), p. 151.
30 Nestorius, p. 350.
31 Malchus, p. 387. 23, Dindorf.
32 Ib., p. 406. 10.
33 See J. Marquart, *Ērānšahr*, p. 105.
34 Constantine Manasses, 2904.
35 John Lydus, *De Mag.* iii. 43 (p. 132). My conclusion in these paragraphs coincides in general with that of Papparregopoulos, edn 5, vol. 11. ii, pp. 251ff. The opposite view is maintained, among others, by Andreades, p. 83, n. 1 (bibliography 6 below), but I have not found his arguments convincing.
36 Zosimus, iv. 32. 3.
37 Zosimus, v. 29. 5ff, from Olympiodorus.
38 I accept in general Seeck's interpretation of this incident, cf. his *Untergang*, v, p. 382.
39 p. 388. 5ff, Dindorf.
40 Ib., e.g. p. 387. 23.
41 Ib., p. 388. 4.
42 Cf. the scholium printed in Maas, l.c.
43 Priscus, p. 326. 32 πάντων δὲ αὐτῷ εὔνοιάν τε καὶ σπουδὴν συνεισφερόντων.
44 The loss of his chief encampment, which Priscus visited, would have cost him little, for it was much less elaborate than is commonly supposed: see Thompson, *JHS.* lxv, 1945, pp. 112ff. Some nomadic peoples even possessed towns of their own, e.g. βακάθ (Bakath) of the Onoguri (Theophylact, vii. 8. 13), βαλαάμ (Balaam) of the Kidarite Huns (Priscus, p. 349. 32).
45 The point is excellently argued by Lattimore in several passages of

his *Inner Asian Frontiers of China*, esp. pp. 330ff; cf. idem, *Geogr. Journ.* xci, 1938, p. 15 to both of which works I am heavily indebted here.

46 Sozomen, ix. 5, cf. *CTh.* v. 6. 3: see pp. 33–4.
47 Priscus, p. 285. 12: see p. 95.
48 See p. 99, and cf. Nestorius, quoted on p. 223.
49 Cf. esp. Socrates, vii. 22.
50 So Seeck, *Untergang*, vi, p. 258. 32, who on this point is certainly right.
51 Evagrius, *HE.* i. 10.
52 Cf. Priscus, p. 283. 26 'with outrages'.
53 Malalas, p. 358. 5, Bonn.
54 *Later Roman Empire*, ii, p. 348.

9 Conclusion

1 Those who approach the Huns from the steppe rather than from the Roman Empire do not agree: see, for example, Lattimore, p. 513.
2 Jordanes, *Get.* xxxv. 180 'is namque Attila patre genitus Mundzuco, cuius fuere germani Octar et Roas, qui ante Attilam regnum tenuisse narrantur, quamvis non omnino cunctorum quorum ipse'.
3 Procopius, *De Aed.* iv. 5. 6.
4 Marcellinus, *Chron. Min.* ii, p. 82, s.a. 447 'The general [magister militum] Arnegisclus was killed in Dacia Ripensis near the river Utus in a fierce battle against king Attila, in which *many of the enemy were slain.*' Marcellinus readily admits the great defeats suffered by the East Romans on other occasions, cf. his entries s.aa. 441, 443, etc.
5 *Ges. Schr.* iv, p. 539.
6 Priscus, frag. 1 *init.*
7 See Prosper, s.a., quoted at ch. 6, n. 75.
8 *De Gub. Dei*, v. 36, *et al.*
9 Amm. xxvii. 5. 7.
10 Cf. the intimacy of Ardaric and Attila, Jordanes, *Get.* xxxviii. 199, quoted on p. 184.
11 See on this point F. Engels, *Origin of the Family*, pp. 177ff.
12 Bury, *Later Roman Empire*, i, pp. 297ff; Alföldi, *Untergang*, ii, p. 88.
13 I say nothing of the part which the Huns play in Bury's theory of the contingent events by which he seeks to explain the fall of the Roman Empire (ib. i, pp. 311ff), for that theory has not won acceptance. It should also be observed that he does not overlook the importance of the events which followed the year 376. See also his judicious

remarks on the significance of the battle of the Catalaunian Plains and of the Nedao, ib., p. 294, and *The Invasion of Europe by the Barbarians* (London, 1928), pp. 149ff, 155ff.

14 Priscus, p. 348. 8–11.

Afterword

1 It is not meant disparagingly that I will not be considering more popular books such as P. Howarth, *Attila, King of the Huns: Man and Myth*, 1994.

2 We may contrast with both, the view of Altheim, *Attila und die Hunnen*, p. 84, who, on the basis of no evidence whatsoever (and against every likelihood), considers Uldin an earlier member of the same dynasty which later produced Attila and Bleda.

3 T. Nagy, 'The last century of Pannonia in the judgement of a new monograph' *Acta Antiqua*, 19, 1971, pp. 299–345; J. Harmatta, 'The last century of Pannonia', *Acta Antiqua*, 18, 1970, pp. 362–9; A. Mocsy, 'Review of Varady', *Acta Archaeologica*, 23, 1971, pp. 347–60.

Appendix A   The Songs of the Huns

1 p. 317. 14: see p. 129.

2 *HA.*, p. 86.

3 Ib., p. 85.

4 p. 76.

5 Priscus, p. 304. 9: see p. 124.

Appendix B   The Causes of the War of 441

1 P.-W., Supplb. v. 665 (correcting *Byz.-neugr. Jbb.* v, 1926–7. p. 3).

2 *CTh.* I. i. 6. 2.

3 *Nov. Theod.* i. 7.

4 p. 276. 30.

5 *Geschichte*, i, p. 435, n. 1.

6 p. 281. 11.

Appendix C   Valips

1 *Revue archéologique*, viii, 1868, pp. 86ff.

2 P.-W. xvii, 1194, s.v. 'Noviodunum' (7).

3 P.-W. i (Zw. R.), 1215.

4 *Geschichte*, p. 119.

5 pp. 43ff.

Appendix D   The Campaign of 441–3

1 *Geschichte*, p. 341, n. 66 *a*.

2 Idem, p. 342, n. 69.
3 *Later Roman Empire*, i. p. 274.
4 *Geschichte*, p. 437, n. 2.
5 *Untergang*, vi, p. 291ff.
6 p. 281. 11.

Appendix E   Chronological Note on the Years 449–50

1 *Untergang*, vi, pp. 286ff.
2 *Later Roman Empire*, i, p. 276.
3 i, p. 364.
4 *Eng. Hist. Rev.* viii, 1893, p. 211, n. 9.
5 *JRS.* ix, 1919, p. 10.
6 *Hist.* vi, p. 612.
7 'Akten d. ephesinischen Synode vom J. 449', *Abh. d. Ges. d. Wiss. zu Göttingen*, xv. i, 1927, pp. 15, 33, 47.
8 Bibliography 8 below.
9 Art. cit., p. 4.
10 Cf. Leo, *Ep.* 75 in Migne, *PL.* liv. 902.

Appendix F   The Site of Attila's Headquarters

1 Cf. Jordanes, *Get.* xxxiv. 178.
2 p. 359, n. 107.
3 p. 86.
4 P.-W. vi. 941, s.v. 'Tigas', and ib. 1470, s.v. 'Tisia'.
5 p. 362, n. 108 *a*.
6 p. 58.
7 Bibliography 8 below.
8 See, for example, Diculescu, l.c.; Patsch, P.-W. v. 1706, s.v. 'Dricca'; Tomaschek, P.-W. v. 1696, s.v. 'Drenkon'; Fluss, P.-W. vi. 1471–2.

Appendix G   The Alleged Gothic Names of the Huns

1 *Later Roman Empire*, i, p. 278.
2 p. 74 n.
3 *Streifzüge*, p. 42, n. 1.
4 The *Vita Lupi*, v, p. 298.
5 Cf. Hodgkin, p. 123, but note that the reading *Hunagaisus* is now abandoned.
6 pp. 39–40.
7 Cf. Jordanes, *Get.* ix. 58 'Romans borrow names from the Macedonians, Greeks from the Romans, . . . and the Goths frequently from the Huns'.

Further Reading

Primary Literary Sources (New Editions, Translations)

Ammianus Marcellinus, Eng. trans. R. C. Scott, 3 vols, rev. edn, Loeb, 1950–2; or W. Hamilton, Penguin Classics, 1986.

R. C. Blockley, *The Fragmentary Classicising Historians of the Later Roman Empire: Eunapius, Olympiodorus, Priscus, and Malchus*, ed. and Eng. trans., 2 vols, 1981–3.

Callinicus, *Vita S. Hypatii*, ed. G. J. M. Bartelink, SC 177, 1971.

Claudian, Eng. trans. M. Platnauer, 2 vols, Loeb, 1922.

Jordanes, *Gothic History*, Eng. trans. C. C. Mierow, 2nd edn, 1960.

Fl. Merobaudes, ed. and Eng. trans. F. M. Clover, *Transactions of the American Philological Society*, lxi, 1971.

Sidonius Apollinaris, *Poems and Letters*, ed. and Eng. trans. W. B. Anderson, 2 vols, Loeb, 1936.

Theodosian Code, Eng. trans. C. Pharr, 1969.

Zosime, *Histoire Nouvelle*, ed. and Fr. trans. F. Paschoud, Budé, 3 vols, 1971–89.

Zosimus, *New History*, trans. R. T. Ridley, 1982.

Secondary Works

F. Altheim, *Attila und die Hunnen*, 1951.

——(ed.), *Geschichte der Hunnen*, 5 vols, 1959–62.

V. Bierbrauer, 'Zur chronologischen, soziologischen und regionalen Gliederung des ostgermanischen Fundstoffs des 5. Jahrhunderts in Sudosteuropa', in H. Wolfram and F. Daim (eds), *Die Völker an der mittleren und unteren Donau im fünften und sechsten Jahrhundert*, 1979, pp. 131–42.

I. Bona, 'Die archäologischen Denkmaler der Hunnen und der Hunnenzeit in Ungarn im Spiegel der internationalen Hunnenforschung', *Ausstellungskatalog Niebelungenlied*, 1979, pp. 297–342.

——*Das Hunnenreich*, 1991.

R. Browning, 'Where was Attila's camp?', *Journal of Hellenic Studies*, 73, 1953, pp. 143–5.

L. Buchet, 'La déformation cranienne en Gaule et dans les régions limitrophes pendant le haut Moyen Age: son origine – sa valeur historique', *Archéologie Médiévale*, 18, 1988, pp. 55–71.

F. M. Clover 'Geiseric and Attila', *Historia*, 22, 1973, pp. 104–17.

R. J. Cribb, *Nomads in Archaeology*, 1991.

B. Croke, 'Evidence for the Hun invasion of Thrace in AD 422', *Greek, Roman and Byzantine Studies*, 18, 1977, pp. 347–67.

E. Demougeot, *La formation de l'Europe et les invasions barbares. Vol. 2: De l'avènement de Dioclétien au début du VIe siècle*, 1979.

C. D. Gordon, *The Age of Attila: Fifth Century Byzantium and the Barbarians*, 1966.

R. Grousset, *L'Empire des Steppes. Attila, Gengis Khan, Tamerlan*, 1960.

J. Harmatta, 'The golden bow of the Huns', *Acta Archaeologica Hungaricae*, 1, 1951, pp. 114–49.

——'The dissolution of the Hun empire', *Acta Archaeologica Hungaricae*, 2, 1952, pp. 277–304.

P. Heather, 'Cassiodorus and the rise of the Amals: genealogy and the Goths under Hun domination', *Journal of Roman Studies*, 79, 1989, pp. 103–28.

——'The Huns and the end of the Roman Empire in western

Europe', *EHR*, 110, 1995, pp. 4–41.

M. Kazanski, *Les Goths (Ier–Viie siècles ap. J.-C.)*, 1991.

M. Kazanski and R. Legoux, 'Contribution a l'étude des témoignages archéologiques des Goths en Europe Orientale à l'époque des Grandes Migrations: la chronologie de la Culture Cernjachov récente', *Archéologie Médiévale*, 18, 1988, pp. 55–71.

A. M. Khazanov, *Nomads and the Outside World*, trans. J. Crookenden, 1984.

Gy. Laszlo, 'The significance of the Hun golden bow', *Acta Archaeologica Hungaricae*, 1, 1951, 91–106.

R. Lindner, 'Nomadism, Huns, and horses', *Past and Present*, 42, 1981, pp. 1–19.

O. J. Maenchen-Helfen, *The World of the Huns*, 1973.

J. F. Matthews, 'Olympiodorus of Thebes and the history of the west (AD 407–425)', *Journal of Roman Studies*, 60, 1970, pp. 79–97; reprinted as no. III in id., *Political Life and Culture in Late Roman Society*, 1985.

——*The Roman Empire of Ammianus*, 1989.

L. Musset, *Les Invasions: les vagues Germaniques*, 1965; Eng. trans. E. and C. James, *The Germanic Invasions*, 1975.

W. Richter, 'Die Darstellung der Hunnen bei Ammianus Marcellinus (31, 2, 1–11)', *Historia*, 23, 1974, pp. 343–77.

B. D. Shaw, '"Eaters of flesh, drinkers of milk": the ancient Mediterranean ideology of the pastoral nomad', *Ancient Society*, 13/14, 1982/3, pp. 5–31.

J. Tejral, 'Zur Chronologie der frühen Völkerwanderungenzeit im mittleren Donauraum', *Archaeologica Austriaca*, 72, 1988, pp. 223–304.

E. A. Thompson, 'The camp of Attila', *JHS*, 65, 1945, pp. 112–15.

P. Tomka, 'Die hunnische Fürstfund von Pannonhalma', *Acta Archaeologica Hungaricae*, 38, 1986, pp. 423–88.

L. Várady, *Das Letzte Jahrhundert Pannoniens*, 1969.

J. Werner, *Beiträge zur Archaologie des Attila-Reiches*, Bayerische Akademie der Wissenschaften, Phil.-Hist. Kl., n.f. 38A, 1956.

T. E. J. Wiedemann, 'Between man and beasts. Barbarians in Ammianus Marcellinus', in I. S. Moxon, J. D. Smart and A. J. Woodman (eds), *Past Perspectives: Studies in Greek and Roman historical Writing*, 1986, pp. 189–211.

G. Wirth, 'Attila und Byzanz: Zur Deutung einer fragwürdigen Priscusstelle', *Byzantinische Zeitschrift*, 60, 1967, pp. 41–69.

Bibliography

(In cases where no confusion would arise, the following works are cited by the author's name only. Several works, which are mentioned in the footnotes but are only indirectly relevant to the Huns, are not included here.)

1 General Histories

Tillemont, *Histoire des empereurs*, Gibbon, *Decline and Fall* (ed. Bury 1897), T. Hodgkin, *Italy and Her Invaders*, vol. ii, Oxford, 1898, and A. Güldenpenning, *Geschichte des oströmischen Reiches unter den Kaisern Arcadius und Theodosius II*, Halle, 1885, are all valuable still. Interesting information will also be found in E. W. Brooks, 'The Eastern Provinces from Arcadius to Anastasius', *Cambridge Medieval History*, vol. i, and in the first volume of the *CMH* generally. But the fundamental and indispensable works are J. B. Bury, *History of the Later Roman Empire*, edn 2, London, 1923 (which does not entirely supplant the first edition of 1889), Otto Seeck, *Geschichte des Untergangs der antiken Welt*, vols v–vi, and E. Stein, *Geschichte des spätrömischen Reiches*, vol. i, Vienna, 1928. For the barbarian world beyond the northern Roman frontier see L. Schmidt, *Geschichte der deutschen Stämme: die Ostgermanen*, edn 2, Munich, 1934, but there is little material relevant to Attila in R. Grousset, *L'Empire des steppes: Attila, Gengis-khan, Tamerlan*, Paris, 1939. A vast quantity of mostly irrelevant information will be found in W. Herbert, *Attila, King of the Huns*, cited here from the reprint in the author's *Collected Works*, vol. iii,

London, 1842, where the reader will also find a lengthy poem on Attila 'calculated to direct the emotions of the mind to the true comforts of religion'. Acknowledgement must be made of the great assistance derived from many articles in Pauly–Wissowa's *Realencyclopädie* (herein P.-W.), chiefly by Seeck and W. Ensslin.

2 The Nomadic Background of the Huns

Ralph Fox, *Genghis Khan*, London, 1936.

L. T. Hobhouse, G. C. Wheeler, and M. Ginsberg, *The Material Culture and Social Institutions of the Simpler Peoples* (The London School of Economics and Political Science: Monographs on Sociology, No. 3), London, 1930.

Owen Lattimore, *Inner Asian Frontiers of China* (American Geographical Society: Research Series, No. 21), New York, 1940.

——'The Geographical Factor in Mongol History', *Geographical Journal*, xci, 1938, pp. 1–20.

E. Parker, *A Thousand years of the Tartars*, edn. 2, London, 1924.

T. Peisker, 'The Asiatic Background', *Cambridge Medieval History*, vol. i, pp. 323–59.

3 Archaeology, Numismatics, etc.

A. Alföldi, 'Funde aus der Hunnenzeit und ihre ethnische Sonderung', *Archaeologia Hungarica*, ix, Budapest, 1932.

——'Archäologische Spuren der Hunnen', *Germania*, xvi, 1932, pp. 135–8.

E. Babelon, 'Attila dans la numismatique', *Revue numismatique*, Ser. IV, vol. xviii, 1914, pp. 297–328.

A. Blanchet, 'Les Monnaies de la guerre de Théodose II contre Attila en 442', *Revue historique du sud-est européen*, i, 1924, pp. 97–102.

E. Gren, *Der Münzfund von Viminacium* (Skrifter utgivna av K. Humanistiska Vetenskaps-Samfundet i Uppsala, xxix. 2), Uppsala, 1934.

Olov Janse, 'Notes sur quelques représentations des bractéates en or scandinaves', *Revue archéologique*, Ser. 5, vol. xiii, 1921, pp. 373–95.

——'Notes sur les solidi romains et byzantins trouvés en Scandinavie', *Revue numismatique*, Ser. IV, vol. xxv, 1922, pp. 38–48.

——'L'Empire des steppes et les relations entre l'Europe et l'Extrême-Orient dans l'antiquité', *Revue des arts asiatiques*, ix, 1935, pp. 9–26.

E. H. Minns, 'The Art of the Northern Nomads', *Proceedings of the British Academy*, 1942, pp. 47–101.

C. Moisil, 'Sur les monnaies byzantines trouvées en Roumanie', *Académie roumaine: Bulletin de la section historique*, vol. xi, 1924, pp. 207–11.

J. Nestor and C. S. N. Plopsor, 'Hunnische Kessel aus der Kleinen Walachie', *Germania*, xxi, 1937, pp. 178–82.

Zoltán de Takács, 'Congruencies between the Arts of the Eurasiatic Migration Periods', *Artibus Asiae*, v, 1935, pp. 23–32, 177–202.

J. Werner, review of Alföldi's *Untergang* (see below), in *Germania*, xviii, 1934, pp. 236–8.

4 The Camp of Attila

K. G. Stephani, *Der älteste deutsche Wohnbau und seine Einrichtung*, vol. i, Leipzig, 1902, at pp. 173ff.

J. Strzygowski, *Die altslavische Kunst*, Augsburg, 1929, at pp. 138ff.

E. A. Thompson, 'The Camp of Attila', *Journal of Hellenic Studies*, lxv, 1945, pp. 112–15.

Ferenc Vámos, 'Attilas Hauptlager und Holzpaläste', *Seminarium Kondakovianum*, v, 1932, pp. 131–48.

5 Attila and the West

A. Alföldi, 'Les Champs catalauniques', *Revue des études hongroises*, vi, 1928, pp. 108–11.

A. de Barthélemy, 'La Campagne d'Attila: invasion des Huns dans les Gaules en 451', *Revue des questions historiques*, viii, 1870, pp. 337–404 (with bibliography).

J. B. Bury, 'Justa Grata Honoria', *Journal of Roman Studies*, ix, 1919, pp. 1–13.

A. Coville, *Recherches sur l'histoire de Lyon du Vme siècle au IXme siècle (450–800)*, Paris, 1928.

Girart, 'Le Campus Mauriacus: nouvelle étude sur le champ de bataille d'Attila', *Revue historique*, xxviii, 1885, pp. 321–31.

G. Kaufmann, 'Üeber die Hunnenschlacht des Jahres 451', *Forschungen zur deutschen Geschichte*, viii, 1868, pp. 115–46.

A. Loyen, *Recherches sur les panégyriques de Sidoine Apollinaire*, Paris, 1942.

T. Mommsen, 'Aetius', *Hermes*, xxxvi, 1901, pp. 516–47, reprinted in *Ges. Schr.* iv, pp. 531–60, from which I quote.

G. Waitz, 'Der Kampf der Burgunder und Hunnen', *Forschungen zur deutschen Geschichte*, i, 1862, pp. 3–10.

6 The East Roman Payments to the Huns

A. Andréadès, 'De la monnaie et de la puissance d'achat des métaux précieux dans l'empire byzantin', *Byzantion*, i, 1924, pp. 75–115, at p. 83, n. 1.

A. P. D'yakonov, 'Vizantiiskie Dimy i Faktsii v V–VII vv.', *Vizantiiskii Sbornik*, Moscow and Leningrad, 1945, pp. 144–227.

C. Manojlović, 'Le Peuple de Constantinople', *Byzantion*, xi, 1936, pp. 617–716.

K. Paparregopoulos, Ἱστορία τοῦ Ἑλληνικοῦ Ἔθνους, edn 5, Athens, 1925, vol. ii, pt. ii.

7 After Attila

W. Ensslin, 'Die Ostgoten in Pannonien', *Byzantinisch-neugriechische Jahrbücher*, vi, 1927–8, pp. 146–59.

H. H. Howorth, 'The Avars', *Journal of the Royal Asiatic Society*, xxi, 1889, pp. 721–810.

——'The Sabiri and the Saroguri', ibid. xxiv, 1892, pp. 613–36.

F. Klaeber, 'Attila's and Beowulf's Funeral', *Publications of the Modern Language Association of America*, xlii, 1927, pp. 255–67.

F. Kluge, 'Zur Totenklage auf Attila bei Jordanes, *Get.* 257', *Beiträge zur Geschichte der deutschen Sprache und Literatur*, xxxvii, 1912, pp. 157–9.

C. A. Macartney, 'The End of the Huns', *Byzantinisch-neugriechische Jahrbücher*, x, 1934, pp. 106–14.

L. Schmidt, 'Die Ostgoten in Pannonien', *Ungarische Jahrbücher*, vi, 1927, pp. 459–60.

E. Schröder, 'Die Leichenfeier für Attila', *Zeitschrift für deutsches Altertum und deutsche Litteratur*, lix, 1922, pp. 240–4.

8 Miscellaneous

A. Alföldi, *Der Untergang der Römerherrschaft in Pannonien* (vol.

i, Ungarische Bibliothek, x, 1924; vol. ii, ibid. xii, 1926).

——'Attila' in P. R. Rohden and G. Ostrogorsky, *Menschen die Geschichte machten*, vol. i, Vienna, 1931, pp. 229–34.

——'L'Idée de domination chez Attila', *Nouvelle Revue de Hongrie*, xlvii, 1932, pp. 232–8.

J. B. Bury, *The Invasion of Europe by the Barbarians*, London, 1928.

——*Selected Essays*, ed. H. Temperly, Cambridge, 1930.

H. M. Chadwick, *The Heroic Age*, Cambridge, 1912.

——*The Growth of Literature*, vol. i, Cambridge, 1932.

E. Darkó, 'Influences touraniennes sur l'évolution de l'art militaire des grecs, des romains, et des byzantins', *Byzantion*, x, 1935, pp. 443–69; xii, 1937, pp. 119–47.

J. Darkó, 'Die auf die Ungarn bezüglichen Volksnamen bei den Byzantinern', *Byzantinische Zeitschrift*, xxi, 1912, pp. 472–87.

C. C. Diculescu, *Die Gepiden*, Leipzig, 1923.

W. Ensslin, 'Maximinus and sein Begleiter, der Historiker Priskos', *Byzantinisch-neugriechische Jahrbücher*, v, 1926–7, pp. 1–9.

——Review of Alföldi's *Untergang* in *Philologische Wochenschrift*, xlvii, 1927, pp. 842–52.

R. Helm, 'Untersuchungen über den auswärtigen diplomatischen Verkehr des römischen Reiches im Zeitalter der Spätantike', *Archiv für Urkundenforschung*, xii, 1932, pp. 375–436.

F. Hirth, 'Über Wolga-Hunnen und Hiung-nu', *Sitzungsberichte d. kön. bayer. Academie d. Wissenschaften zu München: phil.-hist. Classe*, 1899, ii, pp. 245–78.

N. Jorga, *Geschichte des rumänischen Volkes*, vol. i, Gotha, 1905.

O. Maenchen-Helfen, 'Huns and Hsiung-Nu', *Byzantion*, xvii, 1944–5, pp. 222–43.

——'The Legend of the Origin of the Huns', ibid., pp. 244–51.

J. Markwart, 'Kultur- und sprachgeschichtliche Analekten', *Ungarische Jahrbücher*, ix, 1929, pp. 68–103.

J. Marquart, *Osteuropäische und ostasiatische Streifzüge*, Leipzig, 1903.

J. Melich, 'Über den ungarischen Flussnamen "Tisza, Teiss"', *Streitberg Festgabe*, Leipzig, 1924, pp. 262–6.

Gy. Moravcsik, *Byzantinoturcica*, 2 vols, Budapest, 1942–3.

J. Moravcsik, 'Zur Geschichte der Onoguren', *Ungarische Jahrbücher*, x, 1930, pp. 53–90.

R. L. Reynolds and R. S. Lopez, 'Odoacer: German or Hun?', *American Historical Review*, lii, 1946, pp. 36–53.

R. Roesler, 'Zur Bestimmung der Lage des alten Naissos', *Zeitschrift für die österreichischen Gymnasien*, xix, 1868, pp. 843–6.

Kara Chemsi Rechid Saffet, *Contribution à une histoire sincère d'Attila*, Paris, 1934.

M. Schuster, 'Die Hunnenbeschreibungen bei Ammianus, Sidonius und Iordanis', *Wiener Studien*, lviii, 1940, pp. 119–30.

E. Stein, 'Der Verzicht der Galla Placidia auf die Präfektur Illyricum', *Wiener Studien*, xxxvi, 1915, pp. 344–7.

——'Untersuchungen zur spätrömischen Verwaltungsgeschichte', *Rheinisches Museum*, lxxiv, 1925, pp. 347–94.

E. A. Thompson, 'Priscus of Panium, Fragment I *b*', *Classical Quarterly*, xxxix, 1945, pp. 92–4.

Ion D. Ticeloiu, 'Über Nationalität und Zahl der von Kaiser Theodosius dem Hunnenkhan Attila ausgelieferten Flüchtlinge', *Byzantinische Zeitschrift*, xxiv, 1923–4, pp. 84–7.

E. Troplong, 'La Diplomatie d'Attila', *Revue d'histoire diplomatique*, xxii, 1908, pp. 540–68.

A. A. Vasiliev, *The Goths in the Crimea* (Mediaeval Academy of America: Monograph No. 11), Cambridge, Mass., 1936.

NB Priscus is quoted throughout from L. Dindorf, *Historici Graeci Minores*, vol. i (Leipzig, 1870).

Index

Acatziri: Hunnic nation 15; tribal organization, 48 f; subdued by Attila, 84 f, 105 ff, 205, and by Saraguri, 175; ruled by Ellac, 121, 124, 168, 175
Addai, 284 n. 59
Adrianople, 92, 131 f; battle of, 29, 62, 236
Aegidius, 210
Aelianus, 77
Aeschylus, 21, 24
Aesti, 106
Aetius: hostage among Huns, 38, 60; supports John, 40, 55; defeated by Boniface, 71 f, 305 n. 17; relations with Bagaudae, 76 ff, 137 f, 152 f; Burgundians, 72 ff, 139; Franks, 147, 155; Vandals, 79, 86; Visigoths, 75 f, 155 f, 229; sends secretaries to Attila, 122, 138; quarrels with Attila, 139 f, 144; victory in Gaul, 151 ff, failure in Italy, 157 f, 160 f; attitude to Huns, 155, 183, 231; his Western critics, 102, 231 f, 301 n. 75
——Eastern general, 163, 198
Africa, 79, 87, 143, 161, 174
Agathias 20, 56
Agathyrsi, 105
Agintheus, 116
Aignan, St, 154

Alans: conquered and ruled by Huns, 26 f, 66, 68, 84; economy of, 27, 47, 51, 60; fight for Huns, 27, 29, 33, 37, 183; enter Gaul, 33, 236; settled near Orleans, 139, 153; at Catalaunian Plains, 154; at Nedao, 168, 303 n. 111
Alaric, 39, 52, 151, 160, 216, 236
Alatheus, 28
Almus, 170
Alps, Julian, 38, 158, 232
Altai, 176
Altinum, 159 f
Altziagiri, 189 f, 194
Amandus 77
Ambrose, St, 282 n. 10
Amilzuri, 80, 230
Ammianus Marcellinus: describes the Huns, 9 ff, their barbarity, 41, 56 f, economy, 47 f, greed, 62, origin, 19, 24; social organization, 48 ff; trade, 188; women, 185; Roman social organization, 206, 217; historical method, 10, 13
Anagast, 172 f
Anatolius: career, 112, 208 f; Attila's attitude to, 127, 134; first treaty of, 93 f, 98, 141, 177, 195, 214; second, 108, 118, 119, 195; third, 135 f, 142, 156, 273f; treaty with Persia, 96

Angisciri, 172, 202
Anthemius, Emperor, 86, 170 f
——Prefect, 34 f, 40, 86, 100
Antioch, 31
Apollonius, 156, 163, 209f
Aquileia, 18, 159
Arabia, 31
Aral Sea, 84, 176
Arcadiopolis, 92
Arcadius, Emperor, 41, 133, 203
Ardaric, 99, 168, 184, 196
Areobindus, 92, 131
Ariminum, 71
Armenia, 27 f, 31, 87, 96
Armorica, see s.v. Bagaudae
Arnegisclus, 90, 92, 101, 172
Asemus, 37, 55, 93 f, 210 f, 220
Aspar: fights in Africa, 79, 83, 90; Italy, 40; Thrace, 92 f; his truce with Attila, 90, 272; owns Zerco, 129; disgraced, 131
Assyria, 22
Atakam, 85
Athanaric, 28 f, 233
Athaulf, 38, 53, 146
Athyras, 93
Attila: accession, 101 f; attitude to Theodosius' ministers, 209; autocracy of, 178 f; contribution to Hun history, 227 f, 230; death and burial, 164 ff; diplomacy of, 228;